BO RYAN

ANOTHER HILL
TO CLIMB

BO RYAN

Another Hill To Climb

Bo Ryan
with
Mike Lucas

KCI
Sports Publishing

Cataloging-in-Publication Data is available from the Library of Congress.

First KCI Sports Publishing edition: 2008
ISBN-13: 978-0-97987-291-4
ISBN-10: 0-97987-291-X

Book Layout and Design: Nicky Brillowski

This book is available in quantity at special discounts for your group or organization. For further information, contact:

KCI Sports Publishing
3340 Whiting Avenue
Suite 5
Stevens Point, WI 54481
(217) 766-3390
Fax: (715) 344-2668

Photos courtesy of: the Bo Ryan family, University of Wisconsin Athletic Department, Wisconsin State Journal, John R. Wooden Award, University of Wisconsin-Platteville Athletic Department, and David Stluka Photography.

I dedicate this book
to my parents, Butch and Louise,
for creating an atmosphere of
learning through common sense.
And to my wife Kelly,
for being the most thoughtful
and caring person
one could ever hope to know.

FOREWORD

Bo Ryan is my kind of college basketball coach for one simple reason: He's nothing like a college basketball coach.

Exhibit A: Most college basketball coaches have done one thing their whole lives: basketball. They played it from age 2 until 21, at which time they started coaching it and they're still coaching it. They are conversant in two subjects: basketball and midnight basketball. Bo didn't even become a college basketball head coach until he was 37. Before that, he had an actual life. He sold greeting cards, packed mattresses, welded ships, worked construction, helped build bridges, even escorted military prisoners to prison.

"I'd get them on the plane holding a .45," Ryan says. "And I'd always tell the guy, 'Do you know why they gave me this job? Because I won the pistol contest.'"

Wasn't exactly true, of course. He'd never shot anything in his life. "I didn't even have rounds in the .45. I had them in my briefcase."

Stewardess: The prisoner is escaping!

Bo: Okay, would you mind getting my briefcase out of the overhead?

Exhibit B: He's as honest as sodium pentathol. With most college basketball coaches, you need a translator and a lawyer to figure out what they mean. For instance, most college basketball coaches don't start raging against the idiocy of the NCAA until all the tape recorders are off and the pencils are put away.

Ryan does it while they're still out.

"One time, a recruit came on an unofficial visit," he says. "They were walking the campus and just stopped by. They were hot. I reached into our refrigerator to get them a bottled water. But then we realized, 'Wait a minute. Can we do this?' We actually had to call the compliance officer before I could give them a drink of water. And what's the value of a bottle of water? A buck? And the officer said no we couldn't. We wound up having to give them water from a cup in the sink. Now you tell me if that's not a stupid rule."

Exhibit C: Most college basketball coaches have beautiful golf swings because they get the summers off. Not Bo. His swing looks like a man who is suddenly attacked by fleas in the middle of his backswing. He brings it back really low and about a mile outside the plane, gets to the top, then makes a furious lunge at it, as though he were about to bludgeon a muskrat. The divot goes 90 degrees off his target line and as for the ball, it goes squealing off hideously left and then starts slicing right, until, lo and behold, it's in the fairway! And that golf swing is sort of the way he coaches: self-taught, unconventional, unpredictable, kind of ugly, but, in the end, entertaining, beautiful and, as we all know, ridiculously successful.

Exhibit D: Most college basketball coaches have wives who lie about what a great husband they have, how they're always home by supper to tuck the kiddies in, and what a great help he is around the house. Not Ryan's wife, Kelly. They've been married since 1974 and they have this agreement: Ryan doesn't have to cook, make his bed, walk the dog, do the dishes, vacuum, mow the lawn, pay the bills, fix the car or buy her jewelry under one condition: He has to win. As soon as he stops winning — or coaching — all that changes. And they both like it that way.

"I shudder when he talks about retiring," Kelly says. "He'll drive me nuts. The man has too much energy. He'll be climbing the walls."

So do us all a favor will you, Bo?

Don't change a thing.

-Rick Reilly
ESPN.com Columnist

"One of the legacies of Coach Ryan is his ability to get the best out of his players. He gives his players an unquestionable belief in the system that he runs. He encourages accountability to the point that seniors take ownership and communicate exactly what needs to be done to find success. He teaches the game in a way that doesn't leave a stone unturned — paying attention to the details of all possible situations. He's a great basketball coach, and a fine teacher of young men."

-Kirk Penney
Former UW All-Big Ten player

CONTENTS

INTRODUCTION
The Hill

I felt a burning sensation in my thighs when I reached the top.
But it was a good feeling; a feeling of exhilaration and
accomplishment. True, I wasn't having a Rocky moment, jumping up
and down and dancing around like Sylvester Stallone after he climbed
the steps in front of the Philadelphia Museum of Art.

But I was feeling good about myself because I had found what I was
looking for, and I had run it just once. I could only imagine what it
would feel like running it 15 or 20 times in succession. I thought I was
in good shape, too.

Back in the early- to mid-80s, I was still playing full-court basketball
whenever I got the chance, and I was probably 10 to 15 pounds lighter
than I am now. But I'm telling you, I could feel the burning in my legs
when I got to the top. It was like my body was telling me something,
and it spoke volumes for the physical challenge.

Anybody who has ever played college basketball for me knows what
I'm saying. Whether they played at Platteville, UW-Milwaukee or
Wisconsin, they know that I could be talking about only one thing.

The hill.

One of my goals going into every season was to establish mental
toughness, and the hill was going to be the first task the players were
going to face as a measure of their condition and commitment. It also
was going to be an opportunity for them to impress their coaches and
teammates through their resolve and results.

Reputations could be made or spirits broken. In case of the latter, you
know what they say? Sometimes you have to crawl before you can walk.

Or run uphill.

I once had a player crawl.

Literally.

Jon Nedelcoff was on his hands and knees crawling up the hill in Platteville. His legs had tightened up or had just plain given out on him. I was standing at the top, and I could see him grabbing at the grass and the ground. He was obviously laboring, but he was still doing whatever he could to pull himself up the hill, inch by inch, foot by foot.

I said, "Jon, what are you doing?"

He said, "Coach, I'm not giving in — I'm not giving in to the hill."

I guess that's what you would expect out of a coach's kid. His dad, Jim Nedelcoff, was a Hall of Famer who coached basketball for 40 years at Benton and Southwestern High School in Hazel Green. Jon also got into the profession, and I hired him on my Platteville staff. Whenever I needed a good reference point for someone digging a little bit deeper to reach a goal or the top of the hill, I brought up his example.

The hill was much tougher on the big guys.

I don't think many believed Scott Plondke could run the hill. I got to know Scott during my second year on Steve Yoder's staff at Wisconsin. He was a 6-foot-10 center out of Dubuque, Iowa, who transferred to Northern Iowa and then burned out on basketball altogether for awhile. But I talked him into giving it another shot, and he played a role on our first conference championship team at Platteville.

Scott Plondke was coming off an ACL injury, but I didn't make any concessions in conditioning. He had to do what everybody else was doing. "You've got to run the hill, and get up it," I said. "You're not playing for us unless you complete the hill." Plondke was wearing a knee brace while he was running. And he got to the top of the hill at his own pace, dragging his leg behind him.

There were other Platteville players in the Nedelcoff category whose strong will and sheer determination wouldn't allow them to give in to the hill.

Robby Jeter had exercise-induced asthma, and there were days when he was wheezing and really struggling to breathe. He could barely talk. But he never missed a hill.

Billy Freidig was from Belleville and a starter on our '90 conference title team. Someone told him about breathing through a sock to help his condition. So when he was running the hill, he'd pull out the sock whenever he needed it. It was a clean sock.

Then, there was Moose Murphy from Mineral Point. Ever see the movie *Alien*? You know, where the alien would get inside a person and work his way out of the body. There were days when Moose had this growth coming out of his stomach. It was like a hernia. I don't remember the clinical definition. But he was cleared to run as long as he felt comfortable. Moose never gave in, either.

No one ever used the hill as a reason for leaving Platteville. At least not to me. But word got around — spread from one player to the next — that a couple of guys transferred because they couldn't handle the hill. The way I looked at it, if somebody didn't want to make a commitment to your program because of the work involved, it would be better if he went somewhere else, better for everyone in the long run.

As a player, I always felt I could do whatever the coach demanded. As a coach, I always felt it was my responsibility to raise the bar. I wanted to put it out there where the guys were either going to jump over it or slide under it. The hill took no prisoners.

"This is the first opponent," I reminded the players. "But I don't want you looking at it as an obstacle. I want you to look at the hill as an opportunity. This is an opportunity for you to get into very good shape. I promise you this much: Every day we run the hill, the harder you attack it, the better you become as a player."

***

When I got to Platteville, I was too picky about finding the right hill. There was basically one hill to choose from — what later became THE hill, a toboggan hill located on the lower part of campus where they used to do drivers' tests. There's a cemetery and a row of dorms, and the road ends at the foot of the hill.

To be honest, it wasn't the hill that I had envisioned. There was a steady incline, but there were some dips. So we got the people on campus to work on the hill. It was very minor stuff. They took care of the ruts and made sure the wild grass was cut. Late each summer, I'd make sure the holes were filled in.

Walter Payton used to run the same hill when the Chicago Bears were training in Platteville. From what I heard, he believed that it built endurance and increased explosiveness. Payton was a great salesman for this kind of training. He also ran hills near his home in the Chicago area. And he got his teammates to run with him. He was obviously a good model for what we were doing — on a much different scale, of course.

Some Platteville engineers did a study on the slope of the hill, and they suggested that running the hill was the equivalent of going up a 10-story building in 30 seconds. They measured it as an 11-percent grade. That's pretty steep and not conducive for road travel — except for emergencies. We called the ambulance twice.

One time, we had a guy who ate two chili dogs an hour before he ran the hill, and he got cramps so bad his body just shut down. Another time, we had a guy run the hill in combat boots and a weight belt. His dad had been in the service and he wanted to be different, and he wound up collapsing.

In those days, we didn't have a trainer out there, either. But anytime something happened, we were close enough to one of the dorms and we'd just yell for somebody to call 911.

I remember when Joe Chrnelich inquired about the hill. Joe was a four-year starter for us at Wisconsin, the first player I recruited. He was a captain, a 1,000-point scorer and one of our leading rebounders.

There was nothing soft about Joe or his game. And so when he called and asked about what we were doing with our preseason conditioning at Platteville, I invited him over to check out the hill.

Joe showed up with a couple of his buddies, including Mike Douglass, a very good athlete who had played at Platteville. Joe ran the hill six times. We as a team were on 14 hills that day, and Joe looked at me and said, "I could never play for you here."

I said, "No, Joe, you could do this. But it's a matter of building up to it."

That was the bottom line; I wanted a workout program that builds. Not everybody treated it the same way. Some coaches will tell their players, "When you report to training camp, if you can't run two miles under 12 minutes, there's a penalty." Or they'll say, "You have to be able to do this, this and this before you make the team."

My whole thing about conditioning was, "You come to me as your coach, and I'm going to get you in shape." It was as simple and basic as that.

By the time we started practice in the gym, I didn't have to get the guys in shape. They were already in condition and we could get right to the basketball. Other coaches would tell me that it always took them a couple of weeks to get their players to the point where they needed to be physically. From Day One, we were right into it.

That gave me an advantage in coaching and teaching.

I can't tell you how many guys would come back and tell me that they've never been in as good of shape as they were when running the hill. Do you know what it takes to run 21 or 22 hills? We'd be riding back from our workout and I had guys say, "Coach, if somebody would have told me I was going to do 20 of these hills, I'd say they were absolutely crazy. I never thought I'd do 10, let alone 20."

Guys never got out of shape in the summer. They couldn't afford to be couch potatoes. I wouldn't say that the hill was a cloud hanging over their head or anything like that. But they had to come back ready to do certain things — on command — at certain times. I don't think I would call it dangling a carrot out in front of them, either. Some might.

But it was more about a player making a commitment to himself that "I want to play next year, and this is what I have to do." By doing so, he was also making a commitment to the team. And that's what we were seeking to achieve.

When building or sustaining a program, you've got to make sure you've got guys who want to compete, guys who aren't just happy to be on the team. The hill let me know who was competitive and who really wanted to be ready for the season. You could tell by the way they showed up to run, and I used the hill to measure their reaction.

Was it a matter of trying to find out how they handled adversity? No, I didn't look at it that way. I didn't see any adversity. To me, the hill was a challenge, and we were measuring how far they had come. Because we were starting low and building up, it was a progression. Nothing more, nothing less. Aren't our lives a progression?

Mine has been.

***

I was someone who could run all day, not unlike a John Havlicek, who was known for his stamina when he played at Ohio State and with the

Boston Celtics. My sitting pulse was in the high 40s, low 50s when I played in college, and it stayed at those levels my first 10 years out of school. I always had a low heart rate. Guys would ask, "Bo, don't you ever get tired?"

I'm not saying I NEVER got tired. But I rarely got tired. I'm sure you've been around people like that. And it was not necessarily because I had any special talents. I was just lucky with my genetics. In retrospect, maybe I should have been a long-distance runner. I was one of those guys who didn't sweat a lot and could run forever.

When I came to Wisconsin as an assistant coach in the mid-70s, I was always on the run, morning, noon, and night. I had to stay active. If I wasn't doing something — namely, playing basketball every day — I was pretty much a basket case. I'd get into pickup games at the Shell, the Natatorium, the Field House. I even played a little in the Madison city recreation league when the opportunity presented itself.

My running mate in the summer was usually Steve Randall. When picking sides, we'd often wind up on the same team. Steve played baseball for the Badgers, got his masters degree from Platteville and coached high school ball for 30 years. At Iowa-Grant, one of Steve's players was Greg Gard, one of my current assistants. After Steve passed away, his son, Lance, carried on his legacy by winning two state titles at Oshkosh West.

For some of the pickup games in the Field House, the pace was much different, much slower. In general, the play was more suited to the players. As you might expect, these games weren't nearly as intense. The usual suspects were on hand, though, and they represented all walks of life (not that they walked on the court).

If you were picking a team (good luck), you might have a choice of Andy North, the two-time U.S. Open champ; Van Stoutt, a Madison sportscaster; Si Rogers, a local radio account executive; and Jim Scheidler, a booster and longtime friend (as were the others). Jim Bosanny, the UW basketball trainer, was also among the regulars. He would tape my ankles whenever we played regardless of the level of competition.

When we got together over the noon hour, Alan Zussman, a UW academic advisor, would take part, along with Jim Doyle, the Dane County District Attorney. Today, of course, Jim Doyle is our Governor in the State of Wisconsin. When we played, he was sound fundamentally. That's what I remember most about his game: he had some game as a player and, obviously, as a politician.

Nothing, though, compared to our games in the Shell. You wouldn't believe how physical they got. You also wouldn't believe how many fights some of John Jardine's football assistants used to get into with students. It got so physical at times that punches were thrown. That was not for me. I stayed away from the fighting.

On the other hand, in a figurative sense, I was known to fight for my team on the score. I always used to play hard. Even if it was pickup ball, I always thought you disrespected the game of basketball if you didn't play hard all the time. That was the same attitude that I had in the spring of '76 when I played in my first game at the Shell.

What I remember most about that game was one particular teammate. We're running up and down the court, and there was this tall, rangy guy playing good defense, rebounding and getting me the ball.

When the game was over, we were walking across the track toward the exit, and I remember telling him, "This is my first time here. I'm the new basketball assistant. Did you ever play basketball anywhere?"

"A little in high school," he said.

"Do you go to school here?" I asked.

"Just finished up."

"What's your name?"

"Pat."

"You look kind of familiar."

He nodded. And it dawned on me that he had been on the cover of *Sports Illustrated* for breaking the world high jump record in 1971.

My rebounder was Pat Matzdorf.

That really dates me.

***

I always had an appreciation for track athletes. At Sun Valley, my first high school job, I ended up having a guy who made the '80 Olympics in the decathlon. That was the year of the boycott, and he didn't go. I had talked him into coming out for basketball after seeing him long jump and high jump. He was my leading rebounder.

I was pretty quick myself and won some races when I was a teenager.

I also did a little high-jumping, using the scissors kick, never the Fosbury Flop. When I got to high school, I gave up track because I wanted to concentrate on being a baseball player. The irony is that I later burned out on baseball.

My experience has always been that track coaches were ahead of other coaches when it came to conditioning and taking care of the body. I know I'm making a generalization, but I always felt that to be true. I used to visit a lot with Dan McClimon, the former Wisconsin track and cross country coach. Dan died in a plane crash in the spring of '83. But he left a lasting impression on everybody he touched.

We had so much in common. Dan had an appreciation for basketball players, and I had an appreciation for what he was doing in track. We always talked about conditioning trends, quickness, eye-hand coordination drills and how to best maximize the body.

I remember Dan telling me about the Olympics and what the Russians and Cubans were doing to elevate their heart rate during training. One of the things was running hills. It made sense. After all, that's why people raise or lower the level of resistance on a tread mill when working out. It demands a lot more of your body to run uphill.

In general, Dan was against running the stadium steps because of the pounding on the concrete and the wear and tear on body joints. He used to talk about how the Europeans were running hills and how the grass and dirt formed nature's cushion. I enjoyed listening to him, especially since I could relate to what he was saying. After playing on the macadam all my life, I realized my joints were paying for it.

During this time, I had some conversations with my head coach, Bill Cofield, about some of Dan's thoughts on out-of-season conditioning. As a basketball team, we were running the stadium steps twice a week. I can't say that I ever pushed making changes in our routine for basketball.

I didn't feel like we had the type of hill that we needed to make it work. Bascom Hill was considered but not viable because they wouldn't let us run on the grass, and taking the guys someplace else to run wasn't an option.

But I didn't stop thinking about Dan's recommendations.

Later on, I got to be good friends with Ed Nuttycombe, who took over the Badger track program from Dan. Ed and I had some fun together. One day, I was just returning from the Shell, where I had played five or six full-court games. We had won every one of them, and I was feeling pretty good about myself.

I'm telling Ed about the great workout I had, and he says, "Well, Bo, I've been working out, too. I've been doing this and that and I've been running five miles a day."

One thing led to another, and I'm wondering, "Ed, how many miles do you think I'm doing at the Shell during those full-court games?"

Together, we came up with a little formula, taking into account running from the top of the key to the top of the key — even though I'd drive to the basket at times and play defense on my man down toward the baseline — and we factored in how many times the ball was passed. We determined during a 90-minute pickup game, I was running maybe five to six miles. But Ed kept insisting that it was not like I was REALLY running.

The next thing I know, he's talking about entering a half-marathon in Mazomanie during their Wild West Days. "I'm getting in," Nuttycombe said. "Why don't you?"

Fair enough. I was curious enough to accept the challenge. I knew I was in pretty good shape from playing basketball. I was in my early 30s, and I hadn't reached the age yet where all of a sudden it gets a lot tougher to do things. I don't know what age most people realize that. But for me, it was in my late 40s.

So I got into the half-marathon with Ed and my brother-in-law, Greg Beirne. I ran in my basketball shoes since I didn't have any running shoes. And I was feeling pretty good until we got to the hills. I realized then what some of the other marathoners meant when they were talking about the hills on the course.

Why do runners dread a hill? Because it's an obstacle, a physical and mental obstacle when you run.

I filed away my Mazo experience along with what Dan and Ed had told me about running hills. That was supported by the information that I received while attending a Final Four. One of the guest speakers was a University of Oregon track coach, and he spoke about the value of running on grass versus road running.

It wasn't until a decade or two later that many people came to the same conclusion that cross country running and basketball weren't a match. They weren't compatible. Running five miles was not necessarily the best thing to do, not when short bursts and quick agilities were more beneficial.

Rope jumping is an example of quick agilities. The emphasis is on how quickly you get off the floor and you can develop some of that by working on your quick muscle twitch.

In basketball, the farthest you're going to sprint is 94 feet, the length of a court. You're not going to open up and run 400 meters or two miles. Once you get past that aerobic base in conditioning, you want to get to things that are anaerobic and tie in with change of direction and explosive movements.

You have to condition more specific to the sport. It doesn't make sense to train basketball players like cross country runners.

I filed everything away with the thought, "When I get to be a head coach someday, when I'm running my own program, this is one of the things that is going to happen: We're going to challenge our players by running hills in the preseason."

***

When we began running the hill my second year at Platteville, I wanted to make sure we weren't doing anything that wasn't conducive to what we needed to be doing on the basketball floor. In my mind, there was a correlation between running the hill and simulated game conditions. We're only going for about 30 to 40 seconds up the hill, so it's more about interval training, not unlike possessions in a game.

As you're climbing the hill, you're getting your pulse rate to go up, up, up. Coming down the hill, your pulse is still up. But you have some built-in recovery time. We had our players trot or long stride or even walk down the hill. Once they got to the bottom, boom, they're ready to start climbing again.

That's like a game situation when you go to the free throw line. What are you doing? You're standing and waiting for the sub to come in. You're waiting for the shot to be taken. And, then, boom, the rebound comes off the rim or the ball goes through the net and you're sprinting to the opposite end of the court, driving your pulse rate up.

I know some people might have looked at what I was doing in those early years at Platteville as a novelty thing by a first-time college head coach looking for some attention or his own niche. But I wasn't thinking along those lines. Instead, I wanted to make sure my players didn't get stale. I wanted to get them out of the gym.

If you really want to be a good player, think about all the hours that you spend inside, all the hours you spend in the gym during the summer. By running the hill, we were able to change their environment a couple of times a week. Plus, there's nothing like being outdoors in southwestern Wisconsin on a beautiful fall day.

Running the hill was one phase of a one-credit physical education class at Platteville that was open to everybody on campus. Every year we had about five or six students — non-basketball players — sign up for the activities, which also included weight training and pool workouts. To my knowledge, I was one of the first basketball coaches to incorporate aqua-dynamics into their out-of-season conditioning program.

I got pointed in this direction by Jack Pettinger, the former Wisconsin swim coach. Jack used to talk about the rigors of water polo and the type of athletes that it took to be successful in that sport. And he always felt that they might be the best conditioned in the world. What the swimmers were doing in the water — short bursts driving their pulse rate up — was not unlike what basketball players were doing on the court.

That stuck with me.

At Platteville, we went from the hill to the pool, which we shared with the local high school swimming team. We might start with eight hills and five minutes of running in place in the water. And we'd get up to 20 hills and 20 minutes. We had some guys who couldn't swim, so they wore vests or aqua belts.

I was an economics major in college, so I didn't know all the nuances to the workout. But I knew what my players were telling me. We were running Mondays and Thursdays and the guys wanted to make sure we got into the pool, not because they were looking to take it easy, but because they felt so much better afterward.

We weren't running a country club.

When you're in the deep end of the pool, and your feet aren't touching the bottom, you've really got to work hard to keep your head above water. You couldn't use swim strokes. But you had to keep your arms and legs pumping.

The first time I did the workout, I was in the water for 15 minutes and I felt like jelly when I got out of the pool. I'm thinking, "I'm on to something here. That's a freakin' workout."

Especially in combination with the hill.

(We inquired about continuing our pool workouts on the UW campus when we got to Madison but we couldn't book the use of a pool on a steady basis.)

Now for some guys, the hill was like treading water. Some were naturally better able to handle it than others. Some couldn't get enough of it. After the first day or week, they'd say, "Coach, what else do you have for me?" Others were like, "Whew, I'm glad that's over."

The hill weeded out some people.

But safety was always a priority, wherever I coached.

Alando Tucker was competitive as heck. And he was always in shape even though he couldn't run the hill the last few years at Wisconsin because of a stress fracture in his foot. It's important to remember Tucker didn't get injured while running at Elver Park in Madison. Tucker got hurt at the USA basketball trials and it wasn't diagnosed.

We did have a scare at Elver. (We settled on Elver Park, which is on Madison's far Westside, because our strength coach, Scott Hettenbach, felt like the steep sledding hill would meet our needs. My assistants, Robby Jeter and Saul Phillips, ran the hill, like they had at Platteville and Milwaukee, and agreed with Scott.)

Prior to his freshman season, Latrell Fleming blacked out while running the hill. But it could have happened anywhere — in a gym or on the playground. Latrell was diagnosed with a heart condition called hypertrophic cardiomyopathy. I've been told it's the number one cause of sudden cardiac death in people younger than 35. Trust me, I know how fortunate it was that Latrell's condition was detected before it was too late.

In high school, I played with Paul Williams, a Chester, Pennsylvania, native who was a year or two behind me. Everybody called him by his nickname, "Looty." Looty got a college scholarship to Mount Saint Mary's. He was playing in a pickup game there when he went for a drink of water and collapsed and died from cardiac arrest.

When I was recruiting for Wisconsin in the late '70s, I was looking at a kid in Georgia when another player on another team caught my eye. He really jumped out at me, so I watched tapes and saw him play again, and I liked him enough to sign him. His name was Charlie Hill. The summer before his freshman year, I got the news that Charlie collapsed and died after walking out of the gym following a pickup game.

Gabe Miller was a backup point guard on our undefeated 1995 national championship team at Platteville. He was maybe the most well-liked guy on the team, and one of the hardest workers. This was a kid who loved the game, loved to compete and was always positive to be around. One month after we won the title, Gabe was playing touch football when he became ill and had to be rushed to the hospital.

He died from a tear in his aorta.

Gabe was the type of young man who would put his arm around the ballboy and talk to him and play one-on-one with him. I know, because my sons, Will and Matt, happened to be ballboys, along with some Platteville youngsters. The boys were close to Gabe, so close that Will wore his jersey number, 12.

That was his personal response to a tragedy.

***

As coaches we're always asking the same question of ourselves and our athletes, "How are you going to respond?" In our world that's just part of being a competitor — how you respond to things that are happening around you. How do you respond to the hill? How do you respond to things in life? How do you respond to injustices?

I can't carry a jousting stick and go after windmills. But if I see something that I think is wrong, I'll fight it. My dad wasn't going to let anybody walk on him, and I picked up the fighting spirit from him. I'll fight for my rights and my players.

For instance, I was very disappointed with our draw in the 2008 Big Ten/ACC Challenge. When I learned that we were on the road for the second year in a row and the third time in four seasons, I felt it was a slap in the face to our basketball program, the university, and the fans of Wisconsin.

One of my assistant coaches, Greg Gard, handles our scheduling. Since we had traveled to Duke for the 2007 Challenge game, Greg built our '08-09 schedule under the logical assumption that we were going to get a home game at the Kohl Center. Instead, without any notice or discussion, we were sent on the road to Virginia Tech.

That was wrong and should not have happened. Especially since our seniors will have played three of their four Big Ten/ACC Challenge games on the road — at Wake Forest, Duke and Virginia Tech. They're telling us now that they're going to give us two Challenge games in a row at home. But that's only after we complained.

During our spring Big Ten meetings, scheduling was discussed and there was a push for better communication between the coaches, the administrators and the Big Ten office. When these decisions are made, they should be made sooner and on a more practical basis so players and fans get treated to an equal number of home and away games during a certain period of time — say a four-year window.

This is not the first time scheduling questions have been raised. During the '01-'02 season, Ohio State had to play four straight Big Ten games on the road. We got a piece of the Big Ten championship, but there's no way our radio play-by-play announcer Matt Lepay is doing his "For the first time in 55 years" routine if the Buckeyes didn't have to play at Wisconsin, Michigan State, Iowa and Indiana during that four-game stretch.

I told Jim O'Brien, who was then the Ohio State coach, that I would bring up the issue at the Big Ten meetings because I had a similar experience with the WIAC when I was coaching at Platteville. We were playing three and four games in a row on the road before it was brought to the league's attention and the rule was changed — as it has been in the Big Ten — to read that no more than two road games can be scheduled consecutively unless there's an emergency or the schools agree to the arrangement.

I've always believed that it's important to bring about some type of resolution when you're fighting for something. I have never shied away or backed down from a good fight when I felt like I had a good argument. That's the competitor in me. That's the way I grew up in Chester. I was driven by competition.

For instance, if somebody was doing something involving dexterity, like juggling, I'd go home and get some tennis balls or baseballs and teach myself how to juggle. I'd challenge myself if somebody could do something I couldn't do. And if somebody beat me at something, I wouldn't quit until I could beat them.

Just ask Chris Zwettler, one of my former assistants at Platteville.

Chris played basketball and golf for the Pioneers and was inducted into the school's Hall of Fame. He was a good athlete. But after he beat me in badminton, I kept working at the game until I got to the point where I could beat him.

It always came down to the same thing for me. Whether you were playing dodge ball, Monopoly or badminton, would you rather win or lose? Why would the other way even be an alternative? I've never liked losing.

That has always been my response.

***

There wasn't a scoreboard on the hill. But it was a good measuring stick. You've got guys pushing each other and competing. Unlike most basketball drills in the gym, it will not only tell you if someone is going hard, but whether they're going their hardest. The hill will help identify your leaders.

Let me give you an example.

When I was in the Army, we'd go on marches, and I was in charge of the platoon. I had to make sure everybody got back to the barracks. On one particular march at Fort Bragg, my bunkmate just couldn't go any farther. He was kind of a heavy-set kid, and you could tell he had hit a wall. He was exhausted.

So I grabbed his steel pod and back pack, and, with the help of others in the platoon, we got him back. That's what they do in the service. They put you in a tough situation, and they're going to see how you work your way through it, and whether you're going to leave any of your buddies behind.

Having somebody's back is part of being a leader. Same thing with the hill. You've got to make sure everybody gets through it. In these cases, you're always looking for your seniors to be leaders. If that meant they'd run extra hills to make the big guys feel better about what they were doing then that's what they would do, without being prodded.

Think about it this way: I'm the head coach, and I'm standing at the top of the hill and everybody has got to get to me. When I was that age, if it was my coach standing up there, I'd have made damn sure I got to him. There would be no way in the world that I would let him see me not complete the task. That's where teamwork comes in. Teamwork leads to trust — trusting each other — and trusting that what you are doing is right.

When I got to Milwaukee, after taking the UWM job, people kept asking me, "Bo, now that you've finally reached Division I, are you going to change your offense? Are you going to change your defense? Are you going to change how you coach? And, certainly, Bo, you're not going to run a hill here like you did in Platteville."

I'd just say, "Why change anything?"

"Well, this is Division I, not Division III."

I'd say, "Okay, I get that."

"And you're going to have to change your ways. Especially with the hill running because scholarship basketball players aren't going to run hills."

I'd say, "I'm not changing."

And I didn't, and our player response in Milwaukee was no different than it had been in Platteville. You want to play? Show me by the way you run the hill.

In coaching, I never worried about being at a certain level — Division I or Division III — whether it was high school or college. I never worried about where else I needed to be or should be. I always figured that if you're successful, then opportunities will present themselves and then you make a decision.

People say I've climbed some steep hills moving from level to level like I have as a coach. I know I've convinced myself that there really isn't a difference. It still demands discipline, it still demands conditioning, it still demands camaraderie, teamwork and playing off each other. And it's still about getting people to bond, and it's still about getting people to believe in what they're doing.

You can win games with less talent than maybe somebody else. But if you can get talent and have the same kind of closeness as a team, if you can still teach and mentor, you can do extraordinary things.

That was the case with the '07-08 season. I thought we could be solid, but I didn't know we could do 31 wins, including 16-2 in the Big Ten.

Getting them to believe was a part of it. But you can't keep telling people that Good 'N Plenty has licorice inside the hard coating, unless they get to taste it. The road win at Texas might have been our licorice.

That's what motivates me. That's what gets me fired up every morning to come to the Kohl Center. I want to see the faces of these young men and how they react when good things happen. And if they have difficulty with something, I want to be able to help them through it. You've got to give them some rope to get out on that ledge a little bit. And they need to climb, slip, stumble and pull themselves up. All the clichés.

Throughout the process, I'm not their buddy. I'm not one of those coaches who feels like he has to coddle his players. I'm not someone who's calling them up all the time on their cell phones or bringing them into my office for discussion. My approach and style is different, and it's a product of my upbringing.

As a player, I didn't feel like I needed somebody looking over my shoulder all the time. I took pride in trying to do the right things based on what I had learned from my mentors and teachers. My mindset was, "Tell me what you want and I'm going to give it to you. And if I need help, I know where to go."

I wasn't allowed to lack confidence as a high school or college player. More often than not, I was the one expected to take charge because the positions I had gravitated to — point guard, shortstop and quarterback — were take-charge positions.

As a coach, you're never allowed to lack confidence because your players will pick up on that in a heartbeat. Wavering or waffling is a great way to lose your team. The players have to believe in what you're doing, and if they're not sure, you have to keep working at it until you get them to believe.

That applies at every level.

Now if you're asking me if running the hill was a factor in winning national championships at Platteville or Big Ten championships at Wisconsin, I'm going to say it was about cultivating discipline and taking the right mental approach to a challenge. And if you can get your players to accept that in September and early October, you check that off your list, say "Next" and head off to the next hill.

CHAPTER ONE

Who's Got Next?

Playing defense in high school was often a numbers game for me. I guarded players who later had their jerseys retired, and hanging from the rafters. That was a reflection of the competition we faced in southeast Pennsylvania.

Chester was a tradition-rich basketball school in a sports-friendly community — 10 miles south of Philadelphia on the Delaware River.

Chester was the oldest city in the state and home to Joe Klecko, the old Jet; Danny Murtaugh, the old Pirate; and Bill Haley and the Comets, the old rockers.

I grew up listening to the Temptations, the Four Tops, Marvin Gaye, and Chubby Checker.

I grew up dancing the Twist, the Pony, the Mashed Potato, and the Bristol Stomp.

I grew up playing defense.

Playing for the Chester High Clippers, I drew the opponent's top gun, though I got help from my teammates, whether we were playing straight-up or a specialty defense. When we were in a box-and-one, I was the principal defender, man-to-man.

Our league schedule was challenging from that standpoint because of offensive threats like Upper Darby's Bobby Lloyd, who went on to have his college number retired. Lloyd was an All-American, and the all-time leading scorer at Rutgers University.

Outside our conference, I took on Geoff Petrie, who played at Springfield High School in Delaware County before moving on to Princeton. Petrie later had his number retired with the Portland Trail Blazers of the NBA.

(In case you're wondering, I wore No. 42 at home and No. 43 on the road, and the numbers are still available as far as I know. At least they didn't retire my jersey when I was still in it.)

When Chester played Cheltenham, a Philly suburb, their leading scorer demanded extra attention because he was so physically imposing. He was built like someone who had been bench-pressing all his life even though nobody was really lifting weights in the early '60s.

The guy was just chiseled, and he knew how to use his strength and athleticism to slash to the rim. He later had his number retired, too — No. 44 with the New York Yankees.

Reggie Jackson was a natural.

I was a junior when Jackson was a senior. Besides his obvious physical skills, he had a decent jump shot and an undeniable presence on the court. But back then there was none of the hype and marketing that high-profile athletes have today.

So it wasn't like we went into the Cheltenham game thinking, "Oh, no, it's Reggie Jackson." We didn't know who he was going to become. This was long before he became Mr. October with the Yankees.

But you could tell he was destined for fame in baseball. Sometimes things can get fabricated as you get older and you put distance between yourself and the event or moment. The truth can get stretched. But I know this for a fact: Reggie had prodigious power from the left side. He hit a ball against us at Cheltenham, and we all just turned and gawked at how far it traveled.

I don't know if it has come down yet.

Reggie Jackson had a Hall of Fame baseball career. But he went to Arizona State on a football scholarship. He was the best running back in our conference. Cheltenham beat us 33-0. Or something like that. I don't remember the exact score. I played safety, so I was the last guy who had a shot at tackling Jackson. I saved a couple of touchdowns. Not that it mattered. We were terrible.

Baseball was my hobby. Basketball was my passion. But I did love football. When I was 12, I played for my dad, Butch. When we moved to Chester Township, there wasn't a youth program. So he started up a league from scratch, the Aston Athletic Association. There were no uniforms and when the kids were told to bring helmets to practice, they'd show up with their father's hardhats from the shipyards or motorcycle helmets. It was a motley crew.

During the week, we'd practice on a field that was littered with rocks and bottles. I was reminded of the old turf recently when Wilkes College classmate, Joe Frappolli, who went on to become the winningest football coach in South Jersey history at Florence High School, gave me a "Rocks and Bottles" t-shirt. A lot of his kids had played on those types of fields, too.

When I got to high school, I played defensive back and quarterback. Like everybody else in the area, I pulled for the Philadelphia Eagles. My favorite players were Tommy Brookshier, the hard-hitting DB, and Norm Van Brocklin, the strong-armed QB. I really liked playing defense (which should come as no surprise considering my MO as a basketball player and coach). As a quarterback, I didn't have the big gun. And, like I said earlier, we didn't have much of a football team, either.

Chester was a basketball school, period. And that's what every kid grew up dreaming about playing. Ted Cottrell was one of the exceptions. Football was his game. In 1969, he got drafted out of Delaware Valley College by the Atlanta Falcons, and he played a handful of seasons in the NFL and Canada before getting into coaching. That's where he has made his mark as a pro — coaching over 20 years, including the last few seasons as the defensive coordinator of the San Diego Chargers.

Ted Cottrell was my offensive center for two years at Chester, and we were named co-captains going into our final year. But that's when I had to make a choice. Between my junior and senior year, I got the chance to attend a basketball camp on the "outdoor courts of summer" in the Pocono Mountains. The camp was run by Rutgers coach Bill Foster and Temple coach Harry Litwack. It was a big deal to get asked.

There was one problem. If I went to the basketball camp, I was going to miss the first day of preseason football practice. When I explained the situation to the Chester football coach, he responded by telling me that I had to pick one or the other. There was no middle ground. Either I committed to football or basketball. That hurt, because Dartmouth had shown some interest in me as a defensive back.

I even told the coach that if he wanted to punish me, I was more than willing to run extra sprints before and after practice. I'd show up and run at 5 or 5:30 in the morning, if necessary. Whatever he wanted me to do. But he wouldn't budge. There was no ambiguity in what he was saying: Miss practice, and you're off the team. I admired his conviction. He was upfront with me, and I was upfront with him.

(When I later became a high school coach, I had some players who wanted to skip practice so they could go deer hunting. I said, "In life we all have to make sacrifices and you have a choice. If you go deer hunting, I just hope you come to the games this season and cheer on your former teammates." They were all at the next practice.)

What was my choice? It was easy. From the time I was five years old, and my dad and uncle would take me to high school basketball games, my dream was to play for Chester and win a state championship. So I went to the basketball camp at the expense of not playing football as a senior. Every move I've ever made, I've always MADE it the right move. I've never second-guessed anything I've ever done.

It was the right decision.

***

I was born in Upland, Pennsylvania, which geographically was to Philadelphia what Middleton is to Madison, only you would never confuse Middleton for Upland, best characterized by the post-World War II housing for vets — the projects, the row houses and the "Pit."

Some called it a gym, but it was a pit. There were cinderblock walls and two baskets at each end of a concrete floor. They had to make sure the outside doors were latched in the winter, otherwise the wind would blow the snow inside. There wasn't any room for spectators. But there was a broken-down heater in a corner.

That's where my dad would put me. I'd sit on wooden planks above the heater during the pickup games that he would play with his buddies. I was about four years old and my dad would lift me down from the heater between games, and I'd grab a basketball and start bouncing it and dribbling it around. I'd try to get it up to the rim.

My dad was competitive and he had a great hook shot, which he picked up from watching Neil Johnston when he played in the '50s for the Philadelphia Warriors. Butch was a little over 6-feet tall, and that was fairly big for that era. He found a way to score in the post and his teams would win most of the time.

What I remember most about hanging around the Pit, though, was the dirt and all the dust. I'd get home and blow crud out of my nose for hours.

When we moved to Chester, we lived in a row house, where the side walls linked a string of like structures, one next to the other. Cookie-cutter architecture. There were a lot of us under the same roof, at least two families. I shared a bedroom with an uncle, sometimes a cousin. I didn't get my own room until we moved to Chester Township. But I never worried about what I didn't have. I was having too much fun seeing what I could have.

Chester was your quintessential blue-collar town populated by hard-working, tough people. You might use the word "hard-scrabble" to describe it. My dad would take me everywhere, whether he was playing touch football, softball or basketball. That exposed me to kids from different parts of the city and area. I never cared who I was playing with, either, and maybe that's where I learned to be aggressive.

"Hey, can I get a run?"

"Hey, can I play?"

That was a heckuva motivating factor for me. In the neighborhood, the older guys would play and you would have to wait your turn. But who the hell wants to sit around? That was my attitude, so I always wound up playing, even if I was the youngest. When I was 8, I was playing Little League baseball against 12-year-olds. In my first game, I was the lead-off hitter and during my first at-bat, I got beaned in the head with a pitch. It knocked me out. Thank goodness for helmets.

When I was that age, I'd hear it all the time, "Aw, kid, you're too small" or "Scram, you're too young to play." I wouldn't listen. All I needed was a chance. I learned how to catch and bat, and I could spray the ball around a little bit and get on base. It always came down to the same things: figure out a way to get on the diamond, figure out a way to get on the court, figure out a way to get on the football field. I hated the alternative — being a spectator. So, I figured out ways to get picked.

In elementary school, there were always arguments, especially if the 6th graders were on the court, and they wouldn't let the 5th graders play. It was a jungle out there — during recess. If you couldn't play basketball, you had to turn to other things. Like shooting marbles out of circles or flipping baseball cards against the wall. That even became competitive. I had the best collection of marbles and cards in the neighborhood. I had built up my inventory by winning, and some animosity developed.

Even in the fifth grade, the whole idea was, "I'm going to take what you've got — you wanted to get mine, and I wanted to get yours." If you won, you took their stash. And without cards or marbles, it was like losing money. You can't bet money you don't have. That's how we competed, and it was never for cash. It was along the lines of, "I'm trying to run you out of what you have, and trying to send you home with nothing because I know that's what you're trying to do to me."

As a result, it was not unusual to get into some fights on the playground. Especially since the kids who lost at cards or marbles would get a little perturbed, and that's putting it mildly. Remember, though, getting into a scrap with a classmate was not that big of a deal in the mid-to-late '50s. You'd fight — and I was rarely the biggest in the scraps — the playground supervisor would break it up and you'd wind up in the principal's office. My defense? I was just protecting what was mine.

On my Franklin Elementary School report card, I had straight A's and one D — the D was in conduct, playground conduct. That turned out to be a topic of discussion during one particular family gathering at an uncle's house.

Everyone was in the living room watching the *Friday Night Fights* sponsored by Gillette razors. My uncle thought it was funny I got a D for essentially fighting, and he made a correlation with a Carl "Bobo" Olson who was boxing in the next televised bout. (Olson was from Hawaii and the world middleweight champion for a few years in the mid-'50s.)

Out of the blue, my uncle started calling me "Bobo."

Everybody else did, too, over time. Up until then, I was Billy Ryan, short for William Francis Ryan, Jr. From that point forward, I was Bobo — later shortened to Bo. I'm grateful Sugar Ray Robinson wasn't fighting that Friday night.

The first time I went to the Palestra, I was 9 or 10, and I was answering to Bo, not Billy. My dad loves telling the story about how we were sitting next to the band and the tubas, and we stuck toilet paper in our ears to block out the sound. Butch has always contended that the Palestra was a life-changing experience for me because of my exposure to the intense atmosphere and so many star athletes who made a name for themselves there.

During its heyday, the Palestra was called the "Cathedral of College Basketball." It played host to more NCAA tournament games than any arena in the country. For years, it was the home floor for Philadelphia's Big 5: Penn, Saint Joe's, Temple, La Salle and Villanova. (Franklin Field, the home of the Eagles and the Penn Relays, was next door, adding to the rich history on South Street.)

As kids, we'd get to the Palestra early and stand on the baseline during warm-ups. We'd all compete for the basketballs that would roll or bounce off the floor. I would find a player and take care of him by rebounding his shots. He'd shoot, boom, the ball might bounce off another ball, I'd track it down and throw it back.

I watched players like Horace Walker, a Chester High grad, who went to Michigan State; Barry Kramer and Happy Hairston from NYU; Toby Kimball from Connecticut; and Bill Bradley from Princeton. One of the guys that I retrieved for was George Raveling, who played at Villanova and later coached at Washington State, Iowa and Southern Cal.

I got a good taste for the atmosphere in the Palestra.

And it planted a seed.

I wanted to play there.

***

Besides being a Billy and a Bo, I was also known as Biddy Bo. There are still guys who call me that today, including Mike Marshall, an old teammate and no relation to the Major League baseball player of the same name. Whenever we see each other or talk on the phone, it's always, "How ya doing, Biddy?"

The nickname stemmed from my dad, a legendary Biddy League coach, and the success that I had playing Biddy League basketball, which was the age-group equivalent (8 to 12) of Little League baseball. Instead of 10-foot baskets, they were lowered to 8 feet, 6 inches. It was a good way to learn important skills while also learning how to shoot with the proper techniques at reachable rims.

I was the leading scorer when I was 12. But I was never worried about scoring titles. If they had been keeping assists, I know my stats would have been among the best in the Biddy League. That was my job — to get my teammates involved. As I progressed through the ranks, from junior high to high school, I heard the same thing from my coaches, "Man, you can handle the ball. You're going to be my point guard."

I played one season with Mike Marshall on the same Biddy League team. Our sponsor was Guyer's Roofing. We were the starting backcourt when he was 12 and I was 11. We were also the starting guards for the Chester High Clippers when I was a senior and Mike was a junior. (I skipped kindergarten, which accounts for the difference in classes and the fact that at age 17, I was the youngest in my high school graduating class.)

As players, we both came of age at the "Cage."

There was nothing that could match the competition on 8th and Pennell Streets in Chester. That was the site of the Cage, a playground court with steel nets — when they were up — that was kind of a Mecca for ballers. Word spread quickly the day that Lew Alcindor (Kareem Abdul Jabbar) showed up for some action at the Cage. I wasn't there, but Mike Marshall remembers beating Alcindor in a best two-out-of-three. Walt Hazzard and Wally Jones were known to play there, too.

That's where it all started for most of us.

You went to the Cage hoping that you could get into games with the older high school players. By the time I got into the 10th grade, I was one of the guys choosing sides. I had grown to the height I am now: 6-foot. I may have been lacking in size, but I wasn't lacking in quickness. Plus, I had spent a lot of time working on my ball-handling skills. Some of my best teachers were the pros: Bob Cousy, Bill Sharman, Guy Rodgers and Paul Arizin. I loved watching Cousy.

During pickup games at the Cage, if you weren't on the winning team, you had to wait a minimum of a half-hour to play again. Nobody wanted to wait, especially me. You wanted to keep the court. That's where I learned to hate a popular card game in Chester called "Tonk." If you were on the losing team, you would sit at a picnic table and play Tonk — a fast-moving street rummy — until you got a chance to get back out there.

My only thought was, "Find a way to win."

That's when you start realizing what it takes to give yourself a chance to be successful. Most of the guys knew I could score because of my Biddy League reputation. But there's no question that I made myself more valuable at the Cage by passing the ball and playing defense. Nobody wants someone who's going to shoot all the time. There are ways to win pickup games. Don't take bad shots. Get the ball to the right people.

Along with the steals, that played to my strengths, there were times when I had to get into peoples' faces and say, "Hey, don't take that shot." I was never bashful talking to the guys that I was playing with. I'm sure some of them didn't appreciate it, but I had developed a reputation, and the thinking more often than not was "Let's get Ryan on our team."

I used to dive on the macadam without fear or hesitation, and I had scrapes all over my arms and legs. They probably thought I was crazy. But the ultimate compliment was getting picked to stay on the court after your team had lost: "Bo, stay, you're our fifth." I wasn't always the guy they picked. But I got my share of action that way.

Guys were always lined up to play at the Cage, and it was a big hustle. When I would step out of the car, the first words out of my mouth were always, "Who's got next?" That became part of the tradition, too. If you made the last shot, the game-winning shot, you'd go, "Next." It was not a cocky thing, but it didn't sit well with the losing players as they were walking off the court.

You won, they lost.

You're staying, they're leaving.

Next.

***

Ron Rainey moved me up to the Chester High School varsity after I had played three games with the jayvees my sophomore year. Coach Rainey was in his first season as head coach, and I was thrilled, knowing that if he was going to bring up a soph, he was probably going to start him. My timing was also pretty good, since Coach Rainey was actually supposed to take over the team a year earlier. But he was in the army reserves and got called away during the Berlin Crisis in 1961.

Coach Rainey inherited a Chester program that was on the rebound because of sanctions. In 1959, there was a stabbing incident outside the Palestra following the state championship game between Chester and Farrell. As a result, the Philadelphia Interscholastic Athletic Association banned Chester from post-season competition, which was a setback for the school.

But it wasn't enough to deter Coach Rainey from taking the coaching job. He was tough; physically tough. He lettered in basketball and baseball at Penn State. And when he played in some of the faculty games at Chester, you could see that he was a natural athlete. Years later, he kept his competitive edge on the racquetball court and was a nationally-ranked player.

Upper Darby beat us out for the conference title my junior year. That summer, I accepted the invitation to play at Foster's and Litwack's camp in the Poconos. Not only did I have to choose between basketball and football, but I had to earn the enrollment fee, $75.

I found some work as a carpenter's assistant and got the money. I still have my 1964 social security form that says I made about $400. After taxes, and paying for the camp, I didn't have much spending money. But it was worth it. I made the all-star team. Jim Valvano, who would later go on to coach NC State to a national championship, was a sophomore at Rutgers and one of the camp counselors. I think I impressed him with my hustle.

Since I wasn't playing football as a senior, I went to the YMCA every day during the fall months and played basketball. Coach Rainey was a member and we got into some pickup games together. I remember driving to the basket for what would have been the game-winning shot, and Coach Rainey hit me so hard that I bounced off the floor. He clobbered me.

But what the hell am I going to do or say? He's my coach. I couldn't believe what he did. I was stunned. Coach Rainey didn't say a word to me. He didn't have to. I got his message loud and clear: Nothing was going to come easy. Especially winning.

He was testing me, making sure I was going to bounce back up after getting knocked down. He also wanted to see if I was going to come up with excuses. After getting fouled, I didn't say anything. I took the ball out, and I tried to drive on him again. I shot and missed, and he scored two in a row at the opposite end and his team won. Afterward, he said "good game." That was it.

Coach Rainey was my guidance counselor, and he made sure that I was in the top level classes with all of the brightest students, many of whom were going on to Ivy League schools. He didn't want me slipping through the cracks. Instead, he was going to make sure I was challenged academically and got the most out of my high school education.

He saw something in me, and I've always appreciated that.

I was a doer. I always got involved. I was class president at Chester. It was a popularity contest, no question. And I was popular because I played sports. But I had also shown that I was willing to talk with the administrators. I could get things done and that was my persona by virtue, maybe, of the leadership and skill positions that I played. Everything revolved around competition. I never once came home on the bus after school because I was always practicing. I used to do my homework late at night.

Despite the hectic schedule, I was determined to get good grades because I was going to college, the first Ryan to do so. (I was the only boy in the family, and my older sister, Nancy, went through Chester and became a beautician. My parents felt so strongly about me getting a proper education that they pulled me out of elementary school because they didn't think I was getting challenged and enrolled me in Christian Day School. I was one of five students in the eighth grade, and by the time I got to high school, I felt very prepared to handle just about anything.)

Sports were my calling card. My senior year, Chester won the conference title in basketball. We went unbeaten. I was one of the starting guards, Mike Marshall was the other. We were a pretty good backcourt tandem. We were tough to press because we could both handle the ball, and the pressure. As a team, we were also very adept at applying full court pressure.

In the District One playoffs, we beat Woodrow Wilson High School in the quarterfinals. We played the game in the Palestra, my dream. That was 1965. Oh, my goodness, more than four decades later I still get emotional and feel goose bumps on my arms talking about that experience.

I always led the team on to the floor for warm-ups. When I came dribbling out of the tunnel, the Palestra was so loud I turned to my teammates and said, "Don't miss the backboard." I wasn't kidding, I was that pumped up.

We started off with a standard tip drill. I would throw the ball off the backboard and everybody would tip the ball in order until the final guy, who would tomahawk slam. We put on quite a show for the opposing fans because we had so many guys who could dunk.

(Imagine that irony. As a high school player, I captained a team of dunkers. As a college coach, I've had to listen to the experts rip us for a perceived lack of athleticism and dunkers.)

That first night we played in the Palestra, the fans were going nuts after one of our guys threw down a dunk from the free throw line. The other team, at the opposite end of the floor, was watching us go through warm-ups. Right then, we knew we had the advantage.

After beating Upper Perkiomen in the semifinals, we played Nether Providence for the district championship and won easily. At the awards banquet, Saint Joseph's coach Jack Ramsay handed out watches to each of the players. Coach Ramsay was a local icon. It was also special having Jack McKinney, a Chester native, present for the awards ceremony. He succeeded Coach Ramsay at Saint Joe's.

Going into the Eastern finals, we were 25-0 and taking on Steelton Highspire. Some were already looking ahead to a potential showdown for the state championship between Chester and Midland, a Pittsburgh suburb. Norm Van Lier and Simmie Hill played for Midland.

But our run ended one step short of the state finals. We lost 84-82 in overtime. In the closing seconds of regulation, I got a steal at mid-court and passed the ball ahead, and we had a chance to take the lead. But we had a player miss a dunk. There was some irony in that, I guess.

Next. What was next for me? Temple and Rutgers expressed some interest. But they weren't offering a full scholarship, just a partial. I still wasn't exactly sure what I was going to do when Coach Rainey was named the head basketball coach at Wilkes College.

"You want to visit Wilkes?" he asked.

"Wilkes? Where is it?" I replied.

I guessed near Scranton. I was close. Wilkes was in Wilkes-Barre. I kind of knew the cities in the area, but I didn't know much if anything about the school. And that's because they weren't winning in basketball, which is why they had a coaching opening and they came after Coach Rainey.

In the end, I earned a leadership grant to Wilkes, which I was very proud of, and that took care of most of my expenses. I felt comfortable going there knowing Coach Rainey was the coach. One of my Chester teammates, Reuben Daniels, was going to be my roommate.

There was one more selling point for Wilkes College.

I could play as a freshman.

CHAPTER TWO
Wilkes and GI Bo

Before the start of my freshman year at Wilkes College, I had a stock answer whenever anybody wanted to know what I was doing for the summer.

"I'm working at the Sealy Posturepedic factory," I said.

"That's a mattress company."

"Yeah, I know," I'd tell them. "I'm testing mattresses."

I'd pause and add, "I'm sleeping on them."

I think some people actually believed me.

But I was a packer, and it was hard work, believe me, especially since you had to handle the box springs a certain way so you didn't rip the covering. If you weren't getting them off the rack fast enough, your co-workers had to wait. I would never let that happen. That's where my stubbornness and persistent nature comes in. I wasn't going to keep anyone from making money.

Including me.

For two years, I made really good money because I had one of the best summer jobs that any college student in the Philadelphia area could have. I worked at the shipyards as a tank tester. My job was to make sure everything was marked properly in the inner bottoms for the burners, chippers and welders.

It wasn't so much the physical labor that made it so demanding or stressful. It was that you wanted to make sure you didn't miss anything because you didn't want the ship to sink — a little thing like that. So I was always moving as fast as I could. I used my speed to try to impress these grizzled old guys, these long-time employees. Until one day when I got the word.

"You're in college, right?" one of my co-workers asked during a break.

"Right."

"You'll be done here the end of August, and then you'll be going back to school, right?'

"Right."

"You know where we're going to be?"

"Probably working here."

"Right," he said. "We're going to be working here, and we all want to be working here for a long time. So if you don't slow your ass down ..."

He let that sink in before continuing.

"Well, let me put it this way," he went on. "If you don't change your habits and slow down, it's amazing some of the things that can happen to a person around a shipyard."

Sleeping with the fish — not sleeping on a mattress — came to mind.

I understood what he was saying. For these workers, the shipyard was the meal ticket, and they wanted to be working for a long time. It had nothing to do with not wanting to work hard. But whereas I wanted to build the ship in a day, they wanted to stretch out that paycheck. It was more about, "Let's make sure we're doing this right. We're not in a hurry. We need this job."

In piece work, you get paid by the number of inches of weld or how many burns you make or how many inches of metal you chip. That's when everybody appreciates guys who are fast. There was a time and a place when certain things had to happen for a launch at the shipyard and piece work was involved, and you're paid by the piece, not the hour.

This was not one of those times or places.

I got the message.

In coaching, I learned early that you have to understand everybody's motives. Everybody wants to be on a successful team. But with some individuals, it's all about their work ethic, or their play, or their performance. That's what they're most concerned about. Same with the welders, the chippers and burners. Some wanted to do more than others.

I've always appreciated talent, and the shipyard was full of skilled and talented people whose work was judged on quality. I got to see the end result and I was really impressed by how well everyone did their jobs. I can't remember being around too many slackers. We're talking about blue collar workers and American ingenuity at work.

I learned a valuable lesson.

***

My dad always thought I'd make a great Philadelphia lawyer. Butch meant it as a compliment, which I believe was the original intent of the phrase. Today, it has taken on a less than complimentary meaning, although clever and crafty are generally still part of the definition. To me, a Philadelphia lawyer is somebody who can talk himself into or out of, anything.

Funny thing is, when I was in junior high, I was asked, "What's your ambition?" Mine was to be a lawyer. I was always intrigued by doing the right things, and punishing those who didn't. I wasn't thinking about being a trial lawyer — a prosecutor or a defender. I just knew the law was important. It was there for a reason, and it needed to be upheld.

At that age, I was known to be a pretty good debater.

We did some pro/con debates in a public speaking course and the teacher remarked how passionate I was about things when I felt like I was right. I didn't yell to get my point across. I didn't get mad. I just kept hammering away at my opponent.

I still remember her saying, "Because you didn't get upset or flustered even though you felt strongly about what you believed, you didn't let the debate get away from the facts. There was emotion, but not fanaticism, and you were respectful of the other person's opinion."

That matches my treatment of basketball officials.

Most of the time.

When I got to Wilkes College, my interest in the law had waned and I was planning on majoring in accounting. Back then, though, do you know what an accountant did? He sat behind a desk with a pencil in his hand. Times have changed.

But the more I thought about accounting — the time-consuming and tedious compilation of numbers — the more I thought it was not a fit for my personality, so I got into economics and marketing because you could pick areas of concentration.

I've always been fascinated with our system of government and how capitalism and the economic system work. I was infatuated with the concept of supply and demand and people being rewarded for working hard. I was hooked on those ideas through my competition in sports.

I saw the carryover. Like a team, if you're fundamentally sound in your business practices, you can be successful. To this end, my focus academically was on business administration and economics. Wilkes was a good school, and it was a challenge.

Athletically, it was also a challenge because the basketball had been so bad there before Ron Rainey took over. They had won only a handful of games the previous season.

I didn't start every game as a freshman. But I knew that I could compete at that level of competition because of my high school and playground background in Chester.

As freshmen, Reuben Daniels and I weren't overconfident. But we were confident enough that we could contribute to a college team like Wilkes. And we weren't mistaken.

The hardest thing to deal with was losing.

Especially that first year.

On top of the basketball, I was adjusting to the campus experience. In this context, I was out of my element. Reuben and I were first-generation college students, and we found ourselves going to class for the most part with people whose parents had some college background. Many of our classmates had come from boarding schools or prep schools.

It was a totally different environment.

I imagine that first year also had to be frustrating for Coach Rainey. But you wouldn't know it by the way he handled us. Taking his lead, we just tried to play and get better, which we did.

What was it like to be coached for seven straight seasons — three at Chester and four at Wilkes — by the same person, Coach Rainey? I don't know what to say other than there was a comfort zone from the basketball perspective. I knew what Coach Rainey expected out of us, and me.

Defensively, at times, we would hang our hat on the 1-2-2 zone. It was a matchup before people were labeling it as such. I was at the top of the defense and when the ball went to the baseline, I fronted the low post. Guarding big people was nothing new for me, though.

Neither was the way Coach Rainey managed a team because he was a lot like my dad. I heard the same things from both: "Don't make excuses. Play hard. Give it your best effort. Be accountable." That was drilled into my head.

Coach Rainey had a plus and minus system, awarding plusses for scoring, assists and hustle. You could get minuses for turnovers and missing free throws and things like that.

When I became a head coach, I never used that system. I didn't want players worrying about statistics. I wanted them concerned about contributing in any way possible and focusing on what's next. I didn't want them reflecting on what they had done. People can sometimes get too caught up in the numbers, and they don't develop a feel for the game.

There was nothing intricate about Coach Rainey's system. Trust me, it was pretty basic at Chester and Wilkes (and that's why I've never worried about being too elaborate myself). Coach Rainey was big on conditioning, especially running sprints at the end of practices.

I was the type who would never let anyone beat me in anything — in any type of drill or sprint. I remember Coach Rainey running us one day at Wilkes and asking, "Are you guys tired yet?"

Some guys were getting tired. My only thoughts were, "Hey, you've got to be tougher than this. Whatever he gives us, we can handle. He's definitely not going to break me."

Famous last words.

I kept running and running until Coach Rainey realized I couldn't run any more. I couldn't do another sprint, and so he waved it off and had us move on to something else. I think he was protecting me from passing out. But he made his point to me and the team.

Coach Rainey was smart — street smart and book smart. He was also very perceptive. When he was at Chester, the students even saw him as "hip." He knew what was going on, even though he had a 1950 haircut in the mid-'60s.

At Wilkes, he kind of befriended me and Reuben since we were the Chester Trio and all in it together. If I needed to talk to Coach Rainey about something, his door was always open. Except I'm not that type of guy. I'm a very private person and I've been that way for as long as I can remember.

By the time I got to my senior year, I could see the improvement in the program. By then, Reuben Daniels had transferred to Cheyney State, a college division II program, where he played on a national championship team. Besides losing Reuben, we had a couple of other players from the Philly area — really good recruits — leave because they just didn't like Wilkes. That hurt.

I still loved the game of basketball. But it didn't have the same feel as it had for me at Chester High School. The biggest disappointment at the time was that we didn't have a chance to play for a championship at Wilkes College. But we did get the program turned around.

We kept getting better. That was a positive.

My senior year, I had one of those nights against Susquehanna, a school about 50 miles north of Harrisburg. The game was originally scheduled to be played on my birthday, December 20, 1968. But it was postponed because of a snow storm. The makeup was played in February and I scored 43 points.

Near the end of the game, Coach Rainey took me out and yelled at me for passing too much and NOT shooting. I fell a few points short of the school single-game scoring record and my dad brings it up to Coach Rainey at every Final Four.

I saw a box-and-one defense the next time we played, and I'm laughing inside the whole game. I finished with about seven points and we just destroyed the other team. After scouting us against Susquehanna, they probably thought I was going to take most of the shots. That wasn't my game. I've said it before and I'll say it again: I never worried about points, I worried about winning.

That spring, the spring of '69, I interviewed with oil company ARCO (Atlantic Richfield), and I felt like I really nailed it. That summer I got my draft letter. Not the NBA draft, the military draft. While some were groaning, moaning and throwing pity parties for themselves, I said, "All right, this is what I've got to do, so let's get it done." I definitely thought I was going to Vietnam.

***

My first stop was Fort Bragg, North Carolina. I was there for eight weeks, and I'll never forget the motivating technique used by a drill sergeant there. "If you don't do this and this and this," he barked at us while we were going through the obstacle course, "you're coming home one way — in a body bag." That was his central theme; his only theme.

"If you can't keep your weapon clean, you're coming home in a body bag," he would reiterate. "If you can't keep your mess kit from contaminating, you're going to get food poisoning and you're going to come home in a body bag."

We all thought the same thing: we're in the army now.

My next stop was Fort Gordon in Augusta, Georgia, where I was sent for advanced infantry training. That's where I stayed until I got out of the service in 1971. My grandfather was a decorated soldier in World War I. My dad was a bronze star winner in World War II. And I was prepared to go where they told me. I assumed I was going to Vietnam, and I was ready. But I didn't get the call.

How it happened that way, how it played out that way, I'm not sure. My buddies and I would just look at each other and shrug. How did we avoid going to 'Nam? It was kind of like how they schedule teams for the Big Ten-ACC challenge. It was a mystery.

While I was at Fort Gordon, I went to military police school and I won the pistol competition for the battalion. Fortunately, I never had to pull my gun after I was assigned to the 140th company. A few times we had to go into town to bring back guys who had had too much to drink but that was the extent of our "combat."

Throughout my Army commitment, I played basketball every chance I had. During basic training at Fort Bragg, you were limited on what you could keep in your foot locker. But I found some loose boards underneath the barracks and that's where I stashed away a T-shirt, gym shorts, some socks and a pair of shoes — my Chuck Taylors.

We'd get into some pretty competitive games on the post. It was almost like "old home week" because I ran into guys who I had played against in high school and college. After each game, I'd rinse out or wash my stuff at the gym and put it back under the barracks for safe keeping.

When I got to Fort Gordon, we had more freedom to do things. And after I got stationed there as an MP, my goal was to get on the base team, which traveled and played teams from other bases. There was one glitch. I went from the military police to being a correction specialist — my new assignment was to work with the prisoners in the stockade and try to get them back to active duty.

Since there weren't many of us with that title, the commanding officer wouldn't let me play on the team. It made sense. The Army wasn't going to put me through extra schooling and train me to be a correction specialist and then let me play basketball on their time. But it was frustrating. I'm not saying I was that good of a player, but I know I could have played on that team.

But it didn't happen.

Basketball was taken away from me for the first time in my life, and there was a void. I don't know that I had an epiphany. But I do know that I missed the competition, the organization, the camaraderie; everything associated with the sport. And that's when I really decided for the first time that I wanted to teach and coach.

***

ARCO had a job waiting for me when I got out of the Army, but I had made up my mind. I was going back to school to get my teaching certificate; my first step to becoming a coach. My mom was working in the business office at Widener College in Chester, and that's where I enrolled. It used to be known as the Pennsylvania Military College, but it's referred to as Widener University today.

To stay active, I was still playing in pickup basketball games when a couple of guys I knew from Chester asked me to play on a touch football team. I was a defensive back, and one of the receivers that I covered in practice was shifty. He had been an outstanding track athlete at Saint Joe's.

But nobody knew, then, that Vince Papale would turn out to be a living legend, even invincible.

Papale made the jump from touch football — and bartender and substitute teacher — to professional football. He got his first break in the old World Football League and that's how he caught the attention of head coach Dick Vermeil and the Eagles.

Papale, who never played college ball, was a 30-year-old rookie when he made his mark with the Eagles and he went on to be their special teams captain and inspirational leader.

His personal history ended up on the big screen.

While I was at Widener College, I took quite a few history courses. I've always been interested in the origin of things, and I wound up getting my teaching certificate in social sciences.

It really didn't matter to me what I taught — history, world culture, geography, or psychology. I was just anxious to get started on a career path. I didn't have to wait long.

The second semester of that year, the spring of '72, I was doing my student teaching at Northley Junior High School in Aston, when I got an offer to be a history teacher and the head basketball coach at Brookhaven — a small burg in Delaware County, Pennsylvania — whose junior high school was in the Penn-Delco school district.

I jumped at the offer.

I was paid $4,000. That included coaching basketball and baseball — as an assistant — as well as my teaching salary. I taught world cultures and American history, pre-1895. On the court, I taught the importance of taking care of the ball. How do you get more shots? Get on the offensive glass and limit turnovers. That was my emphasis from the start.

Brookhaven had to play against the four Chester junior high schools, which made it tough. We didn't have a very big team, but we had some scrappers. The program had not been very good in the past. But you could see positive things happening during the year and I knew we could get better.

As a first-time coach, I was looking to get better, too.

I remember going to a basketball clinic in southeastern Pennsylvania and listening to a college head coach talk about the principles behind playing winning defense — the positioning, the help, the concept of playing five versus three. He also talked about screening and cutting on offense, but his focal point was defense, and he influenced me into changing my thinking.

I went from coaching some zone and trapping defenses to coaching solid, man-to-man defense. I didn't get a chance to visit one-on-one with the coach at the clinic, but evidently he had done pretty well at Army because he was now coaching at Indiana.

Bob Knight impacted a lot of young coaches.

I was one of them.

***

Lincoln University was located in southern Chester County, and I knew two guys who played basketball there for Bill Cofield. They would turn out to be my link to Coach Cofield, who went from coaching at Lincoln, an NAIA school, to Prairie View A&M to the Dominican

College of Racine.

In 1973, Bill Cofield made history by becoming the first black athletic director and head coach in the country to oversee a department and a program at a predominantly white school, Dominican.

In the midst of assembling his staff, he contacted two of his former Lincoln players and offered them the opportunity to be an assistant basketball coach and the head coach of the baseball team in Racine. Both turned him down. One had just gotten married and taken a job with a company and wasn't interested in relocating. The other had also just taken a good-paying job and was in the process of starting a family. Both recommended me to Coach Cofield.

I was teaching at Brookhaven when I got summoned to the principal's office for a phone call. It was Bill Cofield. The class bell rang, and we were still talking basketball and his plans for Dominican. The principal tells me to stay put and he gets another teacher to cover for my next class. The bell rings again, and I'm still on the phone with Coach Cofield.

Principal Bruce Williams again covered for me. He was a former basketball coach, and he was the one who hired me at Brookhaven. When I finally hung up, he asked me, "Well, what are you going to do?" He knew Coach Cofield wanted to talk to me about coaching with him.

"I'm intrigued," I said.

"How much are they offering you?"

"About $10,000."

"You've got to take it."

I appreciated that. Instead of trying to hold me back, the principal said, "Hey, you're too good to stay here. You've become restless and you've got to go and check this out."

I took the job, but I had no idea the school was so close to bankruptcy.

We couldn't compete at the NAIA level with nearby UW-Parkside which had a great team and a great player, Gary Cole. Cole would later play in the NBA as Abdul Jeelani. We had some pretty good players, but it was all about the freshmen and we finished one game below .500 for the season.

At the end of February, we got the word that the school was going under and only faculty would be paid for the rest of the year. That excluded Coach Cofield's position and my position.

I met with my baseball team — we had been running and

conditioning and hitting in the cage — and I told the players, "Look, I've made a commitment to you, and you've made a commitment to me. I'll coach for nothing. I'm not worried about the fact they're not going to be paying me."

The school thought I would take a hike, and they could just drop baseball.

"Even though I'm not getting paid, I'm not going to treat you any differently," I warned the players. "This isn't going to be some club team and we're not just going to all hang out together at the diamond. On the contrary, we're still going to work hard and play to win."

In preparation for the baseball season, we worked on cutoffs and pickoff plays and all the little things that would help our fundamentals. We hung in there with our opponents, too. We bunted a lot, we made teams field and throw and we probably won some games we weren't expected to win. We definitely competed with everybody, and I was even named Coach of the Year.

But there was an odd juxtaposition to the season — when I wasn't coaching the Dominican College baseball team, I was standing in line, collecting my unemployment checks. I had to eat.

In April, I was contacted by Sun Valley High School in Aston, Pennsylvania and offered the head basketball job. They were going to pay me $12,000, a $2,000 raise. That helped since I was working for two now.

Right after I got to Racine, I met Carol Kelly, a Chicago girl, who was working as a secretary in the Dominican College athletic department. It was the 4th of July weekend and everybody else had abandoned the campus, when I heard some pebbles against my dorm window.

It was Kelly (she adopted her surname as her first name) and a girl friend and they wanted to know what I was doing. It falls short of Romeo and Juilet — none of the dorms had balconies — but the three of us hung out and just talked that night on the lakefront.

I started seeing more and more of Kelly. You could tell there was some chemistry between us. She loved basketball, she really did. She knew the game, and she could shoot free throws. I was the only guy who could beat her. That's what she claimed. I don't know if she let me win or not.

I do know that we hit it off. As a bachelor, I was known to be very picky. I enjoyed my independence, my freedom, if you will. I was footloose and fancy free. But once I met Kelly, those days were over. She was the person I was looking for — the person I wanted to have a family with, the person I wanted to spend the rest of my life with. I could just tell.

I proposed that fall. I said something romantic like, "If you're not doing anything next summer, how 'bout we get married?" So maybe it wasn't Ryan O'Neal and Ali MacGraw in *Love Story*.

But she said yes, and we got married in Chicago the second week of June. A few days later, we spent the second half of our honeymoon on the road, pulling a U-Haul to Aston and my new job at Sun Valley High School. We were financially set: I had my last unemployment check and we were hauling a bedroom set, the extent of our furnishings.

Seriously, I didn't need much and Kelly was low maintenance.

The first thing I did when we got to Sun Valley was get the kids playing in a summer league, so they knew, "This guy is committed, this guy means business."

I wanted to be a teacher and a coach and that's what I was. I taught a comparative political systems class and psychology to some kids who were there only because the law made them go to school. How did I handle them? If you're going to be with somebody for 55 minutes and you're the teacher, you figure out a way to get their attention.

I enjoyed teaching because you can make a difference. You've probably heard the old story about the CEO who made a lot of money and the teacher who didn't. The CEO's inference was, "If you can't do, you teach." So why would you put trust in anybody who would have a lifetime goal of wanting to be a teacher? Especially since the money was so bad.

"You want to know what I make?" the teacher posed to the CEO. "I can make a kid read, I can make a kid read some more, I can make a kid be accountable for being on time and for getting his lessons done. I can make a difference in a kid's life. That's what I make."

That's the way I've always felt. I enjoyed the challenge of teaching when I was in my twenties, and I'm 60 now and still enjoy it. I enjoy getting through to people to the point where they understand that if they want to be part of something special, there are things that they have to do, and dues that they have to pay. But they will be rewarded for their effort in the end.

I grew as a coach at Sun Valley. I got better. That's when videotape was coming into vogue and we taped all the time.

My players weren't very big or tall. They were all around 6-2, so we pressed all the time. I didn't have anybody who was drawing college recruiting traffic. But we had some depth and got to the state tournament. Chester won the league, and we were the wild card.

The first time I coached against Chester — 10 years after I had graduated from the high school — it was really different because it wasn't the same school. It was a new high school, a new gym. As I expected, it was a very competitive game, even though we lost.

While I was at Sun Valley, I was taking administration classes at Villanova. I used to tell Kelly, "I'll coach high school basketball for 20 years and then I'll be a high school principal."

Throughout this period, I stayed in touch with Bill Cofield. After leaving Racine, Bill had hooked on as an assistant with Terry Holland at the University of Virginia. Bill had always told me that when he got another head coaching job, he'd want me as an assistant.

That day came sooner than I thought. "Bo, I just interviewed for the University of Wisconsin job," Coach Cofield informed me over the phone. "Are you ready?"

"Of course," was my eager reply. "I've got my bags packed."

The Sun Valley superintendent tried to talk me out of it.

"This is your second team here and you have some good players coming up," he rationalized. "For two years, you've been building this program. Why would you leave now to take a college job as an assistant when you're a head coach with such a bright future?"

I was almost speechless.

Almost.

"You don't understand, it's the University of Wisconsin," I stressed. "It's the Big Ten."

"Well, guess what? They fire coaches in the Big Ten," the superintendent countered. "You can have the job at Sun Valley for the rest of your life."

"I'm not looking for any security," I replied. "I've got a chance to coach in the Big Ten. I've got a chance to coach against teams I've been watching play on television. I'm going to Wisconsin."

As I was walking out of his office, he had one last thing to say. "You're making a big mistake. I don't think you know what you're doing. You don't know what you're getting yourself into."

Did I know?

I thought so.

But, then, everybody says that.

CHAPTER THREE

Ferociously Persistent

People thought I was crazy.

That was the consensus in the Philly area.

I said Wisconsin, and they said it all.

"Bo, you're going where?"

"Bo, did you say WES-con-sin?"

"Bo, you are definitely crazy."

It was not like Wisconsin basketball had much of a national profile, if any at all in those days. Especially on the East Coast, though the Philadelphia 76ers did take the Badgers' Al Henry in the first round of the 1970 NBA draft. Still, Wisconsin was off most radar screens.

Even my friends wondered if I was doing the right thing because they had heard some of the same things I was hearing: "There's no way that you can win at Wisconsin." That's what people wanted you to think.

I never thought that way.

On March 17, 1976 — St. Patrick's Day — I signed my contract at Wisconsin.

I was going to make $16,000, an upgrade from the $11,800 I was making at Sun Valley High School. I thought I had it made, too, until I saw the price of housing in Madison. But having been in the Army, I didn't have to put a penny down.

We bought the yellow house on the corner of Tokay and Segoe on Madison's far Westside. It cost $42,000.

To this day, I still have a souvenir from my first summer in Wisconsin as a Badger assistant coach — four capped teeth. In honor of Bob Uecker, they're all in the front row.

Along with the coaches from the various other sports, I was in

Monroe for a two-day Badger outing that included golf and plenty of good cheer. The Kublys, the founders of the Swiss Colony company (think: cheese products) and huge Wisconsin fans, had a basketball gym in their home and naturally that's where I ended up.

It started off harmlessly enough — a full-court, five-on-five pickup game. But it definitely ratcheted up competitively and when I went up and blocked a shot on a guy who was driving to the basket, he swung out his arm and knocked me down. My head bounced off the floor.

The damage?

Four chipped or broken teeth.

One tooth pierced my lip.

A football assistant coach, Chuck McBride, got me some ice for my mouth and jaw. Despite some swelling, I still played golf the next day, which endeared me to McBride, a tough son-of-a-gun who had just been promoted from the offensive line to defensive coordinator under John Jardine.

It was nice to have McBride on my side.

We needed all the allies we could find in basketball.

Winning at Wisconsin wasn't easy.

It still isn't easy.

For that matter, it isn't easy winning anywhere in college basketball.

But when Bill Cofield took over the program here in the mid-'70s, we were getting hammered on the recruiting trail — making it even more difficult to succeed.

Recruiters from other schools would talk about how our facilities were outdated. Or how we hadn't won in basketball and there was no commitment to the sport. Or how Wisconsin was a hockey and football school, not a basketball school.

I didn't buy any of it.

Shoot, I felt we had something to sell.

"You've got a chance to play in the Big Ten," I'd tell recruits. "You've got a chance to play at a high level of competition, not only within the conference but outside. Especially since we are upgrading our schedule. Most importantly, you've got a chance to get a degree from a prestigious institution like the University of Wisconsin."

Recruiting was about selling and commitment. There was a method and a madness to it all. You can recruit for positions; focusing on point guards or small forwards or whatever. But you are competing against the other schools, and you don't always get a yes and that can create a roster void in one area or another.

Since we were starting from a little bit further behind at Wisconsin, we had to run a little faster. But you had to be genuine because people can tell when you're not. What else does a good recruiter have to be?

You have to be ferociously persistent.

What do I mean by that?

When I was a kid in Chester, I used to go door-to-door selling greeting cards. It was a way to earn some money to buy the things that I couldn't otherwise afford. If you sold x-number of boxes, you got to pick a gift from a catalog. No matter how many doors were shut in my face, I was persistent enough to earn a camera.

I don't give in easily.

As a recruiter, I was the same way. I was persistent. But I tried not to be overbearing. I wasn't that penny that just kept turning up (you know the old saying). I was that coach who made sure the prospect knew that I really wanted him.

Joe Chrnelich and Bob Jenkins were the first players I recruited who said yes.

Given the timing of our arrival as a staff at Wisconsin — mid to late March — we were playing catch-up against schools that had already done most of their groundwork. And that led to no's from Glen Grunwald, who went to Indiana, and Ronnie Lester, who went to Iowa.

South Milwaukee's Kurt Nimphius and Beloit's Bill Hanzlik were also already locked up. Nimphius went to Arizona State and Hanzlik to Notre Dame. The word was that Chrnelich was going elsewhere, too, after leading Milwaukee Pius to back-to-back state championships. "Joe, you need to be here," I said. "You need to be in red and white."

I kept telling him that he was special, and he was. He had special toughness. Iowa and Oregon were recruiting him. But I don't think he wanted to go far from home. That also held true for Jenkins, who scored 33 points for Milwaukee Washington in a state tournament game.

I thought it was a positive for our program to get two kids from Milwaukee. Coach Cofield had ties to a couple of players from the East Coast: Clyde Gaines from Baltimore and James (Stretch) Gregory from Washington, D.C. And they made up our first recruiting class.

The next year, we got a shooting guard, Dan Hastings, from Drexel Hill, Pennsylvania (just up the road from Chester); a quick point guard, Wes Matthews, from Bridgeport, Connecticut; a big center, Larry Petty, from Power Memorial in New York City; and a power forward, Stretch's brother Claude Gregory, from Washington, D.C. That class got high marks from the recruiting analysts.

When I was coaching at Sun Valley, we scrimmaged against Hastings and Bonner High. He was his team's most valuable player, and all-Philadelphia. He played in several all-star games, including the Dapper Dan Classic in Pittsburgh, the pre-eminent game in the country prior to the McDonald's high school showcase.

Matthews was the MVP of the 1977 Dapper Dan.

We almost landed two in a row.

Bruce Atkins, a 6-7 forward from Wilkinsburg, Pennsylvania, was a heckuva player and the MVP of the 1978 Dapper Dan. I had developed a great relationship with the kid, and we thought it was a done deal. But he was only 17 and his mom refused to sign the letter of intent. When we made the home visit, his mom wouldn't even come out of the kitchen. She refused to talk with us.

Atkins went to Duquesne University in Pittsburgh. He was one that got away — that year. That's the nature of recruiting. You're going to lose some every year. When I was younger, I tried to dance with some ladies who said no. In either case, you go after the 10s first and you probably end up dancing with a few 5s and 6s.

Nevertheless, I tried to make it real tough for someone to say no — knowing full well that some would. I developed personal relationships with the players and made it a practice to under-promise and over-deliver. I didn't think it was right to promise something that I couldn't guarantee.

***

Recruiting rules have changed significantly over the years. I might have been one of the guys that influenced some of the changes, like the number of phone calls that you can make to a recruit.

There were no limits in the '70s and I was calling guys all the time. Not at 3 in the morning, mind you, but I just kept working the phone. I kept a notebook on each kid. That was part of my system. When I called, I wrote down what we talked about. So let's say he tells me, "Coach Ryan, my sister broke her leg," or maybe he says, "My mom is starting a new job."

I would jot that down in my book and the next time I would call that recruit, I'd say, "I really want to talk to you about why you should be at Wisconsin. But, first, why don't you tell me how your sister is doing. Is the leg getting better?" Or I'd ask, "How is your mom enjoying her new job?"

When you have so many different conversations with so many different prospects, it can be easy to forget what you talked about unless you had it written down. That's why I have always asked all of my assistants to keep track of what's going on within the family. Remembering information is extremely important in the recruiting process.

One of my strengths has always been paying attention. I know how it affects me when somebody calls and is working to sell me something and he says at the beginning of our conversation, "Hey, Bo, you know the last time we talked, you were headed to a golf outing. How did you do?"

That always leaves a favorable impression — knowing the other person is actually listening to what I am saying. Was I good on the phone? I'm a Philly guy. Of course I was good. My mom was very quiet, but my dad was outgoing and had the gift of gab. I inherited those traits from him.

Some things never change in recruiting. Like the fact that the recruit's mother is always the key and you have to reach out to her. I always treated dads with respect, too, and I would always "X and O" with the high school coach. I'd say, "Do you have an out-of-bounds play for me?" or "What's your favorite offense against this type of zone defense?"

I never talked down to anybody. I never took them for granted. I'd make sure they knew, "I was a junior high coach and a high school coach and I might be in the Big Ten now as an assistant coach, but I don't know any more basketball than you do."

When you were the leg man on the road, you also had to make contact with the high school janitor or custodian because they would always tell you what was going on.

In this same vein, I'd always go into the corner grocery store or gas station and buy some gum or a soda. I made sure I got to know the people behind the counter. Back then, we wore three-piece suits. And that was much different than it is today when you can advertise with your school logo on your breast pocket.

"I'm Coach Ryan from the University of Wisconsin," I'd tell the person at the counter when I was making a purchase." When I stopped the next time, I'd hear, "Aren't you the coach from Wisconsin? Why sure you are." That opened the door for me to ask about the player I was recruiting.

"Seen so-and-so around lately? How's he doing?"

"He comes in all the time. By the way, Bo, the Pittsburgh coach was here yesterday."

That's how I got information.

It was possible back then to outwork people.

That's what we did with two Cleveland area-kids: Scott Roth from Brecksville and Brad Sellers from Warrensville Heights. Both would play in the NBA. Both were part of our 1981 freshman class, which also included Cory Blackwell, Carl Golston, John Ploss and Jack Hippen. That was Coach Cofield's last recruiting class at Wisconsin.

Roth had some quality choices and narrowed his list to Arkansas, Tennessee, Michigan, Ohio State and Wisconsin. I got to be good friends with Scott's high school coach, Biff Lloyd. How good? After his daughter left for college, they had a room open up in their home and he invited me to stay whenever I was recruiting in the area. He even put up a sign over the door, "Bo's Room."

Meanwhile, there were days when I made myself at home in Brad Sellers' high school. I couldn't talk to Brad, but there was no rule against me physically being there.

I wasn't just present, I was omnipresent. I would just stand in the hallway outside a classroom waiting to make eye contact with Brad.

Everyone in the school knew who I was. Between classes, kids would walk by and say, "Go Buckeyes." Others would say, "Go Wolverines." Most were hoping Brad would go to Ohio State. They were all pretty friendly, and I just smiled and hung out.

Brad would come out of a class, see me standing in the hall, and maybe wink or pump his fist in the air. I never said a word to him. Didn't have to. My presence said everything. I wanted him to know that Wisconsin really wanted him, more so than anyone else who was recruiting him.

Like I pointed out earlier, you could outwork people to get recruits. But some of the things we were doing as coaches started to make less and less sense. Why are we standing in a high school hallway like an ornament waiting for a prospect to walk past? Why are we away from home all the time? Why are we doing some of these things?

Some NCAA rules that would go into effect were the result of hard-working coaches who were just trying to do their job successfully. But the limits were welcome. The limits on how many times you can be in a school; the limits on how many times you can contact a recruit. And so on.

As coaches, we've fought for changes over the years to eliminate some of the stupid things — like camping outside a recruit's door the night before he could sign his national letter of intent. You'd park on the street, along with all the coaches from the other schools, and the next morning we'd all rush up to the porch at the same time and ring the doorbell.

Almost in unison it was, "Who are you going to sign with, kid?"

That can't happen anymore.

How far have we come as a coaching fraternity since then?

Today, instead of dealing with street parking, we're dealing with street agents.

"I'm handling all of the recruiting," the coach is informed.

"Who are you?"

"I'm the third cousin. But everything is going through me."

"Oh, really. That's how it works?"

Thanks, but no thanks.

I don't do real well in those situations.

    ***

Bill Cofield believed in me. He gave me the chance that some very good coaches never get — through no fault of their own — and that was the chance to coach in a conference like the Big Ten. Many of the things that I picked up during my apprenticeship as a Badger assistant helped accelerate my evolution as a coach and prepare me for my next step.

Recruiting was just one facet of my job at Wisconsin. The coaching staffs were much smaller then, and I was doing a little bit of everything, including scheduling. I was setting up bus and plane trips. I was also running the summer camp. In retrospect, my Wilkes education helped me tremendously in organizing the office and prioritizing responsibilities.

During those years, I did my homework. I studied college systems and took mental notes — Things to Do and Things Not to Do — that I filed away for later use. I learned by handling the advance preparation and scouting reports on opponents. That was a great foundation. While breaking down strengths and weaknesses, you're being exposed to a variety of different nuances in strategy.

I was in my late 20s, not even 30 yet, and I was working as a Big Ten assistant. I was gaining invaluable experience on how to handle a pregame, a halftime and a postgame, along with how to handle timeouts and how to counter in-game moves.

Coach Cofield gave me the freedom to branch out — not with the idea that I was going off on my own without reporting back to him. Nothing like that. But he encouraged my growth as a coach, and he would always listen to what I had to say.

During the 1979-80 season, I took over the defense in practice and we did some things that were pretty good. I still remember Jim Mott, the school's sports information director, telling me that our scoring defense matched the lowest in over 25 years or since the early '50s at Wisconsin.

We finished a game above .500 — our only winning record in six seasons.

I thought we had the talent to be better.

We never really developed an identity as a team. We never stayed with the same offense or defense. We never built a system. What are you? Are you a fast break team? A control team? Are you a defensive team? A rebounding team? We didn't have a brand.

It was frustrating because I could see where at times certain individuals felt it was more about them than it was the team, and that's not good. Every player has his own individuality. But you have to get each of them to understand, "We can have a lot more fun if we're doing this as a team."

We didn't have the camaraderie that good teams have.

In that era, the Oakland A's won a string of pennants and World

Championships with players who were always bickering in the clubhouse or the dugout. But all you had to do was watch the A's on the field — watch their relay throws, watch how they backed up bases, watch how they played the game. That told you all you had to know about them.

As teammates, you don't have to be best friends. But when you're on the basketball floor, you have to know, "Do you have my back if I get beat on defense? Can I rotate here? Can I help off my man? Are you going to make that extra pass to get me the shot?"

That's when you can tell whether a team is together — by how they compete. I didn't see much bonding or belief in each other. There was never any question in my mind, either, that Bill Cofield was scrutinized more because he was a minority coach.

In 1970, Illinois State hired Will Robinson, who was the first black head coach in Division I history. Six years later, Bill Cofield became the first black head coach in Big Ten history. That included both major revenue sports in the conference, basketball and football. There were some people who weren't ready for that breakthrough.

All coaches have a burden of expectations.

From my perspective, there was an additional burden for Bill Cofield, which I became acutely aware of before he ever coached a game at Wisconsin. It had nothing to do with winning or losing.

I took it upon myself that first year to sort through his mail. I brought it up to him from the onset. I said, "Look, if you don't mind, I'll keep some of this stuff from getting to you — the stuff that I don't think is necessary for you to see." He didn't mind, and he understood what I was doing.

Some of the letters were cruel. I realized there were a small percentage of people who just didn't get it — who just didn't understand what being a minority was like. Unfortunately, there were a few other things that happened during those years that convinced me that race was a factor in how our program and Coach Cofield was being measured.

There was the Stretch Gregory incident where he was accused of taking an alarm clock. Thing is, I knew of some other incidents with other Wisconsin athletes in other team sports that appeared to be more serious than Gregory's, and they didn't get nearly the play, if any play at all publicly.

But to some this was an example of a minority coach bringing in a minority player who took advantage of a fellow student on campus by taking an object, an alarm clock. I was new to the city and the over-reaction surprised the heck out of me.

I remember speaking to a booster gathering and one guy pulled me aside afterward and asked, "How many blacks do you have on your team?"

I looked him in the eyes and said, "I work with these players every day, and, to be honest, I don't know how many blacks we have on our team. I haven't counted. I couldn't tell you how many white players we have, either. I'd have to check the team picture."

I wasn't trying to be sarcastic.

But that wasn't the answer he was expecting, and he followed up with another question. "Because we have a black head coach, are we going to have all black players?"

Again, I tried to set him straight by saying, "I don't know. It could be. It also could be that we have all white players. We're going after players — the best players — white or black."

There were times when I thought, "What did I get myself into?"

Whenever I felt that way, I reminded myself that it was just a small percentage of people who thought that way and revealed their prejudice by saying those things and writing angry letters.

There were dramatic changes taking place in society and there were different levels of acceptance of what was going on. Some resisted change more than others based on their own frame of reference, whether it was their upbringing and education level or their intolerance and ignorance.

I was a minority in Chester, a predominantly black community. While I never thought I was different than anybody else, I knew that I had to prove myself. But you can do that through athletics. Once you've shown you can play, most people will accept you. I have always looked at sports as a unifier, and I've always felt that you treat others like you want to be treated.

It helps to win, though.

That final season, Coach Cofield's final season, was tough. The shrapnel was coming from all directions. The main thing was to stay loyal as assistants. Did I feel like Coach Cofield had been given a fair chance? Yes. Did I feel like our staff had been given a fair chance? Yes.

Nobody owed us anything, and we weren't looking for special favors.

Bill Cofield resigned with three games remaining in the 1981-82 season. He made the official announcement after a home game against Ohio State. That night we lost by two points on a last-second basket by Clark Kellogg, who just replaced color analyst Billy Packer on CBS's telecast of the Final Four.

It didn't end there. Coach Cofield stayed on through the final weeks of the season and losses to Michigan and Marquette. We finished with a 6-21 record.

I wasn't sure what my next move was going to be. If I wanted to leave Madison, I had some places to go. But I didn't necessarily want to pursue those options.

Plus, I couldn't turn my back on all the young players we had in the program. I tried to hold everything together during the transition, but it wasn't easy. I always felt that they should stay committed to Wisconsin and work with the next head coach, whoever that was going to be.

I had to talk the players out of making certain demands on the administration for me to be the next head coach. I just didn't feel that was something that needed to be pressed at the time. Not because I didn't feel like I could win here. But how's that going to look if the players are determining the future of the program?

I assured the administration that I would keep the guys together and keep recruiting. There were a couple of setbacks. When UW-Eau Claire's Ken Anderson was named as Coach Cofield's successor and introduced at a press conference, I was recruiting in the state of Ohio.

That weekend, I got a phone call from assistant athletic director Otto Breitenbach.

"Are you sitting down, Bo?" he asked.

I said, "No, but I can be."

"Well, you'd better take a seat. Ken Anderson just went back to Eau Claire."

I thought he was kidding. He wasn't. I got back to campus as soon as I could to make sure all hell wasn't breaking loose with the players. Was I totally shocked by Anderson's decision? Not really. I was mature enough to know that people can change their minds.

Ball State's Steve Yoder finally took the job.

I was going to be retained on the staff, but I had a decision to make. Michigan State coach Jud Heathcote called, and he basically said that he had a plane ticket waiting for me. The way it sounded, the assistant's job was mine if I wanted to make the move to East Lansing.

I felt Coach Heathcote was one of the best who has ever coached the college game. Three years earlier, he won a national championship with Magic Johnson. Jud Heathcote was sound. He was tough. He was funny. He was a character. He kind of reminded me of my dad.

Knowing that Michigan State was a potential option, I went into Coach Yoder's office, and said, "What do you have for me, Coach? How are you going to use me?"

I wanted to make sure that he wasn't just keeping me around to continue recruiting Madison La Follette's Ricky Olson and Chicago Vocational's David Miller. Was I being retained just to keep Scott Roth and Brad Sellers from transferring?

Coach Yoder convinced me that I was needed.

He wanted me here.

I heard what I wanted to hear.

The airplane ticket to East Lansing went unused.

Coach Yoder was good to me, and I tried to ease his transition by introducing him to the people who had the best interests of the Wisconsin program at heart. I steered him away from those who just wanted to be a best buddy to a Big Ten head coach.

By then, I had already sifted through the talkers and the doers.

George Chryst was a doer.

That was his makeup.

He got things done.

I first met George in the mid-'70s when he was an assistant football coach at Wisconsin, his alma mater. Prior to that he had a successful run at Madison Edgewood High School, which was also his alma mater. George was a people person. You never had to guess where he was coming from or what his intentions were. He had nothing but good intentions.

George Chryst was the head football coach and athletic director at UW-Platteville while the transition from Coach Cofield to Coach Yoder was taking place.

During Coach Yoder's first season, George came by my office and talked to me about Dick Wadewitz and his plans to retire as the head basketball coach at Platteville. He wasn't sure when that would be, but he was guessing in a few years.

Out of curiosity, I drove to Platteville on my own and looked around. I had been through that area of the state before, but I had never stopped and gotten out of my car. My first reaction was, "Wow, this is different." Different from my experiences as a Philly kid growing up on the East Coast. But it was a college town and there was a basketball program.

That's all I had to know at that point because I was still focused on helping the Badgers win games, and Dick Wadewitz was still on the job at Platteville.

The following year, after Coach Wadewitz decided to retire, George Chryst made it clear that he wanted me to replace him. George was a persuasive salesman.

"Bo, you can build something here, and this is an opportunity to prove yourself as a college head coach," he stressed. "As much as we need you, Bo, you also need Platteville."

That was a powerful selling point. The perks were important, too, like a country club membership. It had nothing to do with my golf game, and everything to do with networking in Platteville. The country club was a vehicle that would give me a chance to meet the doers in the town — the business people who are going to donate to your basketball program and buy tickets.

Many things factored into my decision. Our kids were at the right age to move. We weren't moving out of state. We weren't moving far from Kelly's mom and sisters in Madison. And the move felt right in my gut. So, I called George and said, "The timing is good, let's do it."

George had promised me moving expenses. Little did I know that the movers would be his son, Paul, and some of his buddies on the 1984 Platteville state championship high school football team. During the move, we came up missing a lamp shade. It must have blown off the truck. We still joke that there is a cow wearing a lamp shade somewhere in southwestern Wisconsin.

Today, Paul Chryst is regarded as one of the top offensive coordinators in college football, and we're lucky to have him in Madison calling plays for the Badgers. I still know him as "Heimer." His nickname can be traced, I'm told, to a Mother Goose rhyme — "John Jacob

Jingleheimer Schmidt" — which he always sang on car trips when he was a youngster.

That was not a nursery rhyme I grew up with in Chester.

But I was fond of nicknames. I can't remember anybody not having one in my circle of friends. There was John McClain, who was "Onions." He was fond of them on his cheesesteaks. There was Charles Pierce, who was "Bugsy." He had the look of a boxer if not a gangster.

We also had an "Ace" and a "Looty" and a "Pusshead." My dad's best friend was a "Boogy." And then there was "Smooth Sailing." Only it wasn't for Curtis Canion, Smooth Sailing that is. During his senior year, he joined the naval reserves. I remember the SP's, the Shore Police, interrupting one of our practices to arrest Smooth. Apparently, he had skipped some meetings.

Getting back to Heimer — Paul Chryst — he's fond of telling the story of how he and his dad were on their way to Madison to watch a spring football practice at Camp Randall Stadium when George decided to make a detour to my house.

At the time, George was not only recruiting me for his head coaching vacancy in Platteville, but he was recruiting the Chicago Bears, who were thinking about relocating their preseason training camp to Platteville.

"If I can pull off one of these two things — hiring a Big Ten assistant or landing a pro team — it would be unbelievable," George told Heimer. "And imagine if we get both Bo and the Bears."

George Chryst pulled it off.

What were my expectations for Pioneer basketball?

I wanted to build a program that the community could rally around.

My biggest challenge was finding anybody who believed that I was making the right move. Not many offered encouragement because they were too busy telling me why I couldn't win at Platteville. It was an engineering school. Engineers can't play basketball. How many engineers are playing in the NBA? It was a farm school. How many city players want to play in the sticks?

I heard everything.

Too few malls.

Too few theaters.

Too few girls.

Too few minorities.

If I had a dollar for every reason I heard about why I couldn't win at Platteville, I wouldn't have taken the job because I would have been wealthy enough to retire.

But I was 36 and the energy was there to take on the challenge. Every time an excuse came up, I would respond, "So what you're saying to me is if somebody can go in there and turn this baby around, that would be a pretty good accomplishment. Is that what you're saying?"

I know what George Chryst was saying.

"Bo, it can happen here," he kept telling me.

I believed him, and I knew of only one way to get it done.

Be ferociously persistent.

CHAPTER FOUR

PIONEERING THE SWING

I was a head coach again — for the first time in nine years — and it only cost me $7,000. That was my pay cut for taking the Platteville job. Obviously, I didn't have David Falk, Drew Rosenhaus or Scott Boras representing me as an agent.

I cut my own deal.

George Chryst knew that I made $32,000 as a Wisconsin assistant. And he tried in every possible way to put together the best financial package that he could at Platteville. When he gave me the final number — a one-year salary of about $25,000 — I said, "Thanks, George. I appreciate everything you've done for me. Let's go to work."

I didn't need a lot. Kelly didn't need a lot. We weren't into material things as a family. Plus, I felt that I could eventually make up for any loss of income by running my own summer camps. It was just a matter of hustling and making it work. Before long, we were the biggest camp in the state.

I've never taken a job with the idea that I was going to be there for two years or 50 years. For me, though, Platteville was an investment. I really wasn't worried about what I was making that first season. I was more concerned about what was going to make me and my family the happiest.

As a head coach, I realized that I could control my own hours. I could recruit when I wanted to recruit, and I could teach. I had my certification and even though I didn't have any history classes — I taught basketball theory and racquetball — it kept me in touch with the students on campus.

After signing my Platteville contract, I made a doctor's appointment, but it had nothing to do with my health. The appointment was with Dr. Tom Davis, the head basketball coach at Stanford University.

I first met Coach Davis in 1976. We were watching some high school all-star games at the Palestra in Philadelphia when our paths crossed. I was a Badger assistant and he was the head coach at Lafayette College. The irony is that Tom Davis wanted the UW job that went to Bill Cofield.

"Bo, I'm from Wisconsin," was the way he introduced himself.

I made the connection.

(Coach Davis grew up in Ridgeway. He got his undergraduate degree from Platteville and his masters from UW-Madison. Ever the proud Pioneer alumnus, he was always good to our program, and he bought windbreakers for our guys after we won our first championship at Platteville.)

There was another ironic twist.

In late March of 1982, I was in New Orleans for the Final Four. That was the year that North Carolina's Michael Jordan made the game-winning shot against Georgetown.

Wisconsin officials were still sizing up candidates to replace Coach Cofield, and the search and screen committee's list included Tom Davis, who was then at Boston College.

There was one glitch — all the UW administrators were in Providence, Rhode Island, for the NCAA hockey tournament, and Coach Davis was in New Orleans.

That's where I came in.

My role was to keep Coach Davis from signing with Stanford. My response? C'mon, you've got to be kidding me. I'm going to hold Dr. Tom hostage? In the interim, the Stanford president flew to New Orleans to woo Coach Davis and close the deal. Which he did. In the end, Wisconsin had two swings at him but didn't connect on either.

Coach Davis couldn't have been happier for me or more gracious when I took over the Platteville program in 1984. After telling him that I wanted to pick his brain on some things, he said, "Bo, if you get out here, I'll take care of the rest. This will be my gift, my donation to Platteville."

I ended up spending three days on the Stanford campus in Palo Alto, California, with Coach Davis and his two assistants, Bruce Pearl (who's now the head coach at Tennessee after following me at UWM) and Gary Close (who's now on my staff at Wisconsin).

During our visit, we talked about recruiting, organization, and X's and O's. We all agreed that basketball was not rocket science. Coach Davis tended to keep everything pretty simple. His philosophy was, "Just do everything well." That was no different from what Coach Rainey had preached to us at Chester High and Wilkes College.

Some of the things that Coach Davis was doing with the flex offense were very much in tune with what I wanted to do. Dr. Tom also emphasized the bounce pass on offense and pressure on defense. From that standpoint, he was a disciple of another doctor — Dr. Jack Ramsay, a Philly area icon, who was also a strong influence on the way I wanted to coach. Especially on defense.

I've always believed that if you have depth, if you have a lot of players who were of the same ability (like we had at Platteville), you can play pressure defense, you can harass your opponent. Some years we would double-team more than others. Some years we would "show and go" — show pressure and get back. But it still revolved around playing solid half-court defense.

That has always been non-negotiable and a constant in my coaching.

***

One of my first priorities at Platteville was the locker room, which needed a complete make-over, from the carpet to the locker stalls.

Why was that so critical?

The players have to feel like they're important.

When you're asking them to dive on the floor for a loose ball, when you're asking them to run the hill, when you're asking them to get in the weight room and lift during the off-season, they have to know that you're trying to make it better for them.

Players react differently to demands when they understand that you have their best interests in mind. They listen better and pay better attention. The locker room was a good starting point because it was one way to get better right away.

Coyle Carpeting gave us a good break and one of our incoming freshmen, Joe Theisen, donned the knee pads and installed the carpet. Joe's family was in the carpeting business.

I went to the industrial tech people on the Platteville campus and they made and installed the new lockers and stools. Eastman Cartwright Lumber Co. donated a lot of the wood.

I called Ronnie Krantz, a friend and loyal Badger booster. He didn't even ask how much it would take to get the locker room done. He just wrote out a check.

I grabbed a brush and along with my assistants, Denny Morgan and Todd Kuckkahn, painted the walls. We all thought we knew what we were doing. How hard can it be to paint? We made sure that we didn't splatter on the windows by taping them, sealing them shut.

The longer we stayed in the locker room, which was below ground, and the longer we painted, the more fun we had. We were singing and telling jokes and laughing. I didn't want to stop, but I had to go upstairs to my office to call a recruit.

When I got off the telephone and walked back downstairs, the smell really hit me. So did the reality. I finally put two and two together: we were using an epoxy paint and there was no ventilation in the locker room.

"Whoa, whoa, whoa, we've got to get out of here, guys," I said to Morgan and Kuckkahn, who were still singing and laughing. "We've got to open the windows and get outside."

Whenever a sportswriter uses the phrase that a team has run out of gas late in the season and the players were "running on fumes," it has a whole different meaning for me. I was running on fumes once, and I couldn't stop smiling.

Besides changing the physical appearance of the locker room, we also upgraded the way Platteville traveled. In the past, the school was using station wagons. Usually the managers or assistants drove. Sometimes the players were driving themselves to a road game.

That's just not safe or smart. That's just no way for a basketball team to travel. Especially since I read somewhere that the average car seat is built for someone under 6-feet tall. It was a given that I wasn't going to have the job very long if I didn't recruit players taller than 6-feet.

As it turned out, one of my neighbors was the manager at Hardees in Platteville and I solicited some of their corporate people and local franchise owners and they donated money toward bus travel.

We improved the locker room and our mode of transportation by hustling, by making phone calls, by talking to people, by meeting and greeting. Best of all, the players knew we were doing it for them. "What we're trying to do is have a first-class basketball program here," I explained to everyone I met at the country club. "To do that, I need help from the community."

When I talked to George Chryst about starting a basketball booster club in Platteville, he looked at me funny, chuckled and gave me the bad news.

"Bo, I nearly had a revolt," he said.

"What do you mean, George?"

"Bo, we raised the dues from $10 to $15 for the football booster club," he said, "and I thought I would need an armed security guard because I was sure somebody was going to mug me."

We went ahead with our plans for the basketball boosters, charged $10 and raised the price in small increments. The backing was unbelievable. Platteville isn't very big and doesn't have many businesses. What helped was that many of my friends from Madison supported our program.

After we started winning, some of the most contentious arguments during divorce proceedings centered around who would get custody of season tickets to our games.

But that was on the horizon.

I knew that we weren't going to finish first in many, if any, categories that first season. But if there was a ranking for the hardest floors in college basketball, we'd have to be at the top of the list.

We had a density test done on the floor, and the macadam in the parking lot was softer than the floor in Williams Fieldhouse. At least, we were No. 1 in something.

***

To save expenses, Denny Morgan and Todd Kuckkahn lived with George and Patti Chryst during the week. We had three kids so we didn't have room. The Chryst's called the makeshift accommodations in their basement the Coach-Tel. It was the equivalent of a hotel for my staff. Denny drove home on weekends to be with his family. His wife, Jo, was teaching in Waunakee.

(I have some special memories of Denny Morgan, a Dodgeville native, who was a high school head coach at Middleton, Richland Center and Wonewoc Center. He coached two seasons at UW-Platteville before he was diagnosed with cancer. Denny relocated to the Houston area, so he could get aggressive treatment at the Texas Medical Center, adjacent to the Rice University campus. While he was being treated, he worked as a volunteer assistant for Rice head coach Scott Thompson, a former All-Big Ten player at Iowa under Lute Olson. In March of '89, Denny lost his battle with cancer. Nine months later, we played a game at Rice and we used the guaranteed money to start a scholarship fund for the Morgan children.)

When we first got started at Platteville, I couldn't offer much to my assistants beyond the opportunity to work on their masters degrees while coaching basketball. But that was incentive enough for Denny, Todd and Bo Jensen, a student volunteer. None of us went into this situation blind.

I knew the Pioneers were in a good league — what was then the WSUC, the Wisconsin State University Conference (which is now the WIAC, the Wisconsin Intercollegiate Athletic Conference).

I knew the teams were well-coached, with Ken Anderson at Eau Claire, Augie Vander Meulen at Whitewater, Dick Bennett at Stevens Point, Dewey Mintz at Stout, Burt McDonald at La Crosse, Stan Jack at Rivers Falls, Jim McGrath at Oshkosh, and Chris Ritchey at Superior.

A lot of different people gave me advice about the WSUC.

But, then, I'm the kind of guy who's going to do it his way anyhow.

When I met with Platteville's returning players, I told a few of them that it was probably not in their best interest to come back. I clued them in on what it was going to be like and I could just tell by their attitude that there was no way they were going to mesh with me.

I'll never forget our first day of practice. I've got some guys walking into the gym and taking off their sweat tops and bottoms and putting them on the side of the floor against the wall.

I stared at them and blurted out, "What the hell are you doing?"

"Coming to practice, coach."

"You change in the locker room," I bellowed. "And when you step on this court, your shoes are tied, your shirt tail is tucked in, and you're ready to go to work, you're ready to practice."

I reminded them of one other thing.

"When you hit the floor, you don't just grab a basketball and start jacking up shots."

They needed to get loose first.

Some just didn't get it, though.

"But this is the way we did ..."

I interrupted, "Doesn't matter. This is the way we're doing it now."

***

Freshmen played a majority of the minutes that first season.

I fully understood that we would be judged on our first recruiting class. Why? Human nature. After four years, people are going to take a hard look at your program under the assumption that if you're a decent X's and O's coach, you can be competitive with the right leadership.

What happens if you don't get it done in that time span?

The recruiting gets tougher and tougher.

But all the pieces fell into place for us.

I saw Baraboo High School play in the state tournament, and with all due respect to Darin Schubring, who got a full ride with the Badgers, I thought Steve Showalter was their best player in those tourney games. They also had a good little guard in Jimmy Gilmore, and we took him.

When I watched Wilmot's Randy Kazin play, I was struck by his moxie and his court awareness. He could have gone Division II. He was a perfect fit at Platteville.

Joe Theisen was from Adams-Friendship, and I had seen him compete during our summer camps in Madison. He was a good shooter who ended up being our best defender.

I knew Pulaski's Rock Ripley had battled his brothers — including Rod, who got tendered at Wisconsin — and I knew he would be a tough son-of-a gun for us in the middle, and he was.

Showalter, Kasin, Theisen and Ripley were the building blocks. Among the returning players was Ray Wagner, our lone senior. Iowa Grant's Mark Place was a transfer from UW-Parkside. Tim Hill, a junior, prepped at Racine Park. And we had another transfer, Tim Hopfensperger from North Dakota State. The rest of the team was made up of freshmen and sophomores.

During the recruiting process, other schools were telling these guys why they shouldn't go to Platteville and why they couldn't win at

Platteville. It was a tough sell for us. But, fortunately, they were sold on the chance to build something together.

They practiced hard and played hard.

Those who didn't, got the message, and moved on.

***

George Chryst never asked me what I was going to run on offense at Platteville. He just trusted that I knew basketball. Conceptually, I knew what I wanted to do based on my experience as a player and coach. From that perspective, I knew what was tough to deal with defensively.

As a Wisconsin assistant, I was responsible for putting together some of the scouting reports on our opponents. In particular, I got a feel for what Johnny Orr was doing at Michigan. He had incorporated the John Wooden-signature UCLA "cut" into his offense. Most teams were running it.

At Chester High School, we ran some back screens and some UCLA up screens. But we hadn't put it together as a system. Having to guard the best offensive player from the other team, I got to know which screens were the toughest to handle and where I needed help from my teammates in the rotation.

I never claimed to be reinventing the game.

But there are basic actions and if you can make plays off them, it's basic basketball. The actions were the back screens, the up screens, the fade screens and the ball screens.

In theory, I screen for you and you screen for me. Whatever the action, you read it and make a good decision with the ball. If the defender counters and goes over or under the screen, it's all about what is going to happen after that action. What's next?

UCLA would bring the 5-man (center) to the high post and he would set the up screen for a guard who would make the UCLA cut through the middle and post up. But the Bruins weren't looking to get the ball inside to him as much as they were trying to get to a "duck-in" on the other side of the lane.

I just thought if the guy is open in the post, get him the ball. It was just basic basketball: a big screening for a little and if a guy can catch it in the post and score, why not?

Let me take the time here to describe some terms and actions.

The UCLA cut: An up screen from the post for a guard at the top of the key. It's otherwise known as an inside screen, a big for a little. The decision for the defense? Are you going to switch?

The Flex cut: A back screen for a wing player to cut along the baseline to the post on the opposite side.

The back screen: Any type of screen on one side of the floor where you're cutting a player to the ball from the opposite side.

The fade screen: Freeing up a shooter by screening a help defender who has gotten caught in the middle of the floor. The shooter fades off the screen; an outside-in screen.

The ball screen: A screen for the guy with the ball. You can pick-and-roll, or pick-and-pop off the screen action.

The post-up: Taking a defender into the low and medium post area and trying to get an angle on the player for a post feed and a basket.

The duck-in: When you're in the low post, you're stepping into the lane, a big wide first step, in an attempt to get the right angle to keep the defender on your backside.

Counters: If the defense takes away one thing, what do you have next? It's what you do, depending on what the defense does. It's your next action as a player, with or without the ball, and away from the ball.

Skip pass: If a team is jamming the middle defensively, it's a pass that is thrown over the top of the defense from one side of the floor to the other; skipping players on the perimeter.

Bounce pass: A slower pass. But the ball stays lower, allowing the receiver to keep a wider base so that he can ward off the defender, catch the pass and post.

As we were preparing for our first season at Platteville, I decided to watch a segment of practice from the window overlooking the floor from one end of Williams Fieldhouse. It was a bird's-eye view and perfect for what I wanted to see: the spacing of our players.

As the players executed the back screens and ran their cuts, and as the ball was moving from side to side, it looked like a swing going back and forth on the floor.

So that's what I called it.

The Swing offense.

I've referred to it as equal-opportunity offense that has interchangeable parts and maximizes strengths. Everyone passes into the post, everyone passes out of the post. So it's about receivers and hand targets and how the receiver should always be ready to do something with the basketball.

I've always known that if you can pass and catch the ball, you can compete at any level. That was ingrained in me from the time I was 3 years old. And it was a fundamental truth whether I was playing basketball, football or baseball.

Before we started winning at Platteville, though, other schools were using the offense against us by telling recruits that there was no freedom to improvise or create in the Swing.

I had a kid tell me that once.

"So, you're under the impression you wouldn't have any freedom in the Swing?"

He nodded and said, "Yeah, because you're too disciplined as a coach."

"Too disciplined?"

"Yeah, I had another coach tell me that he would get me the ball on the wing, where I could attack and do my own thing."

"Oh, really. Let's take a look at some film."

Once in the dark room, I pointed to some actions on the screen and said, "What do you think this guy is doing in the swing?"

After a few seconds, he said hesitantly, "Attacking from the wing."

There were misconceptions about the Swing. And they were planted to keep players away from us. Early on, they often succeeded. But once we got on a roll at Platteville, I had recruits tell me, "Your guys are like machines, the way they play off screens and run the offense."

If you were looking at some of our better teams, it was like watching a platoon in the Army — marching in cadence — where you couldn't tell one guy from the other. I had high school coaches tell me the same things about our efficiency. They would call the office or write and request a copy of what we were doing with the Swing. There was nothing tricky about it.

So much of what we do is based on common sense.

Like the post-ups. You're going to get a higher percentage shot the closer you are to the basket. And you're likely to get fouled inside. You're not going to get fouled from 18 feet out. That's why you work on post moves: to get to the free throw line.

How many times have you heard me say this? If you're touching the post, good things will happen. But you have to know what to do with the ball when you get it there.

We've always concentrated on five post moves. Like many coaches around the country, we named each move after an NBA player for the sake of identification and instant recognition.

The Sikma: A reverse pivot where you open up to the basket.

(Jack Sikma was a 6-11 center out of Illinois Wesleyan. He was a seven-time NBA all-star who played for the Seattle SuperSonics and the Milwaukee Bucks.)

The Moses: A drop step, power move. Shoulders square to the backboard.

(Moses Malone was a Hall of Fame low-post player. He played two years in the ABA and 19 years in the NBA with Houston, Philadelphia, Washington, Atlanta, Milwaukee and San Antonio.)

The Dominique: An up and under move. He would use shot fakes to get people in the air and out of position and then if the help arrived, he would cross over with a step.

(Dominique Wilkins was the, "Human Highlight Film." An explosive dunker, and Hall of Famer, he was best known for his scoring exploits with the Atlanta Hawks.)

The Bernie: Shoulder fake one way, turn the other way.

(Bernard King was one of the NBA's most prolific scorers. He played 14 seasons with New Jersey, Utah, Golden State, the Knicks and Washington.)

The McHale: A jump hook.

(Kevin McHale was an All-Big Ten power forward at the University of Minnesota who went on to stardom with the Boston Celtics.)

In drills, I could say, "I want you to Bernie into a McHale."

And there would be no mistaking what I wanted.

I want you to shoulder shake, turn like you're going to shoot and when somebody comes over to block your shot, I want you to use a little jump hook.

Would a player use or perfect all five post moves? No. But he had some options and something to work on with the thought and confidence that, "Any time I'm inside 10 or 15 feet, here's a move that I can use to score." That was our standard.

Everybody who played for me would know the difference between a

Moses and a Sikma, or a Sikma and a Dominique, or a Dominique and a Bernie, or a Bernie and a McHale or a McHale and a Moses. Hundreds upon hundreds of campers were also programmed that way every summer.

As a high school and college player, I had my own favorite move: the Cousy, named after the Boston Celtics' Bob Cousy, a Hall of Famer. On a drive, it was a running one-hander. Extending my arm away from my body — to keep the ball away from the bigger defenders and better jumpers — it was a little flick shot. I would kiss it off the glass with either my right or left hand.

My former players and assistants who are now coaching have carried on the tradition of the Bernie, the Sikma, the Dominique, the McHale and the Moses. Some have adopted their own reference points to more contemporary NBA stars. Like maybe the LeBron or the Kobe or the Dirk. But why would I change? I haven't. Why confuse anybody?

Like I said earlier, it's not tricky.

***

As a coach, I haven't received many technical fouls. There's no trick to that, either. I've never felt there was a reason to get a technical as far as changing the course of a game or the momentum. But there are times when you have to wake up the officials. "Hey, guys, you're sleepwalking," I'd tell them. "You're not giving these young men your best effort."

On those occasions, I'll get up and say something to the officials. Mostly, you'll see me crouching in front of the bench — my catcher's crouch.

I can't tell you how many people have come up to me and asked, "Bo, how in the world can you stay in that crouch position for a whole game without blowing out your knees?"

I've never had to condition myself to be in the crouch, even after three games in three days at the Big Ten tournament. My main objective was to make sure I wasn't standing in somebody's way.

I like talking to my players. I like being able to move up and down the bench. When you're kneeling or crouching, you can do those things without blocking anybody's vision.

I don't like parading up and down the sidelines. And I'll rarely, if ever, leave the coaching box on the sidelines. That's in sharp contrast to what some other head coaches are guilty of doing.

All you have to do is look at the house feeds from the Kohl Center, and you'll see how demonstrative some of these coaches can get. You'll see them dropping to their knees, or stomping on the floor or doing pirouettes and triple salchows and double lutz's.

No technicals.

I raised my hand one time, and I got the T.

I pointed to the floor another time, and I got the T.

Must have been bad timing on my part.

Those house feeds are proof of what others have been getting away with. This isn't sour grapes from me. I've won enough games. I'm comfortable enough in my own skin. I don't have to complain. But you can't convince me that the treatment is the same for every coach.

For the record, I got a technical in the first game I coached at Platteville.

I was sending a message: "If you're going to officiate our games, I want your best. You've got to be on top of things, and what you're doing."

Coach Wadewitz was a very good teacher, a quiet man of the highest integrity. He wouldn't say that much during games. But I had to be true to my own personality and as we were developing our own program at Platteville, I wanted the officials to know it was different now when they came to our place. Things were about to change in the WSUC.

We lost by 13 points at Dubuque when I got that first technical, and I can remember saying to that official, "It's not going to be like this forever." We never lost again to a Dubuque team.

In my first home game, we beat St. Ambrose. In the locker room afterward, I said, "Hey, guys, we can get more of these."

I was talking about the wins.

But we didn't get many more. We went 9-17. We had to emphasize fundamentals and we couldn't turn over the ball or we would have been 0-26. We were young and we made a lot of mistakes, but we were starting to be more sound.

I had to remind myself to be patient.

That said, I'm more patient than people realize.

It's just that certain things are unacceptable.

Like the failure to pay attention at practice. We're there for only a couple of hours and it shouldn't be that tough to listen. You have to learn how to compartmentalize. When you're practicing basketball, you have to erase everything else from your mind. Conversely, when you're in the classroom, you erase basketball and when you're out socially, you socialize.

I thought our first team was starting to get it by the end of the season.

Was I more patient with that team than others? No. I gave the players the same kind of coaching and teaching I've given everybody. But you could see the guys get better.

That year, we competed with some of the better teams in the league and that was a positive sign. The year before, Stevens Point had beaten Platteville by 41 and 26 points. The Pointers had a great player in Terry Porter who would have a solid career in the NBA. Later, he coached the Bucks. Today, he's head coach of the Phoenix Suns.

Our first season, we lost by 10 and 13 points to Porter and Stevens Point. That was a measure of how competitive our freshmen were. That was the beginning. Our young players were starting to believe. They were starting to earn respect. It was just a matter of time, and patience.

In their fourth year, they were rewarded.

They cut down the nets to celebrate a title.

CHAPTER FIVE

Champions Run

In 1985, Milwaukee Bucks coach Scott Skiles was playing at Michigan State, Big Ten Network analyst Shon Morris was playing at Northwestern, *Back to the Future* was playing at the movies and I was playing zone at Platteville.

It was not the end of the world, although many would have you believe that seeing one of my teams in a zone defense would be a sign of the apocalypse.

First of all, there are zone concepts involved in certain man-to-man defenses. That includes providing "help" and cutting different areas of the floor into sections.

Over the years, then, there have been times when we have been basically playing a zone within our system, whether it was at Platteville, UWM or Wisconsin.

Unbeknownst to most, we practiced a 1-3-1 zone during our trip to Italy prior to the start of the 2006-07 season. We used the zone, too, in a couple of exhibition games, including the tour finale against Castelletto Ticino, which featured a proven outside scoring threat in Drake Diener, who prepped in Fond Du Lac and played at DePaul.

Why the 1-3-1? I wanted to experiment with Alando Tucker at the top of the zone, and I wanted to see if we could do some things defensively with our bigs. But if you don't move your feet real well, it doesn't matter if you're in a zone or a man-to-man.

I really had no plans to use the 1-3-1 during the season. We were pretty average in the zone and pretty sound in our man, so we would be doing other teams a favor by playing zone. Plus, there was another overriding factor.

Our program has been built around our man-to-man, half-court defense. If you make drastic changes, you're telling the players, "We're desperate."

My thinking has always been, "Let's just do something better than anybody else. So, let's be the best man-to-man defensive team we can be."

In 1985, we played zone on a whim against Loras College.

Over the summer, I had played golf with the Loras coach and we got to talking X's and O's during the round. "I've played nothing but man defense," I informed him.

One thing led to another and I suggested, "Look, I'm willing to play some zone against your team, at least, until you get 10 points. Then we'll see what happens."

Loras came to Platteville for the third game of the 1985-86 season, and we jumped out to an early lead. But then it was boom, boom, boom from their outside shooters against our zone. We needed a flurry of late free throws to hold on to a nine-point win.

Basketball people who understand me know that I can't stand to see a guy get a wide-open shot without somebody challenging him. That was it for the zone. Curtains.

Our second Platteville team won 16 games, and we made the NAIA district playoffs. That was an important step. Still, we weren't quite there yet.

Going into our third year, we were still adding and subtracting, planting and weeding. I thought the guys were doing what they could to figure it out. But we had some injuries, we had some tough losses and we had some things go against us.

We didn't make the playoffs, finishing 14-11 overall. In a nine-team conference, we were one of five teams that tied for fifth place, or last place (depending on whether you looked at things with a half-full or half-empty perspective).

Platteville was bunched with La Crosse, River Falls, Superior and Whitewater, each 6-10. Eau Claire and Stevens Point went 13-3 and tied for the league title.

Our loss at Eau Claire in the second-to-last game of the season was emotionally draining. But it was a seminal moment in our program, a game that turned things around for Platteville basketball. We never won fewer than 23 games from that point on.

We were 2-1 in overtimes that season, including a triple-overtime victory at Oshkosh and a double-overtime win at Concordia. We played four hotly-contested overtimes at Eau Claire and lost by a basket.

There was no question that it was not a fairly-officiated game. When I showed our athletic director George Chryst the tape, he got upset, too. Max Sparger, the WSUC commissioner, had the same reaction. He agreed that we got the short end of the calls, and those two officials were never again assigned to a Platteville game.

We couldn't dwell on the Eau Claire loss, though. Especially since the league was in a Friday-Saturday rotation and we had a game the following night. That was my point to the team. I said, "We got beat here, we've got Stout next."

I could see by the look on their faces that they were crushed. Had we won, we would have put ourselves in position to make the NAIA playoffs.

"There are two ways you can look at this," I went on. "You can put your head down and moan and groan and feel sorry for yourself over what happened. Or you can use this loss as a measuring stick for how close you are to being at the top of this league."

After bussing to Menomonie that night, we learned that the hotel had overbooked for a youth tournament and we had to be out of our rooms at noon on Saturday. The tipoff wasn't until 7 p.m., so we gathered everybody in a small kitchenette and just hung out.

The players were frustrated.

The coaches were frustrated.

Everybody shared their feelings.

I'm not saying it was a cathartic experience. We lost to Stout. But many of the returning players used it as a rallying point for the following season, especially the guys in our first recruiting class, the seniors-to-be: Mike Hemming, Randy Kazin, Rock Ripley, Steve Showalter and Joe Theisen.

They all realized that they had one year left to make a breakthrough.

***

To open the '87 season, we overscheduled and paid for it against Division II programs that gave out scholarships. We played back-to-back road games on back-to-back days at North Dakota State and North Dakota.

We played poorly and got blown out in the opener in Fargo. We were much more competitive in Grand Forks, and DeAndrae Woods had a shot to tie or win on our final possession. But he didn't make it. (He would get redemption later in the season.)

We were 0-2.

But we weren't down.

In our home opener, we scored the first 22 points and blew away Grinnell. We also won our next two nonconference games before the start of league play. What happened next almost defied logical description and set the tone for the season.

We were down by three points in the closing seconds of regulation at La Crosse. Since we didn't have the ball, we were applying pressure, trapping and going for a steal. But the La Crosse ball handler did a good job of passing out of a double-team.

Game over.

At least that's the way it must have felt for the La Crosse coach, who celebrated his team's execution against our pressure by raising a clenched fist into the air. In turn, the La Crosse player with the ball looked to the sidelines and mirrored the action — holding his fist into the air — thinking that the coach was signaling for a timeout.

He was not.

But the official saw the player's signal and called time. La Crosse should have been shooting free throws to seal the victory, because we would have been forced to foul to stop the clock. Instead, they stopped it for us, and we were still alive. During the timeout, I reminded the guys that if we got the ball back, we needed a 3-pointer.

Believe it or not, La Crosse couldn't get the ball inbounds, we got the five-second call and Joe Theisen hit a 3-pointer to send the game into overtime.

How crazy is that? We wound up winning in double-overtime on a couple of Andy Banasik free throws, and all of a sudden we're 1-0 in the WSUC when we should have been 0-1. There's no way we should have won that game.

Whenever I think about that closing sequence, I have another flashback. Coming down the stretch in regulation, we were tired. Steve

Showalter had just fouled out of the game, and we needed a break —
anything to stop La Crosse's momentum.

I called over Rock Ripley and said, "Start looking for a contact lens on
the floor."

"Coach, I don't wear contacts."

"I know you don't, but nobody else knows that. Start looking."

Ripley turned in an Academy Award-winning performance, and the
officials halted the game and helped him look for the contact lens that
didn't exist. Since we didn't have any timeouts left, that bought us some
extra time.

I might want to use that Missing Contact Lens Trick again.

So that's just between you and me.

Following the Saturday win at La Crosse, we returned home for a
Tuesday night game against Whitewater at Williams Fieldhouse. Once
again, we went into double-overtime. Once again, we made just enough
clutch plays to pull out the victory.

That became a trend.

We didn't lose again until late January.

I had a reporter remind me, "Bo, after starting off 0-2, you've won 13
straight, 16 of 17, and 21 out of 23, blah, blah, blah." I corrected him.
"It's we've won, not you've won, and I really have no idea how many
we've won in a row."

I don't think he bought it. But my focus was totally on the rematch
with Whitewater on their home floor. There was plenty of hype
surrounding the game since both teams were 13-2 in the WSUC. I knew
the championship was on the line.

Since we were so evenly matched, the game fittingly came down to
one shot with the game tied. And it was DeAndrae Woods — the same
DeAndrae Woods who missed a last-second shot against North Dakota
— who made a jumper at the buzzer to lift Platteville to its first
conference title in 13 years, first outright since 1959.

The final play had broken down, and Woods made a great one-on-one
move. That's why we had the ball in his hands at the end of a game,
again.

At Whitewater, we started Woods, a junior, and four seniors: Kazin,
Ripley, Showalter and Theisen. Banasik, a sophomore, and Scott Plondke,
a senior transfer, came off the bench. Through thick and thin, we got

great mileage out of the rotation.

I remember saying afterward that a conference championship was something that our freshmen dreamed about four years ago and that they had to dream it before they could actually live it. And that's what they did — they dared to dream.

Their dream was to win a title, and they did.

Getting to the NAIA national tournament in Kansas City was another goal. But, as a team, we came up short in the district title game — losing in overtime to Eau Claire in Platteville. That snapped a 19-game home winning streak at Williams Fieldhouse.

During the season, we led the WSUC in free throw shooting, making 78 percent. But we made just 12 of 22 in the second half of the title game, and we came up empty on the front end of five bonus situations in the final minutes of regulation. It was a team effort. Everybody was missing free throws, not just one or two players.

Because we were such a senior-dominated team, there was the presumption in some circles that Platteville's run in the WSUC was short-lived. People had already begun to write us off as one-hit wonders. What they didn't take into account were our freshmen. They also dared to dream.

In their fourth year, they cut down the nets.

They celebrated our first national championship.

***

High school players and coaches in the Chicago area had at least heard of our school and program, thanks in large part to the Bears holding their training camp in Platteville. But recruiting is still cyclical, and it wasn't like we had established a pipeline to Chicago as much as we had been able to sign one recruiting class in particular with a strong Chicago flavor.

Robby Jeter was from Quigley South, Delano Brazil was from Brother Rice and Shawn Frison was from Chicago Leo. As freshmen, they were members of our junior varsity or "futures" team. But they didn't complain about a lack of playing time.

Their patience paid off.

Jeter and Brazil became fixtures in the lineup over the next three seasons, starting 89 straight games, while Frison was a valuable contributor off the bench. As seniors, Jeter and Frison were our top scorers. Both shot over 60 percent. That's very rare.

Jeter was relentless and our team leader. He never took a bad shot. He worked hard every day and never had a bad practice. You could always count on him.

Brazil, who had been the leading scorer in the Chicago Catholic League, was tough to handle in the post, even though he was only 6-4.

Frison was a spark, a go-to guy. He had the athletic ability and court IQ to make things happen at key times during a basketball game.

Their graduating class included Sean Poole, Mike Jones and Tim Decorah. At 6-7, Poole had a good touch for his size. He was a terror on the glass. Jones was a transfer from Iowa; a wiry kid who was really competitive. Decorah didn't play a lot of minutes off the bench, but he never hurt us when he was on the floor.

Two juniors rounded out our starting lineup: Robby's brother, Carlton Jeter, and Brian Gilmore, another transfer. Our point guard was a sophomore, T.J. Van Wie. I remember saying then, "T.J. has a strong desire to be a part of positive things."

As a high school sophomore, Van Wie and his Wisconsin Dells team won the Class B state title. He never got cheated on the basketball floor. That was our goal, too.

Going into the 1990-91 season, we were transitioning as a program from the NAIA to the Division III level in the NCAA. I had no problem with the move.

My first goal was still to win the league title. Since we were the defending champion, we were the preseason favorite to repeat because of our returning personnel. But my comment was, "Your experience is only as good as the effort. I've seen other teams with seniors that don't always play as well as they did the year before."

These six seniors didn't let anybody down. On the contrary. They were the road map for a team that won our first Division III national championship.

In the title game, Jeter and Frison combined for 38, and we beat Franklin & Marshall, 81-74, in Springfield, Ohio. Throughout the season, we had exhibited good shot selection while averaging 98 points. We didn't take many bad shots, period.

What else does it take to win a national championship? You've got to have depth, and you have to catch a few breaks along the way. But you also have to be solid defensively because that will always give you a chance.

Many talk about winning a championship, and when it doesn't happen, they're resigned to saying things like, "Well, we tried" or "Well, we came close."

This group could say, "Well, we got one." They backed up the talk by winning it all and that kind of set the tone for everybody else who followed in the program.

My first thought? Okay, that was fun. But there are more titles out there to get.

I didn't go into some rah-rah act with the guys coming back. I quoted an old cliché, "Success has a thousand parents and failure is an orphan."

In other words, everybody loves a winner.

A lot of people were now on the bandwagon at Platteville. That was good. We became THE ticket in town. We were selling out our conference home games, standing room only, naturally piquing the interest of the fire marshal.

The bar was raised and a target was on our back. Wherever we played on the road, we drew the largest crowds. That's a great feeling because you know that you're getting everyone's best shot. That's why the '91-92 season really stood out.

We lost most of our minutes and most of our points from the national championship team, and it was supposed to be a rebuilding year. But everybody did their part and we got back to the Final Four. We wore down opponents by substituting freely and going nine deep with only one player, T.J. Van Wie, averaging over 30 minutes.

We were very inexperienced. But the older players, like Carlton Jeter, were willing to share and teach. They took the younger players, like Ernie Peavy, under their wings.

Peavy redshirted as a freshman. He looked like he was about 12 years old when he got to Platteville. He was short and skinny — about 5-9, 155 pounds. But he grew four inches and put on over 30 pounds during the time he was in our program.

Peavy was a great listener and a quick learner. He used his tools better than just about anyone I've ever coached or seen. Defensively, Peavy was a force to be reckoned with. So were we as a team. We went

27-4.

One of our more impressive wins was over Maryville, Tennessee, in the sectional finals. We played them on their floor and they had two or three D-I transfers. They were very athletic, very talented. But we took them into overtime, and won.

Although we lost in the national semifinals, we bounced back and won the third place game over Jersey City State. That was very rewarding.

When the guys were running the hill back in September and October, I could just see it in their eyes that they felt like they had something to prove. That was true of Jeter, Van Wie, Peavy, Tim O'Connell, Pat Murphy, Billy Reid and everybody else who suited up.

Some things just came with the territory, and Platteville was a marked team from the start. We were not only the defending national champion, but we opened the season with victories over Division II opponents: Bellarmine and Central Missouri.

Once the first Midwest rankings came out that season, we were No. 1 and everybody was shooting at us. But that high ranking was a sign of respect. One of the coaches on the selection committee said, "Bo, you've got something going at Platteville."

Our program was established and going places.

After two second-place league finishes, we tied for first with Stevens Point the following season. The '92-93 team didn't get to the Final Four. But I thought the players — talent-for-talent, size-for-size — performed better than any team I had coached.

Getting a piece of that conference title was special because we dedicated it to George Chryst, who had passed away the previous December. George was a strong believer in winning league championships and his spirit was always with us.

The best way to pay somebody back is to get the job done. Actions speak louder than words. Building a successful program was our way of saying thanks.

To reiterate: George Chryst was one of the most influential people in my life. He convinced me that Platteville was the right job at the right time. He was right.

***

I usually trust my instincts. But they're not always right.

After a preseason scrimmage against Loras College, I went home and confessed to Kelly, "I really don't think we're going to be as good as I thought we could be."

In '94-95, we went 31-0 and won our second national championship.

So much for first impressions.

A more accurate barometer of what kind of team we might have was the game that we played against North Dakota in late November. I couldn't get them to play at Platteville, but they agreed to face us in Madison at the UW Fieldhouse.

They had some Wisconsin kids on their scholarship roster, and they wanted to showcase them against a non-scholarship program.

We drilled them.

We won by 29.

It got back to me that when one of their players was asked why he didn't consider going to Platteville, he was fairly dismissive of our program, saying something to the effect, "Why would I want to go there?"

The exact words of his dad were, "We're going big-time instead."

I didn't bring that up to my players. I didn't have to.

My guys believed they could step on the court and beat anybody.

And that's what they did — they beat everybody.

That included Manchester (Indiana) in the national championship game at the Buffalo Sports Arena. Manchester was coached by Steve Alford, the former All-American from Indiana, and it was the first time in NCAA history two undefeated teams met for the title. We scored the first basket, and never trailed. We were the aggressor from start to finish. I'm not sure we could have played much better than we did.

Possession for possession, we excelled defensively.

We had three players make first team All-WSUC: Ernie Peavy, Tim O'Connell and Aaron Lancaster. We also had three engineering majors in our starting lineup: O'Connell, Scott Borroughs and John Paulsen. That was pretty unique in itself.

From the first day of practice the players kept improving and getting better. They were sound defensively, moved the ball well and didn't make a lot of turnovers. They could score, they could defend, and they could rebound. That combination made us very tough to beat.

On top of that, they had an unbelievable work ethic. They made a statement every day just by the way they practiced. The upperclassmen were making sure the newcomers understood, "This is who we are, this is our level of intensity."

We had some good players who weren't playing much, but they realized that their time was coming and they needed to wait their turn.

What did it feel like to get on an undefeated roll?

I never talked about a winning streak or a losing streak. The players know what they're doing as a team, one way or another. Their friends are telling them. Their fellow students are telling them. Their parents and significant others are telling them.

Why should I tell them something they already know? Instead, I was telling them what was important and what was not important as far as getting ready for the next game. I always kept it that way, kept them in the present. I reminded them, "This is what you have to do today to prepare for tomorrow."

After going unbeaten in '95, our profile began to change — regionally and nationally — because of the attention our program was generating. People would come up to me in the preseason and ask, "Looking forward to the finals, Coach?"

"Finals? What finals?" I'd ask.

"You know, the finals. The NCAA finals. Where are we going this year?"

"Where are we going this year?" I'd repeat incredulously.

We hadn't even played a game yet and they wanted to plan their trip.

Those were the outside expectations. They were changing, but I wasn't. I don't change a lot. Winning never gets old. But it is habit forming.

So, we weren't about to make any changes, not even after winning five straight league titles in the mid-to-late '90s. Nobody had ever done that before in the WSUC.

The run included the '97-98 team that went unbeaten and won Platteville's third national championship. Some of the guys had been around for our second title in '95, like Ben Hoffmann, who came off the bench and gave us a spark against Manchester.

Hoffmann was now a senior, along with Travis Schreiber and Ryan Fuhrman. Both were engineering majors who redshirted as freshmen and paid their way to Buffalo for the Final Four. The other senior was

Andre Dalton, who worked his way into the rotation after not even making the first road trip of the season to Coe College.

Andre overcame a lot of things. His brother was shot and paralyzed in a drive-by shooting over the summer. After he left school, we didn't even know if Andre was planning on coming back. But he did, and I told him, "I'll give you a fair chance to make the team, but you've got some ground to cover here."

Throughout the season, Andre kept doing all of the little things that helped make us successful. And when he got on a roll offensively, he was tough to defend. In our semifinal win over Williams College, he scored 31 points.

In the finals, we beat Hope College from Michigan. Our leading scorer was a sophomore guard, Merrill Brunson, who had 15 points. That spoke to our balance.

In retrospect, that might have been the most balanced scoring team to ever win a national championship at any NCAA level, men's or women's. We had nine guys averaging from 6 to 13 points per game.

Hoffmann was a tireless worker and a first-team All-American. I likened him to a Division III John Havlicek. He averaged 12 points. Dan Wargolet was first-team all-conference. He averaged nine points. He was our second all-league player to average less than double-digits during the time we were in Platteville. Aaron Lancaster was our first.

That became a recurring theme in our program.

We didn't have any head cases at Platteville. We had unselfish players who didn't worry about getting a certain number of shots per game. They just worked their butts off. Especially on the defensive end. The '97-98 team led the nation in scoring defense, allowing less than 50 points per game. Another recurring theme.

To be able to do what this group did — the fourth league title in a row broke Eau Claire's record of three straight — says a boatload for their presence and perseverance, especially given the caliber of players and coaches and schools in the conference.

I know Gabe Miller was on the minds of our players. He was still a part of the Pioneers. After his untimely death — one month after we won the '95 national title — I said that Gabe would be a part of every team that ever plays a game at Platteville.

He was with us every time we took the court.

And he was with us every time we cut down the nets.

***

Our fourth national championship caught most people off guard. Nobody gave us much of a chance of repeating as WSUC champs, let alone NCAA champs.

But we achieved both goals during the '98-99 season.

We only lost twice, once within the conference, now known as the Wisconsin Intercollegiate Athletic Conference (WIAC).

In late December, we lost a one-point game in the final seconds at Hawaii-Pacific. The following day, we soundly whipped Evergreen State, a NAIA team. We were a long ways from home and to bounce back like we did helped build our resiliency.

Prior to taking that trip, we won our league opener on the road at Oshkosh. That was also a defining moment. We were down by three with about 23 seconds left in regulation when Dan Wargolet was fouled attempting a 3-point shot. He made all three free throws and we escaped with an overtime victory.

We had another character-builder about 10 days later at Whitewater. We trailed for most of the game before rallying for the win behind Mike Jones, Merrill Brunson and Dan Wargolet. It was a good example of our persistence as a team.

To win those two road games against rivals — Oshkosh and Whitewater — that were expected to compete for the league crown made believers out of our guys. They just believed that it was going to happen for them, like it had for the national championship team the year before. They didn't brag about it. They just played.

During the course of the season, I think 10 of our 15 wins in the conference came down to the last 10 possessions. We won the close ones. That made the difference. That was the storyline in the Division III finals against Hampden-Sydney.

We won by a point in double-overtime.

Colin Gassner's backdoor layup was the game-winner.

This championship was special because the expectations were so much lower, and we had to overcome many of our own shortcomings. Merrill Brunson was not only the most outstanding player of the Final Four, but he was D-III national Player of the Year.

Usually, our guys don't have the inflated numbers necessary for such awards. They don't average 25 or more points. Merrill averaged 18. And that was probably the lowest scoring average for a player winning that recognition in its 25-year history.

Brunson was smart, competitive and strong. He was a solid all-around athlete — first-team All-WIAC as a centerfielder. He could hit a baseball a mile. Like most of our point guards, he could score. But he took care of the ball and played both ends.

How important is the pitcher in baseball? How important is the quarterback or the middle linebacker in football? That's how important the point guard is in basketball.

When you think about some of the point guards that we had at Platteville — Kazin, Woods, Freidig, Van Wie, Peavy, Hoffmann, and Brunson — they each had their own personality off the court. But there was a common denominator. They didn't want to lose.

Most players will tell you that they don't want to lose. But these guys did something about it. They worked hard at what they did, and they always got better. That was passed down from one point guard to the next, from one team to the next.

Once we got the program rolling, it wasn't hard for them to realize, "This is why we've won here in the past and this is what we have to do now to sustain the success."

The key to the development of any team is what happens after the players leave the practice floor. What are they saying to each other in the locker room? What are they saying to each other while they're together on campus?

As a coach, you know you've got something going when they're saying "Hey, guys, we didn't have a good practice today. We need to work harder tomorrow."

More than once, I've commented, "I don't think the players at Duke work any harder than our players at Platteville. The parallel is that both programs have young people who are committed to success."

As a head coach, I've stayed young by coaching players who have refused to do anything but get better. That's why our victory against Hampden-Sydney was so exhilarating. To win a game like that — the first double overtime in the 25-year history of the Division III finals — was the fountain of youth.

I felt like I was 30 again.

I was 51.

And, for the first time, I was looking for another challenge. Believe me, I wasn't bored in Platteville. My own son, Will, was going to be a sophomore and our starting point guard. Nobody knew the swing offense better than Will. But it was time to see if what I was doing at Division III would work at Division I.

I felt strongly that it would.

CHAPTER SIX

Making the Jump

Joel Maturi didn't mince words.

"Whenever I get a Division I job as an athletic director," he kept assuring me, "you're the first one I'm coming after."

Joel Maturi, at the time, was the associate athletic director at Wisconsin. For nearly a decade, he had worn a variety of different hats for the Badgers, ranging from compliance, to facilities, to game management, to overseeing as many as 10 sports.

Joel was ambitious and trustworthy, a winning combination.

Then and now.

Joel Maturi is now the athletic director at the University of Minnesota, where he has been at the forefront of returning Gopher football to an on-campus, outdoor stadium. He also scored a coup with the hiring of Kentucky's Tubby Smith as his basketball coach.

Back then, the late '80s to mid-'90s, he was working at the UW with the goal of running his own athletic department someday. In 1996, it finally happened for Joel when he was named the AD at the University of Denver. And he lived up to his word.

He came after me the following spring.

Denver was in the process of moving from Division II to Division I in basketball and I was intrigued by the prospect of starting and building my own program.

Plus, I respected Joel.

We had been friends for over 20 years, dating to my first tour of duty at Wisconsin as an assistant. We first met when he was a successful basketball and football coach and administrator at Madison Edgewood

High School.

Over time, I got know him better through my association with Platteville athletic director George Chryst, a former Edgewood coach and a mentor to me and Joel.

I interviewed at Denver in March of '97. You know sometimes when you're in the presence of somebody and something just doesn't feel right?

That's how I felt while visiting with the school's chancellor. He had his own ideas on the type of coach that he wanted for the Denver job and I really didn't fit that description. To be honest, I thought he was clueless about basketball.

After spending 21 years in the UW system, I wasn't about to make a move based on what I was hearing. Their chancellor didn't give me a good reason to leave Platteville. I thanked Joel, and withdrew my name from consideration. Joel understood.

Denver wasn't the first school to contact me about a coaching vacancy. I had conversations with Drake and Northern Iowa. But it never got serious.

I did meet one-on-one with Wisconsin athletic director Pat Richter in March of '92 when the Badgers were seeking to replace Steve Yoder.

I thought I was much better prepared to interview for the UW position than I was 10 years earlier when I didn't have any experience as a college head coach.

I thought I was ready, but Stu Jackson got the Badger job. I felt like I was given a fair shake, and I didn't lose a wink of sleep over not getting it.

But I was ready.

I didn't get an interview with Wisconsin in 1995 when Pat Richter hired Dick Bennett to take over for Stan Van Gundy, who had been a one-year interim coach after Stu Jackson left for the NBA. Everything happened so quickly.

But I didn't have any problems with how it played out. Dick Bennett worked his way through the ranks, and paid his dues as a teacher and coach.

I've never been one to network for a job. I haven't had people call people on my behalf. But I did get a call from Wayne Embry while I was at Platteville in the early '90s.

Wayne was the general manager of the Cleveland Cavaliers and he wanted me to consider the possibility of being an assistant to the Cavs' head coach, Lenny Wilkens.

I must admit that I did think about it briefly, since it had crossed my mind in the past: "What would it be like to coach in the NBA?" Maybe it was the Philly connection of Jack McKinney, Jimmy Lynam and Matt Goukas that aroused my curiosity.

McKinney was a head coach with three NBA teams and an assistant with a couple of others, including the Milwaukee Bucks. Goukas played for the 76ers and later coached them, while Lynam also coached the Sixers and two other teams in the league.

When I talked with Wayne Embry about the assistant's job, it was presented in the context of, "Maybe there was something there." Maybe not. We didn't talk again.

Once I got to Platteville as a head coach, once I got to paint instead of just carrying the brushes, it was difficult for me to think in terms of being an assistant again. Not that I thought that I was above being an assistant. Especially an NBA assistant.

But I still wanted to call the shots at the college level.

That was my niche. Especially the Division I level. I was never really attracted to Division II because of the uneven way the scholarship money was distributed between players. You had X-number of dollars to work with, and you had to divide it up.

I wanted all, or none.

I wanted to work at D-III, where none of the players were on scholarship.

Or I wanted to work at D-I, where all or very close to all were tendered. You do have some walk-ons, but they know what they can and can't do, or earn.

Denver was transitioning to Division I, but it wasn't what I was looking for.

Wisconsin was what I wanted, but it didn't pan out — twice.

In 1999, though, Nancy Zimpher opened the door, and gave me the chance to call my own shots at a D-I program. She believed in me. So did Bud Haidet and Doug Beard.

Nancy was the chancellor at UW-Milwaukee. Bud was the athletic director and Doug was the assistant AD.

I still wasn't convinced that I wanted to leave Platteville for UWM until I walked into Nancy's office and we talked. I thought it was going to be your standard interview.

It was not.

She closed the door, we sat down and she immediately cut to the chase when she said, "What's it going to take to be our head coach?"

I smiled from ear to ear.

She had done her homework.

She had talked to a number of different people.

And she basically said, "You're our guy."

She showed me that she was willing to do some things to upgrade the program. And I could sense in her commitment that she was giving me the autonomy that I needed to do my job. She was going to support me and give me a chance to hustle and outwork people and do whatever I had to do to rebuild the UWM program. Bud Haidet and Doug Beard were just as supportive and committed to me.

Still, some questioned my sanity for even considering the job.

After all, the media kept dwelling on the negative: the last winning season was 1993 and UWM had lost 20 or more games three times in the last five years.

That's what I was reading and this is what I was hearing from others: "You can't do this, you can't do that, you can't win there."

I didn't believe any of it, and I wasn't about to point fingers on why the program had not been successful in the past. Ever hear of a sleeping giant?

No question, I felt that UWM could be a winner. That's the input I got from a couple of friends in the coaching profession, Lon Kruger and Pete Gillen.

"What would you do if you were me?" I asked them.

"You've got to be kidding," they both said. "You've got to take the job."

I had already made up my mind.

The word got around Platteville very quickly that I wasn't coming back. And it was very emotional. I didn't even have a chance to savor the win over Hampden-Sydney and our fourth national championship. I hadn't even seen the replay of the game.

The one statement that I heard repeatedly was, "Bo, we were

surprised that you stayed this long in Platteville. We thought you were going to make a splash — win a championship — and use this job as a stepping stone to go somewhere else."

Even my brother-in-law thought that way.

But we were raising a family and we liked the idea of our kids growing up in a community like Platteville. I felt we could start a tradition that could last for a long time. After our first seven or eight years, people still couldn't believe I hadn't moved on.

Now I was leaving, I was going somewhere else — 15 years later.

***

You can't get it done without players, good players; a universal truth in sports. But I've always maintained that you don't necessarily have to have the best players. You need to have good players who have the right qualities.

I like developing players. I like having them around for four years, sometimes five years. I like giving them that time frame to develop and improve.

When head coaches make the jump from Division III to Division I, they are subjected to questions about their recruiting ability and philosophy.

When athletic directors are evaluating prospective coaches, they sometimes miss the boat on what it takes to be a successful recruiter at the Division III level.

You've got to sell, sell, sell.

You've got to recruit numbers. But how are you going to entice players to your school? You don't have anything to give them financially. Instead, you're offering them a chance to get an education, while playing a game that most of them love.

That's stressed. You have to love the game to play at D-III.

I recruited guys to Platteville, who ended up going to Division I schools. When I started recruiting them, they weren't D-I players. But as they matured as juniors and seniors, they became more marketable and the scholarship programs jumped on them.

I never complained when they went somewhere else.

As far as what we were asking the players to do in conditioning — and in many other aspects of our program — there was no difference between Platteville and any Division I school in the country. We just couldn't give them a penny.

The same questions tend to be raised about Division III coaches.

Can they recruit the blue-chipper?

Can they relate to the big-time athletes?

It can be a moot point, depending on the Division I job.

Let's face it, you don't have to be that good of a salesman or recruiter at some schools and you're still going to get good players because of the program's basketball history or tradition and the school's location and intangibles.

But there was often a stigma attached to Division III coaches — the perception that they wouldn't recognize real talent because they haven't been around real talent.

Get real.

I played with some guys in high school who could play with anybody, anywhere. They just didn't have the grades. Or they couldn't stay out of trouble.

Maybe one of the top five players I've ever seen was from Chester. His name was Emerson Baynard. He was right up there with Horace Walker, who went on to be an All-American at Michigan State.

Baynard was probably better than Walker; maybe even better than many of the guys who are playing right now in the NBA. In the late '50s and early '60s, Baynard was dunking from the free throw line and turning heads with his leaping ability. He once scored 60 points in a high school game and averaged 32 for the season.

Baynard had some issues outside of basketball and he was incarcerated for awhile. His last hurrah came while playing for Sunbury in the old Eastern League.

Let me put it this way: there was no shortage of talent in Chester.

I have been around talented players all my life.

In 1993, I was an assistant to Pete Gillen at the U.S. Olympic festival and I was around talented collegians like Jacque Vaughn from Kansas, Jeff McInnis from North Carolina and Gary Trent from Ohio University. All moved on to the NBA.

In 1995, I was an assistant to Lon Kruger on Team USA, which competed at the World University games in Fukuoka, Japan. Talk about talented players?

During drills, I worked a lot with the guards: Allen Iverson from Georgetown, Ray Allen from Connecticut, Kerry Kittles from Villanova, Chucky Atkins from South Florida, Charles O'Bannon from UCLA and Jerod Hasse from Kansas.

Iverson had different speeds during practice, like he was saving himself. But when we scrimmaged, he was all-out. What a competitor, what a will to win.

I was really impressed with Tim Duncan, the All-American from Wake Forest. He had so much poise athletically, and he was so sharp intellectually. When you're putting together an all-star team, sometimes it's hard to get everybody to buy into the same things. Some guys have their own agendas. That wasn't the case with Duncan.

Overall, it was a good learning experience. I was put in a much different environment at a much higher level of competition. And I wanted to make sure that I did a good job of not only representing Platteville, but all of Division III.

Talk about talent? Believe it or not, Ernie Peavy could have played defensively with that group. Believe it. He was that good by the time he left Platteville.

As a coach, you're reminded, "At every level, we're still all the same. The strategies and X's and O's might differ. But we're still all about getting guys to buy into what we're selling and teaching. We're still all about finding ways to motivate players."

That's no different at Division I, or Division III.

Don't get hung up on the Roman Numerals.

I never have.

Don't get me wrong, either.

A Division III coach has obstacles. The biggest is the marketability of that coach to the decision-makers who are involved in the hiring process.

That coach can be a hard sell to the boosters, the money people who may prefer to have an assistant from a high profile program or a national power team.

A lot of guys can coach at D-III. They know their X's and O's. They know how to run practices. They know how to motivate their players and manage a game.

But can they schmooze fans and booster groups? Can they handle all the things that factor into running a D-I program? That includes media.

Does that athletic director or chancellor feel like they can market that D-III coach to his or her constituency?

There are a lot of good Division III coaches who are content to stay where they're at, and they're not particularly interested in the limelight, so to speak.

That's not why I wanted to be a Division I coach. Like I said earlier, I was curious to see if what we were doing at Platteville would translate somewhere else. I knew the answer. But I needed to get to a school where I really wanted to be, Wisconsin.

There's a progression for many coaches, not unlike many teachers who aspire to be professors. You might teach in a junior high with the objective of moving up and teaching at a high school. Once there, you might set your sights on teaching at a small college with the ultimate goal of teaching at a major research university.

Happens every day in America.

Just like the bagboy at a grocery store, who works his way up the ladder from bagger to the manager of the store to the manager of two or three stores to an upper management position with a big chain of stores to the title of CEO.

It happens.

If you're a newspaper writer, what does it take to move from the Cuba City *Tri-County Press* to the Baraboo *News Republic* to the Wisconsin *State Journal* to the Milwaukee *Journal Sentinel* to the Washington *Post* or the New York *Times?*

It takes writing skills, and good timing. But it also takes someone to believe in you. That's what you need to make the jump from Division III to Division I.

One other thing.

You need to be successful.

Here's what I tell D-III coaches: Figure out where you are on your lifeline and take care of that first. Build your resume. Do a good job with the people you have. Don't spend all your time wishing that you were somewhere else. Live in the moment.

The best advice of all?

Win.

If I was at Platteville for 15 years and I was a .500 coach, I wasn't going to get the UWM job. We were 60-2 over the last two seasons.

Now, is there an age at which you can't lead people to success? After leaving Platteville for UWM, I was asked if I had the energy for another rebuilding project.

I was 51.

John Chaney was 50 years old when he left Division II Cheyney State for the head coaching position at Temple University. And let's not forget about Winston Churchill, who was 66 when he was named the prime minister of Great Britain.

Churchill never went to "war" at Eau Claire's Zorn Arena or Butler's Hinkle Fieldhouse or Michigan State's Breslin Center. But he did say a few things that had application to basketball coaches. Such as, "The pessimist sees difficulty in every opportunity. The optimist sees the opportunity in every difficulty."

That's how I looked at the UWM challenge.

History will be kind to me, for I intend to write it.

That was Churchill again, not Ryan.

***

What's the first thing we did? We spruced up the locker room.

There are different ways of putting on a new coat of paint. What UWM needed at that time was a scrape job that would take off about 10 layers of paint before we could put on that new coat. We knew that we were starting from scratch.

Facilities were an issue. But we thought UWM was underselling itself. So we started changing that culture by stirring up interest on campus. From that standpoint, the Klotsche Center was perfect. Especially after approval of a $2 million renovation.

They were playing some games at the MECCA, the historic arena in downtown Milwaukee where the Bucks and Marquette used to play. But it was too big for our purposes. There's nothing wrong with creating demand — making it a tough ticket.

A lot of the students who lived in the dorms and apartments were able to walk right out their door and into the Klotsche Center. You just wanted to make sure the game was exciting so they weren't worried about what kind of seat they were sitting in.

What were we giving the ticket-holder?

We weren't going to change what was successful at Platteville. We were going to be aggressive; and pressure the ball with our cat-and-mouse game. But our half-court defense was still going to be our blood-and-guts.

On offense, of course, we were running the Swing. We were the easiest team in the world to prepare for once we got it going at Platteville, because we were going to do the same things, and force our opponent to stop them.

I'm a firm believer in staying true to your strengths.

I remember listening to an interview with an elite tennis player, whose playing style came under question because it wasn't considered flashy or sexy. He just went out and hit ground strokes and beat opponents with sound, fundamental play.

When he was asked about the lack of flair and excitement in his game, the tennis player said that he derived satisfaction from "hitting the same old boring winners."

I'm going to do things a certain way, too.

I'm not going to outthink myself.

And, to me, it's never boring. Winning, that is.

When I met with UWM's returning players, I told them, "If some of you want to make a change now, feel free to do so because this is the best time for it. We're going to work you a lot harder than maybe you've been worked before."

There were some guys in the program that we quickly eliminated or they eliminated themselves. I wasn't trying to run anybody off. I was just letting them know what it was going to be like with a "My way or the highway" speech.

They knew that I wasn't going to change very much because the game doesn't change. On offense, it's about taking care of the ball and getting good shots. On defense, it's about not giving up easy layups and making each basket a struggle for the other team.

Now, how can you make the game anymore simple than that?

I closed by telling the players, "It's not that I won't change. But this is just the way I am. I want guys who want to play. And I want guys who play with passion."

We knew that we had to roll up our sleeves and get busy. We knew the situation needed work. But we needed to get people to believe in what we were doing. Beyond that, the first part of any turnaround is being competitive within your league.

That was the Midwestern Collegiate Conference.

Can you beat a Butler or a Detroit? There were a few teams in the league that were head and shoulders above the rest. How do you change that pecking order? You just keep plugging the holes while getting your guys to learn the system and grow.

We started off on the right foot. In our season opener, we beat Central Michigan on a 3-point buzzer beater by Clay Tucker. With four seconds left on the clock, Kalombo Kadima inbounded the ball and Tucker dribbled to the opposite end of the floor and hit the game-winner from the top of the key for a one point win.

The following Monday when the television crews showed up for our practice, I gathered the players and staged a re-enactment of that final possession. I got the idea from something that we did in 1979 when I was an assistant at Wisconsin.

Claude Gregory had drained a 35-foot shot at the buzzer to beat Northwestern. The following day, I had Gregory attempt the same shot for Van Stoutt and his film crew from WISC-TV in Madison. Swish. Claude hit the shot again.

I couldn't resist the temptation to reset, if not rewrite some history at UWM. But Clay Tucker missed the shot with the cameras rolling at practice. "Don't worry about it," I said. "Hey, we're 1-for-2, but the one counted for a W."

We got 15 W's that first season at UWM. We went 15-14 with young players. We had eight freshmen on the roster, including three starters (Tucker, Kadima and Ronnie Jones) and three key reserves (Dan Weisse, Jason Frederick and Justin Lettenberger).

Chad Angeli, a junior from Wausau, was rugged inside and our No. 1 offensive threat. Despite being blind in one eye, he never let it affect how he worked or competed. Shaun Fountain was our only senior starter and our third-leading scorer.

As a team, we were picked to finish last in the league.

We ended up tied for fourth place.

Going into the second season at UWM, I knew we still had some things to learn. As a player, when you reach your sophomore year, the expectations are just different.

Tucker, Frederick, and Angeli each averaged in double figures. Four others averaged six or more points: Weisse, Jones, Kadima and James Wright.

Again, we won 15 games — 15-13 overall, 7-7 in the league. We scored 106 points and lost in four overtimes at Illinois-Chicago. But our guys bounced back the very next game to win in double-overtime at Loyola of Chicago. That showed me something.

One of our most frustrating losses was against Butler at their place. We lost in overtime at Hinkle Fieldhouse in Indianapolis. That was the team and program that you kind of measured yourself against in the MCC. We felt like we were on track.

We had a better team that second year at UWM. But the element of surprise was gone. We weren't sneaking up on people. And the schedule was tougher. Revenue games — or guaranteed paydays — are a fact of life when you're coaching at a mid-major.

Our first season, we played at Iowa State, Cincinnati and Utah. Does it help you prepare for the league playing against bigger, stronger nonconference opponents?

It does. It helps you get better. At Platteville, I never shied away from scheduling Division I and Division II schools. I saw it as a reward for your players.

At UWM, we had to raise X-number of dollars for the athletic department, not just for men's basketball, and that's why we were playing the money games.

Our second season, we played at Iowa, Illinois and Wisconsin. We faced the Illini and the Badgers in back-to-back games. Big Ten commissioner Jim Delany was prepared to invite me to their conference luncheon if I had scheduled that fourth Big Ten school.

Besides the revenue guarantee, we knew that we were getting good experience from playing good teams in good venues. We also felt we could beat them.

You know the playground mentality? Even if you're playing the Kings of the Court — you still have a chance of beating them every once in awhile.

My coaches knew the drill, in a manner of speaking. Robby Jeter, Greg Gard, Saul Phillips and Duffy Conroy also knew the game and what we needed to accomplish at UWM.

My assistants were responsible for communicating with the players and breaking down an opponent's strengths and weaknesses through the scouting reports. I also wanted them to go out into the Milwaukee community and connect people to our program.

Some are better at networking than others.

Some work crowds and boosters better than others.

Still, I believe that you have to hustle and "work it" a little. I'm not saying you have to run for Governor. But you have to promote your game, and basketball program.

You can't sit back and think, "I'm just going to coach and everything else will take care of itself." It doesn't work that way. You have to be a good-will ambassador. And that's what we were during our two seasons at UWM.

I felt good about where we were. I felt within four years we were going to do the same things in Milwaukee that we had done in Platteville. I felt we were either going to win our league championship or, at the very least, be in that battle the last week or two.

In the end, we didn't get a chance to be a part of it because we had moved on. But that was our expectation for Clay Tucker, Ronnie Jones, Jason Frederick, Dan Weisse, Justin Lettenberger and Dylan Page, among others.

In that fourth year, Butler hit a last-second shot to edge out UWM for the regular season title in what was now the Horizon League. Under the guidance of Bruce Pearl, the Panthers won their conference tournament — by beating Butler in Milwaukee — and advanced to the NCAA tournament for the first time in school history.

I couldn't have been happier or more excited for Coach Pearl, and the players. I know that he told the press that he was the beneficiary of some terrific groundwork. But he deserves the credit for doing what we all knew he could do at UWM.

He just needed someone to believe in him.

Like a George Chryst, a Nancy Zimpher and a Pat Richter believed in me.

***

"Bo, are you ready?

"Pat, I've been ready."

That was pretty much the extent of my phone conversation with Pat

Richter, the UW athletic director. He knew me better than anyone could imagine, and he said that he never had any doubts about whether he was getting a guy who can coach.

So when Pat said that he felt the timing was right for me to take the Wisconsin job, I knew that he wasn't going to make that kind of decision haphazardly.

I never asked if he was serious about hiring Rick Majerus after the decision was made to not bring back Brad Soderberg with the Badgers.

It didn't matter. I knew Coach Majerus, and I knew his name came up for job openings all the time. That was his nature, and the nature of the business.

After the Majerus thing kept surfacing, I remember telling someone, "I don't know if I was my wife's first choice, either. But we've had a good marriage."

Was I ready to be a head coach in the Big Ten? You always feel like you can do what you were trained to do. Why else would you be in the profession?

It wasn't like I was dentist, and I was getting ready to perform open heart surgery. I was a basketball coach, and that's what I've been training to be all my life.

Remember, when I played sports, I was the point guard, the shortstop, the quarterback. I don't think I fell into those positions by accident.

I never thought I was better than anyone else.

But whenever I got involved competitively, I usually ended up in a leadership role. When people believe in you — especially at an impressionable age — you believe in yourself and what you're setting out to accomplish. My goal was to coach.

What else can a guy do to prepare for a job? Not many, though, get the chance to go back to an institution and conference — Wisconsin and the Big Ten — where they coached as an assistant and the program didn't have success or live up to expectations.

I was the opposite of the prodigal son, the repentant sinner, who comes home poor and tired and says, "I made a mistake."

I went out into the coaching world to learn the things that I needed to learn to be able to come back and finish some unfinished business.

After spending six years with Coach Cofield and two years with Coach Yoder, I firmly believed that this program could compete for Big

Ten supremacy.

How was I different as a coach on my second tour of duty at Wisconsin? Competitively, I was the same person who hated to lose.

But I was more experienced because of each year that I coached at Platteville and UWM. In the coaching profession, you're learning every practice and every game and you're constantly tweaking. But you don't change your values or principles.

I've never changed how I believe the game should be played.

I was convinced, too, that I was brought to Wisconsin for a reason. When I was asked at my introductory press conference about my goals, I made it clear what that reason was. "We're here to compete for the Big Ten championship," I said.

I wasn't just saying that for the media in attendance or for all our friends who had shown up at the practice gym, the Nicholas-Johnson Pavilion, to welcome us home.

"Don't let the gray hair fool you," I cautioned the crowd that day, my first day on the job. "Energy is not a problem. Recruiting is not a problem. We can sell. We have a lot to sell. To be a Badger is great. To be a successful Badger is even better."

This isn't an ending, I added, this is a beginning.

I meant every word.

The photo appeared in a local publication and the cutline read, "Typical American kids." Meaning we were a pain in the butt. At least I think that's what they were trying to say. My big sister, Nancy Catherine, was 5. I was 4. She was a July baby, '46. I was December, '47.

My first day of class — 1952 — at Upland elementary school. The joke was, "I don't eat graham crackers, and I don't take naps." That's because I was a first grader who skipped kindergarten. I was 4.

As a 12-year-old, I played for Guyer Roofing in the Biddy League, which is akin to Little League baseball. I'm wearing the shiny pants in the top row — second from the left — and I'm standing next to my coach, Sam Ferrrante. We won the championship that year.

I was only a ninth grader at Pulaski junior high school, but I looked tall for my age, even when kneeling for this team shot. Per usual, I made sure I had a piece of the rock. My coach, John Laszek (far left) was one of the all-time greats at Chester. He's still a very good friend today and I see him whenever I go back to the East Coast.

During my senior year of high school, I got most of my steals off the top of our 1-2-2 zone defense. I'm scoring here on a run-out against Lower Merion, a Philadelphia suburb, which later produced Kobe Bryant. I've got the shoes I'm wearing, the Chuck Taylors, in my office at home.

Like any good point guard, I always kept my eyes on the basketball, even when we were posing for a photo. Ron Rainey was my coach at Chester High School and Wilkes College. When he would give us the scouting report, he would go over our opponent's strengths and emphasize what we had to take away defensively. We always trusted him when he said, "So-and-so is their sixth

man and he will do this, this and this when he comes off the bench." That's why our scouting reports have always been pretty thorough at Wisconsin. My assistants can tell you how an opposing player gets off the bus, whether his right foot or left foot touches the ground first.

I'm not sure I went anywhere without a basketball in my hands. That comes with being a point guard, I guess. I still socialize with Coach Ron Rainey and many of my former Wilkes College teammates: Herb Kemp, Wally Umbach, Bob Ockenfuss, Richie Davis, Jay Riemel, to name just a few. They'll show up whenever we play

at Penn State. Or, we'll meet in Atlantic City over the summer and reminisce about playing for the Wilkes Colonels, a college division program in the '60s that didn't have athletic scholarships. The NCAA didn't adopt Roman Numerals until the '70s. Wilkes is now D-III.

Susquehanna				Wilkes			
	g	f	pts		g	f	pts
Boblick	10	3	23	Reimel	2	0	4
Dale	0	0	0	Grick	5	0	10
Miller	7	2	16	Umbach	7	2	16
Freeland	3	2	8	Ryan	18	7	43
Llewellyn	7	6	20	Kennedy	0	0	0
Schere	5	5	15	Frey	0	0	0
Meriwether	0	0	0	Jannuzzi	0	2	2
Mroz	1	1	3	Kurosky	1	0	2
Trembulak	0	0	0	Kemp	11	2	24
Roessner	2	1	5	Davis	5	2	12
				Weizel	0	0	0
Totals	35	20	90				
				Totals	49	15	113

Halftime score—51-46 Wilkes leading.

The Susquehanna game was originally scheduled on my birthday (Dec. 20) and I was mad when it was postponed because of a snowstorm. Two months later, when the teams finally played, they were in a zone and so was I. As a junior and senior, I averaged between 12 and 14 points. But this was just one of those special nights, where I was getting baskets off steals, off put-backs and off the offense. I was 18 of 25 from the floor and 7 of 7 from the free throw line. Coach Rainey still has the shot chart and he estimated that I would have scored over 50 points if there had been a 3-point line.

When I later had this photo framed and sitting in my office, I'd jokingly point to it and tell my players, "Now make sure you always find the open guy." That's me playing for Wilkes College in 1968, and scoring — 1 vs. 5 — against Upsala College.

In 1970, I was inducted into the Military Police. I always wore uniforms playing sports, so wearing a uniform wasn't that big of a deal. Unlike Bill Murray in *Stripes* I never saw a Louise or Stella during our training or in our unit at Fort Gordon in Augusta, Georgia.

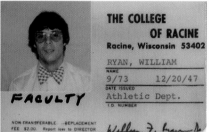

THE COLLEGE OF RACINE

Racine, Wisconsin 53402

RYAN, WILLIAM
NAME
9/73   12/20/47
DATE ISSUED
FACULTY   Athletic Dept.
I.D. NUMBER

NON-TRANSFERABLE —REPLACEMENT
FEE $2.00. Report loss to DIRECTOR

Since Dominican College morphed into the College of Racine, which folded shortly thereafter, my faculty ID is somewhat of a collector's item. I had been coaching basketball at Brookhaven junior high when I joined Bill Cofield as an assistant on his Dominican staff. I taught a class in Racine, and I was also the head baseball coach. But it was a short run.

Jay Holliday was my college roommate for three years at Wilkes. Even though he bears a facial resemblance to Larry Bird in this photo, football was his sport. He was a defensive back on Wilkes teams that lost just once in four seasons.

On a typically windy day in Chicago —
June 15, 1974 — I married Kelly. We
had seen the movie the *Great Gatsby*
together and I told Kelly that
I wanted to wear a white suit in our
wedding. I don't think anyone will
confuse me for Jay Gatsby (Robert
Redford), though.

Since we didn't have any money, we had
our wedding reception in my mother-in-
law's backyard. On top of that, she
cooked all the food. That's Mary (Kelly's
mom) on the far right. My mom, Louise,
is on the far left.

My dad must have thought he was Peter Fonda wearing the shades. From left to
right, that's my mom, Louise; my dad, Butch; Kelly; me, my sister Nancy; and her
husband, Ray. You won't find two bigger Badger fans than Nancy and Ray.

Being an assistant coach under Bill Cofield at Wisconsin (left) shaped me in many different ways. Coach Cofield was one of the best recruiters I've ever seen. He was well-spoken and always presented himself well in the home. My job was to establish the relationship with a prospect to make it real tough for the kid to say "no."

As a recruiter, I had a solid relationship with Madison La Follette's Ricky Olson who committed to the Badgers on the very same day that Steve Yoder (far left) was introduced as the school's head coach. I was retained as an assistant on the UW staff — joining Rick Bowen (second from left) and Brad McNulty. Years later, I crossed paths with Coach Bowen when I was at Platteville and he was running his own program at UW-River Falls.

Robby Jeter (left) was one of my best players with the Pioneers and a member of a national championship team. I called him "Snake" because of his ability to slither to the basket. Robby was a point-forward or what was the equivalent of having a point guard at the 3-spot or small forward. He was bright, attentive, and competitive — all the qualities that you'd like to have in a head coach, which he is today at UW-Milwaukee.

George Chryst was not only the athletic director and football coach at UW-Platteville but he was one of the most influential people in my life. He convinced me that I needed to be a head coach and Platteville was the right destination for me and my family. He was right. George's legacy has been carried on by his sons: Paul Chryst, the offensive coordinator at Wisconsin; Geep Chryst, the tight ends coach for the Carolina Panthers; and Rick Chryst, the commissioner of the Mid-American Conference.

It's not what you think. Even though I'm holding up three fingers on my left hand while pinching the net between my thumb and index finger, I wasn't consciously signaling our third national championship at Platteville. It just turned out that way after we beat Hope College in the finals at Salem, Va. We finished 30-0.

Saul Phillips, a senior captain on our undefeated 1995 team at Platteville, is showing off the Division III national championship plaque in the company of former Gov. Tommie Thompson. Among our seniors present was Ernie Peavy (far left) who was named the post-season tournament's most valuable player. In the finals, we beat Manchester (Ind.), which was also undefeated and coached by Steve Alford. By the way, Saul Phillips at UW-Platteville, Matt Ryan at UWM and Tanner Bronson at UW are on my list of all-time scout team captains. Saul is now the head coach at North Dakota State.

A funny thing happened on the way to playing a late January road game at Iowa. I had a court renamed in my honor at Platteville. It was a very touching and emotional day — Jan. 27, 2007 — for me and Kelly and the kids. That's son-in-law Matt (far

left) and oldest daughter Megan. And that's Platteville chancellor Dave Markee (far right) who presided over the half-time ceremony and had some very nice things to say. He mentioned that our Platteville teams became an extension of the community; extending well beyond the court and the game of basketball. That was one of our goals, along with raising a family and building a program everybody could be proud of. It should be noted that we won our game the following day at Iowa making the excursion even more meaningful.

When I was introduced as the head coach at UW-Milwaukee, I said, "If people want to tell me what can't be done here, I'll listen to them and walk away and go, 'So what?' I don't see anything here that can keep us from building a strong program. How far we can take it, I don't know. But I don't dwell on negatives." I was 51 — going on 31 in my mind — and I was ready for another challenge with the Panthers.

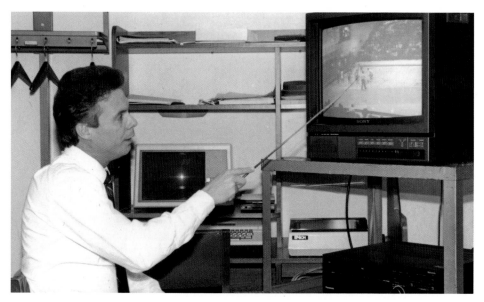

What we're trying to do with our video sessions is present some visual bullet points on the screen that we can use as teaching points for our players. The tape doesn't lie. We'll point out where they might have made a better decision. We'll also point out their good decisions—with the hope that it resonates with the other players, especially those who aren't getting minutes, because they need to learn, too.

Throughout my journey as a coach, I've had people believe in me and Wisconsin athletic director Pat Richter was among them. At my introductory press conference, Pat pointed out that I had waited patiently for this opportunity to coach the Badgers. He was right. I wouldn't have left UWM for any other school. Because I was 53 when I returned to the UW, people have proposed, "Can you imagine the record you might have had if you had been given the job earlier in your life?" No, I can't imagine because I was busy doing what I was suppose to be doing at Platteville and Milwaukee. Could I have done it when I was 35 or 40? Sure. My principles didn't change, my values didn't change and how I saw the game being played has never changed. You're learning every day as a coach, and you're tweaking, but you don't change your values. At least I never have.

Alando Tucker was confident without being arrogant and one of the strongest leaders I've ever had a pleasure to coach. That's why it was such an honor for our school and Alando to be among the top vote-getters for the 2007 John Wooden Award. He was most deserving of sharing the national spotlight with the other finalists. From left to right, Ohio State coach Thad Matta and Greg Oden; Tuck and me; former Texas A&M coach Billy Gillispie and Acie Law; and Kevin Durant, the first freshman to win the Wooden, and Texas coach Rick Barnes.

Devin Harris was the fifth over-all pick in the 2004 draft. It was a little complicated in that Washington and Dallas had earlier arranged a deal. So the Wizards drafted Devin and traded him to the Mavericks along with Jerry Stackhouse and Christian Laettner in exchange for Antawn Jamison. During the draft, itself, I was sitting behind Saint Joe's Jameer Nelson, a Chester native, who was taken 20th by Denver and traded to Orlando. Devin, who's now with the New Jersey Nets, has always been able to see the big picture. He has just been so right-on with so many things in his life, whether it involves his future and investments, or giving back to his folks and the game of basketball that he so loves.

We didn't see the Pope — he was at his summer place — but our 10-day exhibition tour of Italy was an unforgettable experience for our travel party from Wisconsin. Before the start of the 2006-2007 season, we visited Rome, Florence and Lake Como. We went 5-0 on the trip, and I really thought it brought everyone closer together.

I'll never forget how pleasant and outgoing these USA all-stars were during the 1995 World University games. I hate to single out any one person, because it was such a great group, but Tim Duncan was special. He'd sit down at a meal and start talking like you were a long lost friend.

When the Badgers played at Penn State during the 2003 season, we had a Wilkes College basketball reunion in State College. From left to right, Herb Kemp, Rich Davis, me, Wally Umbach, and Jay Riemel.

Sharing the stage with greatness. My former Chester teammate, Mike Marshall (left), was a first-team prep All-American in 1966. He once scored 58 points in a game. Meanwhile, Fred Pickett was a Hall of Fame coach, winning three state championships, eight district titles, and 331 games during his 13 seasons at Chester.

The Ryans vacationing on the Jersey shore. We've only missed a couple of times in the last 30 years. I'm holding Mairin, who's about seven weeks old. Megan is wearing the 1991 Platteville national championship T-shirt. Will is on the far left, while Matt is holding Brenna. Kelly, of course, is behind the camera.

This was a gathering of the Ryan boys — Matt, Butch, me and Will — at the 1991 Final Four in Indianapolis. That was the year that Duke and Mike Krzyzewski beat Kansas and Roy Williams in the finals. That weekend, I received my Coach of the Year award after winning our first national championship at Platteville. Even though I was coaching the Pioneers, my dad was still wearing Badger gear from my first stint in Madison.

You're looking at three generations of William Francis Ryans: a William Francis Ryan, Sr., a William Francis Ryan, Jr. and a William Francis Ryan, III. They answer to Butch, Bo and Will. A William Francis Ryan, IV, was not in the offering. The string ended when Will's wife, Emily, gave birth to Owen William Ryan. I told Will that you better have a lot of money if your last name is attached to the Roman Numeral IV. Will and Emily are living in Fargo, where Will is an assistant coach at North Dakota State.

The Ryan kids hamming it up with a team huddle. From left to right, Brenna, Matt, Megan (Kaiser), son-in-law Matt Kaiser, Will and his wife Emily, and Mairin.

Kelly has been at my side through thick and thin — for all of our triumphs and championships, whether they were national championships at Platteville or Big Ten championships at Wisconsin. It probably sounds like a broken record, but I won the lottery with Kelly, who has always been there for me and our family.

CHAPTER SEVEN

From Bud to Bo

R on Rainey was my prep coach in Chester and my college coach at Wilkes. The last time I played for him was 1969. But I still address him as Coach or Coach Rainey.

Bill Cofield hired me at the College of Racine and the University of Wisconsin. To me, he's still Coach Cofield whenever I reflect on his memory.

Tom Davis coached at Boston College, Stanford and Iowa. He had an influence on my thinking as a young head coach at Platteville.

Today, if we were golfing together, I might address him as "Tom." But if I was directing a question to him, it would be, "Coach, what do you think about this?"

That's the way I was brought up. I never referred to any of my friends' dads by their first names. It was always Mr. Smith, or Mr. Jones or Mr. Gamble.

Why the formality? Why the professional courtesy? Why not? A coach should always be addressed as a coach, just like a doctor should always be addressed as a doctor.

It's old school, it's John Wooden, it's why *They Call Me Coach* is the title of one of Coach Wooden's books.

Have any of my players ever called me Bo?

Not that I can remember.

But I'm sure they've called me a few other things.

I don't answer well to S.O.B.

I had a good idea, though, what the players were saying about me and the Swing offense after our first four games at Wisconsin. And it probably wasn't flattering.

We opened the 2001 season with a loss at UNLV and that was followed by two losses in three games at the Big Island Invitational in Hilo, Hawaii.

Some players were upset. But they didn't come to me, which is what you want as a head coach. You want them to talk to your assistants. When I worked for Coach Cofield and Coach Yoder, I had players tell me things that they wouldn't tell anyone else.

In this instance, some players went to Robby Jeter, my lead assistant, when we were still in Hawaii, and they said, "Hey, this system isn't going to work. The Swing isn't going to work. What Coach Ryan is doing isn't going to work."

That was not surprising to me. I kind of expected that reaction. So did Robby, who summarily enlightened the players: "Guys, he ain't changing, so you'd better change. Work at it. Either you're changing, or you probably won't be playing for us."

Another assistant, Greg Gard, was at the meeting and backed what Robby was saying. You see, some of the players felt like there was only one way to do things. And they were right. There was only one way to do things — our way. You can't waffle.

Usually, it takes time for players and coaches to get a feel for one another. What I basically had to do was get people to understand what we wanted. At first, they didn't know how to take my criticism in film sessions. They didn't know what to expect.

I don't know too many human beings who are brought into this world saying, "Oh, I wonder what somebody can tell me today that I'm NOT doing right?"

Truth is, I'm straightforward. I can even be biting at times. But I can also be complimentary when it's warranted or needed. I informed the players, "If you're sensitive, you need to lose that in a hurry.' It was, 'Hey, guys, we still love you, but ....'"

The tapes don't lie.

We got home from Hawaii on a Sunday night. And we were back on a plane Tuesday for a flight to Atlanta and our game against Georgia Tech in the Big Ten/ACC Challenge. The guys were physically and mentally tired. Who wouldn't be?

Obviously, there were extenuating circumstances. We had eight scholarship players. Five had never played more than 13 minutes in a college game. Roy Boone, Mark Vershaw, Andy Kowske, Maurice Linton and Mike Kelley were gone. And they were the core of the Final Four team in 2000.

Two others transferred (Ricky Bower and Julian Swartz). Two others were lost before the season opener (Latrell Fleming and Andreas Helmigk). We were playing three freshmen and two sophomores in our rotation at Georgia Tech.

Mike Wilkinson hadn't played yet at Wisconsin. But he was stronger than your normal freshman because he practiced and lifted weights during his redshirt season.

Devin Harris was a true freshman and you could mold Devin into what you wanted. Neil Plank was a true freshman who saw limited minutes off the bench.

Freddie Owens and Dave Mader were sophomores who hadn't played much the season before. They each averaged less than four minutes a game.

I saw Kirk Penney as a one-dimensional outside shooter. Kirk was a junior, and I had to convince him that he had to change his game to play in our system.

When Kirk asked why, I said, "Because I get to be the coach."

I knew he would do well because he was not afraid to work and he enjoyed what he was doing. It was neat to be around that type of a person. He was the opposite of the guy who wants to tell you how tough his job is, and how terrible his life is.

My parents always reminded me that when you meet somebody, you don't always remember what he said, but you do remember how he made you feel.

Charlie Wills and Travon Davis were our two seniors. Charlie was a tough guy who seemed to react pretty well to our ways and what we were doing. So did Travon. I kept hearing the same expression, almost ad nauseum, that they "bought into it."

But you know what they did? They took advantage of an opportunity. That's where you have to give them credit. Some might say, "Well, you had to play them because you only had eight scholarship players."

You had to play them? You know what? You don't have to do anything. As seniors, Charlie and Travon took advantage of an opportunity, knowing that we believed in them as players and we were encouraging them for the right reasons.

We had to establish that trust factor with everybody. That was our first challenge — getting them to understand that we were doing things for a reason, we were doing things for them. When you're going into a new classroom or taking on a new team, as a teacher or a coach, you've got to get them to know that you're going to be firm, you're going to be fair, you don't have favorites and you don't have cliques.

All we wanted to establish was that foundation of trust, a foundation that everybody was going to be treated fairly. We told them, "You make a commitment to us and, as a coaching staff, we're definitely going to make a commitment to you."

No questions.

No ifs, ands or buts.

You can't fool young people.

We knew that there would be some adversity, some things out of our control. And we knew that they were hearing from people outside the program how tough of a season it was going to be for the Badgers. So we took the opposite stance. From the start, we coached them with the idea that we were expecting them to be successful.

Our point guard, Travon Davis, was the key to the season. He had heard all the stuff about being a "one-man turnover" and how he couldn't do this or couldn't do that. When you keep on telling someone what he can't do, there will be a point where he's going to get the chance to prove what he can do. Travon got that chance.

I thought he was very sincere; he was someone who recognized that he wasn't going to be a 20-point scorer or realize some of the dreams that he may have carried into his college career. He was more of a realist than anyone else. He understood what he had to do to help make us successful as a team, and he did it.

At Georgia Tech, Travon Davis had 14 points in the first half. As a team, we were clicking, we were carving them up on defense, and we had a 20-point lead early in the second half. I later watched the TV copy of the game, and the ESPN announcers, Brad Nessler and Brad Daugherty, kept saying Tech had no answer for the Swing offense.

Georgia Tech coach Paul Hewitt admitted to me afterward that he was having trouble believing that we were in our first season at Wisconsin because of the way we were running the offense. He said it looked like we had been together for years.

Coach Hewitt also acknowledged that he was counting on us to run out of gas knowing what we had just gone through — the long flights and travel from Hawaii to Wisconsin to Georgia and the multiple games in multiple time zones. He had it pegged.

We lost the big lead and the game, though we had a shot to win on our final possession. But I didn't use fatigue as an excuse. We didn't have much experience — as far as minutes played — at the guard position. We didn't have anybody on the floor who had handled pressure, and it showed. We didn't answer the challenge that night.

When we returned to Madison following the Georgia Tech loss, I was anxious to see how the players would react in practice. They could have gone in a number of directions. If I sensed that they were starting to feel sorry for themselves, I was going to rip them. But they didn't take the easy way out.

They came back and worked harder than they had worked before. There was no letdown. They showed me that they were committed, and they wanted to get better. While the results weren't want we wanted, we were learning something from each game and grasping something new from each practice.

I could sleep at night.

We just needed to keep our heads above water, despite playing eight of our 13 nonconference games outside of the Kohl Center, including five road games in 12 days to open the season. But I was encouraged because the players didn't blink. Not even when we were 1-4 and our only win was over a Division II opponent, Hawaii-Hilo.

I knew what I was getting myself into. And I knew we needed to show some resolve and patience. That's what I talked about with my coaches — Robby Jeter, Tony Bennett, Greg Gard and Saul Phillips. But it was easier said than done, especially after one game that was particularly frustrating offensively.

"What about showing them the highlight film?" one of them suggested.

"I think the guys would be shocked if they saw it," another chimed in.

My assistants were talking about a highlight film that we had put together on the Swing offense. Up until then, I had refrained from making Platteville references to our Wisconsin players. I was proud of those teams. But it was not something you bring up.

I hadn't.

But the timing seemed right.

We were 2-5. (A friend was calling us the "Wisconsin Possums" because we played dead at home and got killed on the road. Some friend, huh?)

So, I walked into the locker room and said, "Guys, I didn't want to do this, but I'm going to show you this highlight film for a reason. I thought we ran some pretty good offense at Georgia Tech. And you're starting to get the hang of things.

"But I want you to take a look at these clips. I want to show you how simple the Swing offense can be when you square up, you get the angles, you make the cuts.

"Forget about the color of the uniforms. Forget about the name on the jersey. Forget about the markings on the floor. I want you all to watch the basketball and what happens away from the ball. Here's what it can look like."

There wasn't a sound in the room, and it was not because they had all fallen asleep. They were mesmerized by the passing, the cutting and the timing of what they were watching on the highlight film.

They could see that each Platteville player was in tune with the Swing because they knew the nuances and they were reading and reacting off each screen — and each other — and orchestrating the offense like a symphony.

As I was walking out of the locker room, Travon Davis came up to me and said, "Coach, I'm embarrassed. That was a clinic. And I know we can do that."

I thought we'd be okay from that point on, and we were.

***

When I huddled with Pat Richter and Chancellor John Wiley and we talked about some of the challenges that I was inheriting at Wisconsin, I asked them about the school's self-imposed sanctions relating to The Shoe Box investigation.

Initially, the basketball program was slated to lose one scholarship from the 2002-2003 recruiting class. The penalties also reduced the number of assistant coaches who could recruit off-campus from two to one.

The NCAA later announced additional punishment, which included extending the basketball sanctions from one season to two. When I was quizzed on how that might weaken the program, I said, "It is too early to tell how the limits might affect us. Our stick will just be a little bit smaller and we'll have to swing a little harder."

Not only did we have one less assistant on the road than everyone else, but there was a change in the recruiting calendar, reducing the July evaluation period from 24 days to 14. So, we were recruiting short-handed and now we had less time to recruit.

Knowing the head coach still has to be a closer, we had to be creative with our scheduling. It was like we were running a relay race in track and handing off the baton to the runner on the next leg. When I came off the road, somebody would take my spot, either Robby Jeter or Tony Bennett, who were working in a tag team rotation.

My flight might return to Madison at 2 in the afternoon, and we'd have either Robby or Tony out of the office at 2:15 or 2:30. They were both tenacious recruiters who had inquiring minds and understood what we were looking for and what we needed.

With the tender limitations, we had to run a little faster. I spelled it out to my assistants: "Develop relationships. Get to know everything you can about the player in his environment. Do everything the right way and kill them with kindness."

The guys who were identified early were down to a small number of schools by the time they were going into their senior year. Realistically, anybody who was a good player going into his sophomore year had already taken some unofficial visits and had developed a relationship with certain schools and coaching staffs.

What we were trying to do was recruit players who were going to be seniors — some late bloomers who we felt had a high upside. It was going to be hard for us to gain an edge on established seniors, so we were focusing more on sophomores and juniors.

You've heard the cliché — recruiting is not an exact science. You hit on some, you miss on some. There were some guys that we didn't recruit or couldn't recruit because we didn't have scholarships and they went on to have good careers elsewhere.

There were also guys that we took that other people didn't want, and then when they developed into pretty good players, you had people asking, "What did you see in him?" That happens at every school.

What do you want in a player? They're all a little different. But, in the end, you want competitors who have an eye on a championship. They want to play on a winning team, but they also know the sacrifices that are involved.

I'm not one of those coaches who believe that he can change anybody, regardless of his skill or work level. I'm not that committed in my own mind, in my own beliefs, to say, "I can convert anybody into being the type of player who will do X, Y and Z."

I've never shied away from guys who are into their personal stats. My rationale has been, "If you can score 20, let's get 20. But let's not give up 22 at the other end."

You can recruit scorers or shooters. But if they're not on the floor, how can they shoot or score? You tell them, "If you want to be out there, you better play some D."

So, you have to find players who are committed to playing at both ends and who are willing to do all the little things, like rebounding, taking charges and setting screens.

As a head coach, you have so many demands on your time that your assistants have to do much of the legwork in recruiting. Can you tell right away from watching a prospect on tape whether or not he will fit into your program? You can get an idea. But you can't say it's an absolute simply by watching tape.

That's why you have to bring the kid onto your campus. You have to talk with him and see what he's like, what he's about. Sometimes after we've seen how he acts and handles things, we've said, "No, we're not recruiting so-and-so anymore because he just wouldn't be a good fit with our program. So why make it tough on everyone?"

I don't pay any attention to the recruiting lists or "the experts." We have our own list and evaluation. I don't worry about how a recruiting analyst might rank a player. If we think that he can play, then we'll recruit him.

Some guys are more high maintenance than others. They need all the attention and they drain all your energy. When it takes 80 percent of your workload to take care of 20 percent of your players, you have a bad ratio that's never going to work.

There are some kids who can look really good in a pickup game or a glorified scrimmage in Las Vegas. But it's a lot different when you put them in a team environment with a structured offense and defense and they have to produce.

Just because someone can run and jump definitely doesn't qualify him at Wisconsin. It's still about going to class, getting grades and being a total person. Basketball is still an extracurricular activity. In my mind that never changes.

***

When I got to the UW as a head coach, we were still practicing the same way we did at Platteville and UWM. We hadn't changed much at all. The level of competition varies from year to year, but each practice was pretty much structured the same way.

Passing and catching and ball-handling drills were a must. We also emphasized footwork, rebounding and shooting drills, whether it was with a partner or working alone on post moves. Transition defense was another must in every practice, along with drills for help and recovery, chasing and hedging.

You'll always hear me talking about passing and catching in the same breath because the attentiveness of the receiver has a lot to do with keeping turnovers to a minimum. We talk about hand targets and positioning when the ball is caught.

We also talk about maintaining good balance — making sure someone can't wheel around you and swipe the ball away or bump you into a travel with aggressive defense.

Our players know that they're being held accountable in practice.

What's wrong with being held accountable?

When we're scrimmaging against the scout team, I have a manager standing at my side charting possessions. We'll generally break it down to increments of 10 possessions each. There are usually 10 possessions between media timeouts.

We're trying to develop good habits during these segments with the players in our rotation, the starters and reserves. If we're at nine points on 10 possessions, we're stopping practice and the players are running. Or if we're giving up 12 points on 10 possessions, they're running. They have to learn to play through good and bad spurts.

It's all about being efficient, responsible and accountable.

I read where teams averaged about 68 possessions per 40 minutes during games in 2007. Going into the NCAA tournament, we had the second best efficiency margin in the country behind only Kansas, the eventual national champ. We averaged 1.09 points per possession, while limiting our opponents to .91.

That tells you, more than any other statistic, on whether you have been successful or not. Very rarely will you ever score more than a point per possession and not have a successful season. Conversely, if you're keeping teams to .95 or .90 and below, the chances are that you will also have a very good year.

During practices, I'm not one of those over-caffeinated coaches who are expending tons of nervous energy on every possession while shouting out instructions to their players on everything they're doing. That's fine for some. But that's not me.

In a game, the players don't have a voice in their ear telling them what they can or can't do. I'm a big stickler for simulating game-like situations when we're practicing. The other thing is, if I have to spur on someone to get him to play hard in practice, what's he going to do in a game? I just don't think that's how you should teach.

If I was giving advice to a young head coach on how to structure a practice, I would tell him, "Stick to the basics. Do things that are important and do things that guys can identify with as far as how it's going to help them be successful."

It doesn't make any sense to do stuff just to do stuff. So you organize practice in a way where everything has a purpose and everything is related to the game.

How important is practice? Do you play like you practice? Your body gets training through repetitions. It's a learned behavior. If you've taken any kind of classes in behavioral sciences, it's pretty obvious why you practice and why you train.

Someone asked me once whether I relied on my instincts as an experienced coach to determine how hard we practice from day to day, and week to week during the season. My response? You always go hard. That's non-negotiable.

The length of a practice is negotiable. But whatever we're doing is going to be with the same amount of intensity, whether it's the day before a game or five days before a game. I don't know if every coach treats it the same way, and I don't care.

If you're on the floor, you're there for a purpose.

I'm there for a purpose.

Early in his career, Devin Harris came up to me one day and said, "Coach, let me get this straight now — you expect me to play hard on every possession in practice?"

"I wouldn't expect anything less," I confirmed.

Devin is a pretty sharp young man, and he said, "Okay."

That's all that had to be said.

His eyes were open, his ears were open, his mind was open.

If you're going to practice something, if you're going to work at something and if you're going to try to do something as well as you can, why would I ever accept someone not doing it the right way in practice?

Our teams have always been among the nation's leaders in fewest fouls committed. That also is a learned behavior and comes through repetition in practice. Discipline is important. So is positioning and attention to detail with your feet.

Rather than trying to make the great defensive play by reaching from behind or reaching in when it's not advantageous, why not make the sound play? We teach digging, or tipping up with your hand, instead of slapping down.

More often than not, if an official sees that type of motion — a player bringing his arm down on the ball — it's going to be a foul. Defense is all about discipline and persistence and not giving people something easy. You're teaching not to foul.

But basketball is an aggressive game and sometimes you just get called for more fouls. Sometimes you just foul because you're tired and you take a shortcut.

Do you think every employee goes to work every day in the same frame of mind? Do you think your body always gets the same nutrition and same hours of sleep?

My point? There are some nights when you can't move your feet on defense. There are some nights when you're guilty of reaching in and fouling, and you can't explain the mental breakdown. Why did I do that? Doesn't matter, but you have to survive; you have to take the good with the bad and the bad has to be the exception.

We didn't have any margin for error that first season at Wisconsin.

Because we had so few bodies, I had two of my assistants — Robby Jeter and Tony Bennett — suit up and practice every day with the team. Out of necessity, they played that role.

Tony was an All-American at UW-Green Bay, and one of the great 3-point shooters in college basketball. He played professionally and so did Robby after he left Platteville. He played in Europe. Robby and Tony were each 32 years old.

But they were still very competitive and they made our practices better. They both knew the game. That was the key because it made their participation even more meaningful to the development of our young, inexperienced team. They were always talking to the guys and teaching while they were mixing it up with the players.

Tony used to tell me that Robby was one of the most competitive people that he had ever been around. There are people who think that I am, too, so imagine that? I knew Robby had a sense of purpose when he competed. So did Tony. Was it a luxury to have assistants practicing? You can win without it. But why not use them?

That was a no-brainer.

***

I'm more familiar with Joe Wolf than Thomas Wolfe.

Joe was an All-American from Kohler who ended up at North Carolina. He played in the NBA and now he's coaching in the league with the Milwaukee Bucks. Thomas Wolfe was a novelist who wrote, "You can't go home again."

You didn't have to tell that to Steve Yoder, who faced his old school — Ball State — in his first season at his new school — Wisconsin. I was an assistant on the UW staff, and I remember how emotional it was for Coach Yoder to return for a homecoming game in Muncie, Indiana, where he had coached the six previous years, five as the head coach.

Although we were young and inexperienced, we had an upside. Consider the starters we put on the floor at Ball State: Cory Blackwell, Brad Sellers, Scott Roth, Ricky Olson and Greg Dandridge. But we still lost to a fired-up opponent that was led in scoring by Ray McCallum, a former UW assistant, who's now the head coach at Detroit.

Given my frame of reference, you didn't have to tell me how tough it can be to play a homecoming game. Like Coach Yoder, I faced my old school — UWM — in my first season at my new school — Wisconsin. We not only played in Milwaukee at a sold-out Klotsche Center, but my son, Will, was on the Panthers' roster.

Two days earlier, we had Christmas dinner together.

We exchanged presents, not trade secrets.

There are no secrets when you have a matchup of state teams because most of the players have a familiarity with each other through their summer ties or AAU ball.

Do I envision the day when Wisconsin, UWM, UW-Green Bay and Marquette will all get together on the same floor for an in-season tournament?

It will never happen. We wouldn't be opposed to it at Wisconsin. But where are you going to play the games? And who is going to get the revenue?

When we were at Platteville, we had some teams who could have competed favorably against the Badgers, Marquette, Green Bay or Milwaukee. Over the last few seasons, we've been scheduling some of the state university programs for exhibitions at the Kohl Center for the exposure and the overall good of the game in Wisconsin.

After we rallied to beat UWM, 81-79, on Devin Harris' steal and layup in the closing seconds, I pointed out to the media corps, "This was the best thing for basketball in the state, and I'd say that if they had beat us by one, two or 20."

I still believe that.

I also believed that winning the way we did in Milwaukee — by finding a way to get on the left hand side of the score in an emotionally-charged environment — would pay dividends and help us win somewhere down the road in the Big Ten.

And it did.

Nobody gave us a chance to win at Michigan State. And that was understandable since the Spartans had won 53 straight games at the Breslin Center in East Lansing. But we rallied from a 10-point deficit in the second half and hung on for a 64-63 win.

The referee, Tom Rucker, correctly ruled that Kelvin Torbert had caught the ball, instead of tapping it with .2 seconds left on the clock. So his basket didn't count. I had already hustled my players off the floor before they made it official. The guys were so excited that they dumped water on me once we were in the locker room.

I was excited because they were excited and that's always a good thing.

Freddie Owens scored the game-winning shot. I had talked to Freddie about looking for and attacking the gaps. "If they're squeezing people at other places and over-playing certain guys," I said, "you have to be able to make a play."

I tell everybody the same thing: when you're looking to score, you need to put yourself in a position to create action so you might possibly end up at the free throw line.

When Freddie attacked the gap, there was a little bit of contact, but he still got the ball up and off the glass because he was so strong to the rim.

At halftime, I told him that he was shooting 28-footers from 25 feet in the corner, and that wasn't helping the team. You're not going to be effective offensively and your points per possession aren't going to be very good if you're taking those kinds of shots.

He listened.

Why wouldn't he?

Whatever I say to one player in the locker room, I say to the group because the group needs to be listening. It's good working knowledge for the others because they don't want to be in the same position to hear the same things.

It's expectations. It's what I try to get the players to expect in their behavior by reinforcing certain things. It's not what you say, it's what you emphasize. And I try to emphasize the things that aren't that difficult to comprehend about the game.

Like good shot selection.

It was not an issue in our next road game.

We didn't get many shots because we turned over the ball so much. Less than two weeks after winning at Michigan State, we lost by 32 at Illinois.

"Did you ever have your bleep kicked?" I posed to the press afterward. "I have and I always went back to the playground the next day. I couldn't wait to play again. My players are like me. They're going to be okay. They can't wait for the next game."

To say the least, Illinois was great and we weren't very good. The year before, I experienced the same thing in Champaign with my UWM team. We lost by 41.

They were outletting 60 foot passes and scoring on fast break layups. Someone on our bench brought it to the attention of my coaches that they were still playing certain starters and fast breaking with only a few minutes left in the game.

I have never, ever questioned anybody else's tactics or what other players were doing on the court against one of my teams. If they're out there, they're out there to play hard for a full 40 minutes. And if they feel they still need to attack the rim, or they feel they still need to do whatever, guess what? It's our job to stop them.

We lost two of our next three games before we got things turned around at home with a win against Ohio State. Devin Harris and Mike Wilkinson did most of the work from the free throw line in overtime. We shot 46 free throws, and they shot 32 in what was the highest scoring game in Kohl Center history. The final was 94-92.

"Nobody blinked," I said. "That's a heckuva demonstration to play the No. 1 team in the league that many minutes and come away with a W. That's gutsy play."

That was the first of four straight road games for the Buckeyes, whose three losses during that demanding stretch dramatically impacted the league race.

We didn't lose another game during the regular season — a six-game winning streak that included a win at Indiana and the end to another long losing streak.

The last time a Wisconsin team won in Bloomington, Indiana, was 1977.

Bobby Falk hit an 18-footer from the deep right corner with three seconds left for the game-winner. I saw it with my own eyes. I was a Badger assistant back then.

After snapping that 25-year, 22-game losing streak with a 64-63 win over the Hoosiers, I got doused with water in the locker room again. What it told me was how much these streak-busting victories meant to the players, who had grown tired of hearing about how they hadn't won here or there in X-number of years or X-number of games.

Instead of dwelling on it, they went out and did something about it. We still needed some things to happen with Ohio State and Illinois, but we were now in a position to think about playing for the championship if everything played out.

And it did.

Indiana and Ohio State, the co-leaders, lost on the same night. That left four teams tied for first place: Indiana, Ohio State, Illinois and Wisconsin. If we were able to beat Michigan on our home floor, we would be assured of at least a share of the Big Ten championship for the first time since 1947.

It had been a long wait — 55 years.

I've always said, "If you always execute the basics, you always have a chance. If you do the ordinary — extraordinary things can happen."

Someone sent me a list entitled — Bridging the Gap from Bud (Foster) to Bo (Ryan) The Last Time It Happened.

Harry Truman was the President of the United States; Jackie Robinson was breaking the color barrier in Major League Baseball with the Brooklyn Dodgers; and the Big Ten was the Big Nine or Western Conference, minus Michigan State and Penn State.

That was the last time it happened — Wisconsin winning a conference title.

I wasn't around for that one.

The Badgers won it in March.

I was born the following December.

Did any of this history change how we prepared for Michigan? Absolutely not. We showed the clips of our first Michigan game in Ann Arbor, an 11-point loss. And we talked to the players about the things that we did well and the things we needed to do better.

My pregame speech was really no different. I encouraged the guys to "act like you've been there before, and just play."

We stayed within ourselves, and nothing changed. We were better than Michigan for 40 minutes and we capped the season by cutting down the nets in the Kohl Center.

I embraced Kelly and hugged every member of my staff.

Addressing the Kohl Center crowd, I said, "For all the players who have played here for 54 years, this is for you ... I can't tell you how nice it is to see this many people in one place with a smile on their faces."

Among those in attendance was Fritz Wegner, who was an assistant coach on Bud Foster's Big Ten championship team in '47.

I had a great relationship with Fritz dating to when I was a

Wisconsin assistant and he was running the Nat. That's where we conducted our summer basketball camps and he took a liking to me because he knew I was a disciplinarian with the kids.

During that period, I met Bud Foster a couple of times, too.

When I came back to Wisconsin, do you know how many times I heard, "Am I ever going to see a Big Ten championship in my lifetime?"

That's why there was no bigger thrill for me than when they brought out the Big Ten trophy after the Michigan game. And that's why I made sure to thank the boosters and anyone who had worn a Badger jersey and had ever dropped sweat on the floor.

What were my preseason expectations? I felt we could compete for the top half of the league. Almost everybody picked us for 9th or 10th place. But you just never know when something like this can happen when you get a couple of close wins — like our miraculous wins on the road at Michigan State and Indiana.

It made all the difference in the world.

If we lose one of those games, we're tied for fifth with the Spartans. If we lose both, we're in sixth. That's the bottom half. An 11-5 record doesn't get it done very often in the Big Ten. But it did in '02. How did we do it?

We didn't waver on principles and we stayed ferociously persistent in concepts and ideas. We also went undefeated at home, and we beat every team in the conference.

Around town, I kept hearing, "How 'bout them Badgers?"

That's not a bad thing to hear ringing in your ears.

After we lost in the first round of the Big Ten tournament, I thought it was crucial for the younger guys to get a win in the NCAA tournament, which we did against St. John's. I thanked the team afterward for letting me be a part of it.

The prize? We got to play Maryland in front of its home crowd at the MCI Center in Washington, D.C., 10 miles from their campus.

The Terps had an NBA lineup with Chris Wilcox, Juan Dixon, Lonny Baxter, Drew Nicholas, Byron Mouton and Steve Blake. To no one's surprise they whipped us and went on to win the national championship — beating Indiana in the title game.

But I knew we'd learn from it.

We had our players right where they needed to be.

Now they believed.

CHAPTER EIGHT

Can We Do It Again?

Jim Rome?

Jungle karma?

I'm not someone who listens to radio that much. But I had heard of Jim Rome, a nationally syndicated sports talk show host whose fictional lair was the "jungle."

More so than anything else, I remembered Rome from that much-publicized incident in the mid-'90s when he goaded NFL quarterback Jim Everett into attacking him on the set of his ESPN2 television show.

Rome kept calling him "Chris" — purposely confusing Jim Everett for tennis player Chris Evert. Rome got the reaction that he wanted, and it all kind of smacked of pro wrestling when Everett tipped over a table, pushed Rome to the floor and hovered over him until they were separated. It made for good TV.

In light of this, I wasn't sure what I was getting myself into when I agreed to take part in Rome's tour stop at the Dane County Coliseum in early December of 2002.

I was on a guest list that included UW football coach Barry Alvarez and one of his former players, Mark Tauscher, who had moved on to the Packers. A couple of Green Bay legends were also present — Jerry Kramer and Fuzzy Thurston — along with Madison's very own pro golfer, Jerry Kelly, and Brewers manager Ned Yost.

I'm sure Rome had no idea who I was. But it didn't hurt that we had played and beaten UNLV earlier in the day at the Kohl Center. Many in the Rome crowd of nearly 10,000 sounded like they may have been at the game because I got a warm reception when I was introduced. People were pumped. Rightly so.

Alando Tucker, a true freshman, introduced himself to Badger fans by scoring 24 points and grabbing 18 rebounds, including a school-record 11 offensive boards. In his first career start, he certainly was active enough on the glass — and activity often creates good things. Especially when you have a 37-inch vertical.

That was a very athletic UNLV team. They had one guy, Delron Johnson, who was getting a lot of press, and another, Marcus Banks, who's still in the NBA.

Still, we won by 17 points, thanks in large part to Alando; and I knew that he would just keep getting better as the year went on. You could see that he was the type of player who never changed expressions. He didn't get rattled. He just went out and played.

One of his best qualities?

Alando Tucker listened.

***

Not everyone listens the same way.

Not everyone hears and sees the same things.

Pete Brey was a senior captain at the University of Wisconsin when I arrived as an assistant coach in '76. Over the years, we became good friends.

When Pete was coaching high school basketball at Brentwood Academy in Los Angeles, my son Matt was the junior varsity coach. But my favorite Pete Brey story revolved around his experience coaching his daughter's basketball team in Madison.

Trailing by a point with only a few seconds left on the clock, Pete called his final timeout. In the huddle, he talked about what he wanted the girls to do on the out-of-bounds play. He wanted a pick, a cut, a pass and a shot.

And that's how he explained it to each young lady.

You take the ball out.

You pick.

You cut.

You throw the ball in.

You catch and shoot.

Piece of cake.

But nothing happened the way it should have happened. Pete's team never got a shot off, and lost the game. As the dejected players were walking out of the gym, Pete went up to one of the girls and asked the obvious question.

"The whole play was going to start with your pick ... what happened?"

"Mr. Brey," she replied innocently, "what's a pick?"

"You know, when you screen for a teammate."

"Screen? Why didn't you tell me to screen?"

Pete Brey couldn't help but laugh to himself.

I've never forgotten that story. As a coach, you can never assume anything. I've tried not to take things for granted, even if that means using the same terminology day after day after day — year after year after year. People like to call me old school after watching one of my teams play, and that's fine by me.

If by definition old school is repeating the same things over and over again to your players — if old school is using the same terms so that everyone understands exactly what you want done, then I'll be old school for the rest of my life.

It really goes back to what I was saying earlier about people not listening or hearing things the same way. That also applies to players. When you're teaching or coaching, you have to make it easy to understand what you're saying by how you're saying it. That's my job as a teacher and coach — to get rid of all the ambiguity.

Talk to anybody who has ever played for me and you will never hear, "We didn't know what coach wanted or we didn't understand what he meant."

When situations arise during a game, I want my players to feel like they've already been through a similar situation in practice, and because they've practiced that way they know what to expect and can react accordingly. Especially since everything happens so quickly at game speed. You have to play the percentages and keep it simple.

Our game days are like that.

Simplicity.

In the coaches' locker room, I'm always moving because I know I'll be squatting on the sidelines during the game. I've got to make sure I'm stretched and warmed up.

In the players' locker room, I'll write the matchups on a whiteboard.

I'll put down the opponent's last name, his number and who's matched with him. I don't put up 15 different buzz phrases like "Block Out" or "Rebound."

If I've got to remind my guys before a game to block out or rebound — fundamental things — I didn't do a good job of teaching or coaching during practices.

About an hour before the opening tip, I will address the team for 10 to 12 minutes. The players will sit in front of their lockers or in the chairs that are set up for them, and I will talk about the only things that are important for the game.

These are the things that we talked about during the week, and the things that we practiced: what we're trying to do, and what we're trying to take away.

I make sure they understand what we're here for. Nothing else matters.

I don't play the "win one for the Gipper" card. Or the "These guys haven't shown us any respect" card. I don't coach that way. I don't think I put anybody to sleep. But you can't have them bouncing off the walls, either. I don't get into things that we don't have any control over. I've seen that backfire on too many coaches.

Knute Rockne was known for the "Gipper" speech. But he didn't have to motivate his Notre Dame football team 30-plus times every season. If I deliver that message once, what am I going to do the next time? And the time after next?

You don't want to suddenly morph into a wacko in the locker room. You don't want players saying, "Man, look at coach. He's really out of it today."

So you can't give the "Apocalypse is Now" talk every time you play, or your players will have no reaction. They're all jacked up anyhow. It's pretty hard not to be when you're playing basketball in the Big Ten: Great arenas, great crowds, great energy.

While I'm talking to the team, I'll reiterate a few things from the scouting report: "Don't forget to look for so-and-so going down the right wing in transition." Or "Don't let so-and-so catch the ball here."

As they're looking at the matchups on the board, they ought to be able to connect the last name to what the opponent does, and how he does it: "Force him to chase. Don't let him change direction on the baseline.

Make him work on the defensive end. Nothing in transition. Make him put the ball on the floor."

All of these things should come to mind without prompting. If someone is accustomed to coming off single or double stagger screens, we should know that already because the scout team has been running the same staggers for two days in practice.

There should be no surprises. If an opponent is going to change its offense before playing you, that's okay. It should be to your benefit because they're getting away from their strengths and system and doing something they haven't done as much.

When our players take the floor for their pregame warmup, I'll stay behind in the locker room and review the scouting report and game plan with my assistants.

Some head coaches will sit at courtside and watch their opponent run through the layup lines. I tried that my first year at Platteville and I discovered that too many people wanted to come up behind the bench and visit. Nothing personal. But there are just certain things that I want to be focusing on, and I'm not interested in small talk.

Somebody asked me once if I had my "game face" on.

I never thought about it. I don't know what that means. I remember Bob Knight fielding a similar question about "putting on his game face," and he proceeded to contort his face in multiple ways to reflect different expressions. Or game faces.

As a coach, can you tell if a player is ready to play? There have been times where I'll be looking at a guy in the locker room and I'm not sure if he's paying attention to me, at least not 100 percent, and he'll go out and have a great game.

To be honest, I haven't coached many guys who have seemed disinterested because it's all based on what you've done leading up to playing an opponent.

In practice, you may notice a kid who's disinterested and you'll tell him, "Hey, we don't stand for that around here. You have to be attentive. You have to have your eyes, ears and mind open. You talk, I listen. I talk, you listen. It's simple and it works."

Throughout the game itself, I'll make observations to the players on the bench. They need to be listening, too, because that's learning time. Too many players waste their time on the bench by having their minds on other things. Sitting on the bench is a great opportunity to get a lot smarter — as long as you're paying attention.

My assistants can communicate with me anytime during the game. But you won't see me conversing with them out on the floor during timeouts before stepping into the players' huddle. A lot of coaching staffs follow that protocol. I never liked the idea.

I just don't know how it works. I've seen huddles where four people are talking at the same time, including the head coach. I've seen assistants yelling at each other and the head coach has to step in-between and separate them.

I know what's on my mind and what I want to convey. My assistants always have input. But I'm not going to make a show out of a timeout sequence. I'm not going to put on the charade of walking 25 feet out on the floor. I'm not going to put my assistants in a position where they feel like they have to say something.

During the timeouts, I want the players to get water and catch their breath. I always encourage them to communicate with each other. I also expect our point guard to take charge. But they know once I step in the huddle, it's time to listen.

Now that the media timeouts are so much longer, I might seek feedback from certain individuals: "What are they doing on this screen? Are they looking to slip? Can we over-hedge? Are they playing under?"

I save timeouts for special situations at the end of tight games. I'm not taking a timeout just to take a timeout. I like my players to have timeouts to use when they need them, not because somebody on TV thinks the coach should use a timeout. We have proven that you don't need to call one every time somebody scores two baskets in a row.

That's why our teams are known for playing every possession like it's the last possession. If you play hard through every possession, you can't always be looking around for a bailout. Sometimes, if you're looking for a timeout or anticipating one, you may give up another basket because you're not focused on what you should be doing.

There are coaches who are control freaks who try to control their players so much that everything is mechanical, and there are coaches who just let their players do whatever they want, and there are a variety of coaches that fall somewhere in between. Meanwhile, the players are managing the game based on how they've practiced. I'm just making sure they don't fray.

When the TV analysts are blabbering about a coach's ability to do likewise — manage the game — you should always remember this: you manage things, you don't manage people as much as you think they do, even though they get away with calling them baseball managers.

How does that translate to how a game is officiated? There are some nights when an official might call more fouls than he normally does because maybe he's tired or a little frazzled from all of the traveling that some of these guys do during the season.

But it's a misconception to think that a certain official will referee a certain type of game every time he steps on the court. That's why I don't worry about it. We get the list of officials before we play, but I don't look at it. Never have.

In managing the game, does a coach try to establish his turf early with the officials? Absolutely. And the officials also have to establish that they're in control. There is a give-and-take to everything. And the players have to be aware of it.

If not, we'll remind them at halftime.

After leaving the floor at the end of the first half, the players will have some time to themselves before the coaching staff comes into the locker room. As a team, we'll go over some of the different things that have happened and what we're still looking for.

Have I ever gotten mad at halftime? Sure. But it's not an act when I lose my temper. If you have good players, they know why you're upset, and they're going to do something about it. As we're preparing to return to the floor for the second half, our message is upbeat: "Listen up, guys, this is what we have to do to be successful ...."

You get the unpleasant things out of the way first.

You eat the spinach before the steak.

***

Alando Tucker must have eaten his spinach before playing UNLV as a freshman because he flexed his muscle on the boards and sure played like Popeye. That I changed our starting lineup — Tucker replaced Dave Mader — was rare for me.

It might have been only the second time in my 30-plus years of coaching that I made a lineup change for reasons other than an injury.

(The first time was at Platteville when I inserted freshman Ernie Peavy at small forward for Billy Reid. Once we started the rotations, Billy was the first sub. With his flexibility, he could play shooting guard, small forward or power forward. He had developed such a knowledge of the program that he could help at a lot of positions.)

I made the lineup change with Alando because his game was better suited for UNLV's quickness than Dave's. When Tucker took over at power forward, Mike Wilkinson, a rawboned sophomore from Wisconsin Heights, moved to center.

We felt that we could mesh Tucker with the guys who got their first real playing time the season before: Mike, Devin Harris and Freddie Owens.

Outside of our program, I know they were calling our first season a fluke, an aberration, a once-in-a-lifetime miracle. I know they were also writing locally that our Swing offense would no longer be a surprise to opponents and that we would have trouble being competitive in the league because the Big Ten was so much stronger.

We were a flash in the pan.

Can we do it again?

So they wrote.

So they tell me.

How are you going to replace Travon Davis at point guard?

How are you going to replace Charlie Wills and his toughness?

"I don't know," I said. "We'll work at it."

We had Kirk Penney coming back as a senior, and I recognized how much better he had gotten as an overall scorer and defender. We had Devin and Mike coming back with all that valuable experience. Devin started 32 games and averaged more than 34 minutes. Mike played in all 32 and averaged more than 28.

And along with Freddie and the freshmen — maybe I should have called them "Freddie and the Dreamers" after the old British band from the '60s — I knew that we would be competitive in the conference despite what others were saying.

I thought the key to our second season was what took place during our first season. Kirk Penney, Devin Harris, Mike Wilkinson and Freddie Owens got a taste of a Big Ten championship. And it tasted pretty good.

What were my expectations? I go into every season with the same thoughts. It's not about showing off a trophy. It's not about fans storming the court during a victory celebration. It's about the individuals and how they can help us, collectively, become a good team. Everything we do — every practice, every drill — is based on that philosophy.

As a sophomore, Devin Harris was making the transition from shooting guard to the point. And I wanted him to do the same things Travon Davis had done: take care of the ball, involve people, and find the shooters, namely Kirk Penney.

With one year of seasoning under his belt, Devin was ready to be our point guard. It was his time. He had quickness and vision, shooting and slashing ability, and quick hands on defense. And, like Tucker, he also listened.

You have to understand, there are a lot of players who have natural talent. But they don't always make the most of what they have. Devin Harris always did.

During that second year, I remember we were doing possessions in practice, and Kirk was firing up shot after shot after shot. If his shot wasn't going down, he would just shoot more and more and more. Especially in practice — which isn't all bad.

There was a whistle and a foul. While play was stopped, Devin came walking over to me with this half-smile on his face.

"Coach, I just wanted to know if I will be able to do that next year?"

"Do what, Devin?"

"Kirk hasn't passed the ball the last 10 times down the floor," Devin pointed out, "and I want to know if you will let me take 10 shots in a row?"

"You'll get that chance," I assured him, "next year."

He looked me in the eyes and nodded. Devin knew exactly what was going on. He knew we needed Kirk to shoot. More importantly, he knew Kirk needed confidence in his shot. Devin just understood what was needed — when, what and why.

During his sophomore year, I kept working with him on improving his communication skills with his teammates — to mix with them a little more before, during and after games. That's something I've always asked our point guards to do without directly telling them what to do. But you do drop little hints.

If your point guard is throwing the ball away or if he's not in tune with the game, it will spread to other players. If the position isn't steady, the dam will break.

In practice, we'll work through different game situations: Let's say we're up by four points with a minute to go. Or, we're tied with only seconds remaining.

In either case, you're sending a message to every player on your team. But the guy who needs to make sure he's really listening is your point guard.

For the most part, we're breaking down a defense from the wings and 45-degree angles, and we're going through the post with just about everything. So it's not like we just have one guard with the ball in his hands and he's the only one creating offense.

But we do count on our point guard to do some things when the shot clock is running down. And when you get into those tight situations, when the outcome of the game is on the line, if he has strong self-esteem, he will perform and succeed.

That was the case when Devin Harris — a big-time player — made a big-time play, and we ended up beating Illinois, 60-59, at the Kohl Center for the school's first outright Big Ten championship since 1947, a 56-year wait.

In the conference opener, Devin had the final shot of the game blocked by Michigan freshman Daniel Horton, and we lost by a point. It looked like Horton might have gotten a piece of Devin, but there was no call. We licked our wounds and moved on.

The situation was very similar against Illinois.

Coming out of a timeout, Devin created the action. Illinois was overplaying, or forcing him to his right, and he used an extra dribble to influence the defense. He darted back to his left. Dee Brown was forced to foul Devin to prevent him from scoring.

With four-tenths of a second on the clock, he missed his first free throw but made his second, and shortly thereafter, we were cutting down the nets again — marking the first time in 79 years that Wisconsin had earned back-to-back Big Ten crowns.

Speaking for our players and coaches afterward, I said, "I certainly hope everyone else enjoyed it as much as we did. I can't believe I'm allowed to do this — coach — for a living, and the great part about it is that I got this job at the right time."

All we need, all we ever look for in life, is a chance.

You ride a roller-coaster sometimes, but you have to keep an even keel. It's easier to talk about than it is to do. But our guys kept their composure throughout the season, especially when things were getting away from us against Illinois, and we hung on.

Some were saying that we were overachievers.

We achieved. That's what I said. Everything else is interpretation.

Following the Illinois win, I remember sitting next to our New Zealand import, Kirk Penney, during the press conference. "We bought into what Coach Ryan was teaching, and he made us believe," Kirk told the assembled media. "We believed and he believed in us, and here we are now — enjoying this amazing experience."

I leaned over, tapped Kirk on his forearm and said softly, "Thanks, mate."

I felt like a kid again myself and thought, "Here we are, out there just playing a basketball game in T-shirts and shorts. How sweet is that?"

The sweetest part? The players were the ones who started believing in September, and now they had a conference title to show for it in March. I was so proud of them.

I was asked, "Was it sweeter to win the first Big Ten championship at Wisconsin? Or defend it? Which of the first two titles was the best?"

You can't answer that.

I wouldn't answer that.

But if you were a player, you'd have to be living in a vacuum if you didn't know you could come to Wisconsin and have a chance to win a championship. That's what it established. And that does make a difference in recruiting.

***

For the second year a in a row, we won all of our Big Ten home games. Our average attendance (nearly 17,000) led the conference. And, for the first time in school history, we sold out the student section before the start of the season.

That was a far cry from the days of the Faithful 5,000 in the Field House.

There was probably a time when I knew everyone's name in this core base of 5,000 fans who were loyal to the team during the bleakest years at Wisconsin. Despite the losing records, they continued to root for their Badgers.

Although the Field House was about half full for most games, it could still be a very intimidating building for opponents. When it was full, you couldn't hear yourself think because of the noise. Otherwise, it was just small, dark and smokey.

At the start of second half, the smoke would hang over the court from all the people who would light up cigarettes at halftime and smoke in the concession areas. Many left their seats at halftime to towel off after having soda drip down on them from the upper balconies during the first half. There were long lines at the bathrooms, and few amenities.

It wasn't fan-friendly.

Nor opponent-friendly, at times.

That's the oddity about the Kohl Center.

We'll face a Coastal Carolina or a Gardner-Webb, and the head coach will be baffled after playing us: "Wow, you've got an unbelievable home record. But the building is really nice. It's not a pit, and there's nothing really intimidating about it."

That's a compliment to a beautiful facility.

Truth is, everyone has a better home record than road record in college basketball, and our record at the Kohl Center can be attributed to the work of our players and the support of our fans. It goes hand-in-hand. The Grateful Red student section has been a hit, even though we don't have nearly as many students seated at courtside as some other venues.

We haven't beaten ourselves very often at home, and when we have lost it was because of costly turnovers. We've usually given ourselves a chance to win by making the other team play from behind. But we've also shown the ability to rally from deficits.

No matter how many points we may be down, our players believe that they still have a chance to come back. That belief is fueled by the energy that our fans give us.

A lot of times we have been trailing in the second half. That's when the crowd can have more of an impact on us than the opponent. There's no question that when we're down the fans can give us an adrenaline rush.

It's like they're saying, "C'mon guys, we're here for you."

How do you pay back people who believe in you?

You win. Our home record is a testament to that.

What's the most intimidating building I've ever been in?

Zorn Arena in Eau Claire has to be near the top of the list because it was so small. The size of the gym — not even 2,200 could squeeze into Zorn — was really disproportionate to the student enrollment on campus. Whitewater was not as tough an atmosphere as Eau Claire. But it was tough because they had good teams. So, obviously, did Eau Claire.

I've only practiced twice with crowd noise prior to playing on the road. Once was when I was a high school coach at Sun Valley. That was right before we were going to play at Chester. Talk about a tough place to play.

The other time I used taped noise was at Platteville. I think it was before we played Whitewater or Eau Claire. Maybe it was before a postseason game.

The more I thought about it, the more I realized that I was creating something superficial for my players. What I wanted them to do was learn how to process things, physically and mentally. If I made a big deal out of the noise, they were likely to make a big deal out of it.

That was the end of the experiment in taped crowd noise.

You won't get me to pick one arena over the other in the Big Ten. I just believe it's a heckuva deal if you can consistently win half of your conference road games. Especially since the Big Ten annually leads the nation in attendance.

Trust me, you're doing pretty good if you can go into these hostile environments and win at least four out of eight every season. Who has the best road record in the Big Ten over the last seven years? Look it up. But I think you'll find that the same teams that have been winning at the Kohl Center have been winning on the road.

What's our road formula? Our players have to stay true to the game and true to the task at hand. Same as at home. Before we had that 2003 showdown with Illinois in Madison, we had to win challenging road games at Iowa and Minnesota. That was huge.

I'm constantly reminding my players of the same things. "Home or away, you respect the game and you respect your opponents and their ability."

I have never made it "us against them."

That would be counter-productive. In no way do you gain any kind of an advantage by waging in your own mind a psychological battle with an individual or a particular school. It clouds your vision. So I don't do it.

I kept the personalities out of it as a high school and college player.

You've got a job and you've got to get it done. In a competitive situation, you've got to know the strengths and the weaknesses of your opponent during the contest. They're doing the same things. They're walking in the same shoes as you are.

I've also kept the personalities out of it as a coach.

As a Big Ten assistant, I'd watched what head coaches were doing, and what they could get away with doing at times. Because I broke down a lot of film, I could tell by watching how a team played what the coach was all about. The players and how they play, after all, are an extension and expression of that coach.

If you're in the profession, you try to go to school on other coaches. You can pick up some things in game management and how they use their timeouts. But a coach really does all of his teaching in practice. I like to see people in that environment.

Still, every coach is an entity unto himself. Some guys like more attention than others. I've got my own game plan. I don't know about the other guy, but I know what I want to do. Does it always happen the way you want it to happen? No. But I'm still more concerned with the things that are happening on the court as opposed to anywhere else.

At the same time, I don't try to control other people's emotions. I know my assistants and my players feel certain ways about certain teams. But when they're around me, they always share the same perspective: "Let's respect everybody."

After a game, you shake hands.

That's the way I was raised.

"Hey, good to see you."

"How ya doing?"

It's not that hard.

As a coach, I'm only worried about one thing: getting my guys better as people and players. That's always No. 1. Secondly, it's about winning a championship — starting with the league championship and extending to winning a national championship.

If your mind is on something else, if your mind is fixed on another person or another school, how in the world is that productive? If you're thinking about one school too much, then there's a good chance you're going to get beat by another school.

Let the fans get excited about the rivalries. That's great.

But people should know by now that I'm oblivious to how many games I've won against a certain opponent or how many games a certain opponent has won against us.

I can only coach one team, my team. I don't worry about other people.

When I was coaching at Platteville, I had an opposing coach put his starters back on the floor late in the game just so they could score 100 points against us.

We didn't hold the ball on them. But we ran good offense to prevent them from reaching that mark. Our guys were smart enough to get very selective with their shots, while trying to get fouled. I never said a word after the game. Why should I?

My whole focus was on my team. If somebody was getting well over one point per possession, and nearly scoring 100, then you'd better improve your defense for the next game, and you'd better show your players what they need to work on.

I would never bring up the opposing coach in a scouting report. That just wouldn't happen because it would take away from your preparation. Just the facts, Jack. That has always been my approach, despite what others might think.

If you ask me about my relationship with Michigan State coach Tom Izzo, I'm going to tell you it's the same as it is with every other coach. Except I probably have more contact with Coach Izzo because we're on the NABC board of directors. In fact, I've been around Coach Izzo more than anyone else in our league.

I've never talked to Coach Izzo about Alando Tucker's dunk in the closing seconds of our 2003 game against Michigan State at the Kohl Center.

What's there to talk about?

I never felt the need to broach the topic.

***

I wanted to get back to the University of Wisconsin to prove that you could win Big Ten championships here. That always burned inside me.

Do I coach with a chip on my shoulder?

You always want to prove that what you're doing is right.

And the best way for me to thank everyone who has helped me is by doing well and winning games. That's my chip. Every time we have a little success as a team, everybody who has ever been connected to our program is sharing in that victory.

In order to sustain success, you have to keep getting good players who have a good work ethic and who are good student-athletes. You also have to make sure that they're competitive people who want to uphold the winning tradition.

Obviously, you have to build something first.

I talk to the upperclassmen about tradition because I want them to make sure that younger players know what's around the corner and down the road. How things are done within our program is passed down from class to class, from player to player.

The way you show respect is by competing and outworking somebody. If I'm a senior, I want to welcome a freshman to the program by beating him in a pickup game.

How does a younger player thank an upperclassman? By getting better and by beating him, or at least by making every drill or scrimmage more competitive.

If players are really going hard against each other in the off-season, you have a chance to keep it going once you get them in the fall and start building the team.

As the tradition grows, the players feel better about themselves. It also means they tend to be even more determined and more resilient because they feel like they're part of something important.

That all factors into the team building.

In the end, our second team proved our first team wasn't a fluke at Wisconsin.

Our second team, like our first team, also lost in the first round of the Big Ten tournament. I can't say that our guys let down. But sometimes it's hard to win a title and then compete in the conference tourney. It's such a quick turnaround.

That's why I felt it was good for us emotionally to win a couple of games and reach the Sweet 16 of the NCAA tournament to cap our

2002-2003 season.

The Tulsa victory was quite the capper, too.

After ending Weber State's 17-game winning streak in our first-round game of the Midwest Regional, we drew Tulsa, which had won eight straight.

At halftime, we were down by five points, and I informed everyone in the locker room that if they played "one year smarter" we could still win the game.

There was a point in the second half where, during a timeout, I mapped out the comeback. "Guys," I said, "this is how we're going to get it done."

We talked about trapping on defense. When you're behind, you've got to have something to use to get back into the game. With our lack of depth, we weren't the kind of team that could pressure for 40 minutes. But we were able to rattle Tulsa.

We talked about scoring with the clock stopped. In this context, we also talked about the staples of our offense: touching the post and getting to the free throw line.

You've got to make your breaks as you go along, and we did. We forced some turnovers and got some easy baskets. Meanwhile, they missed some shots.

With a little over four minutes left, we were down by 13 points.

But there was no quit in our team huddle.

"Guys, we can still win'" I kept reminding them, "if we do this and this."

You have to have a plan.

Alando Tucker told me afterward, "Coach, I heard what you were saying, but I didn't know how or if, we could come back. But you had us believing that we could."

That's all that counted.

We finished the game on a 16-2 run — punctuated by Freddie Owens' 3-point shot from the deep left corner with just one second remaining on the clock. It was not only a big shot by Freddie, it was a big play by Devin Harris to get him the ball.

After the memorable 61-60 win, I admitted to the media, "I don't know if any opening statement can describe this feeling of togetherness that our guys pulled within themselves. The way they came back is something that only happens once in a while."

I liked what Freddie Owens told a reporter. "This is the stuff that you'll remember the rest of your life; this is something you can tell your kids and grandkids. This is what you live for — to see the smile on all of your teammates' faces."

I was smiling right along with them.

Can't beat that karma.

Jungle or otherwise.

CHAPTER NINE
Sustaining Success

"Who's the quickest player here?" I ask.
A few hands shoot into the air.

I choose one.

"Back in the day, son, I was pretty quick myself."

That usually draws a dumbfounded look.

"Seriously, I could move pretty good."

Dramatic pause.

"Still can."

I'm stretching and loosening up.

He's rolling his eyes.

"Tell you what, let's race."

That gets his attention. He's sizing me up and grinning. And I know exactly what he's thinking. "Are you kidding me? I can beat this old, gray-haired dude."

We're both standing on the baseline.

I station a coach at half court.

"Whoever gets the basketball to him first is the winner."

I bury the hook a little deeper.

"Of course, I'm not as young as I used to be ...."

Now the kid is really revving up his motor.

He can't wait to beat my butt.

Ready, set, go.

He takes off dribbling.

I throw a baseball pass to half court.

"Guys, remember this," I say, delivering the moral to the story. "You can always move the ball quicker with the pass than the dribble."

For years, I've done this stunt at basketball clinics. I've also pulled it off with some of my own basketball teams at Platteville, UWM and Wisconsin, though you can't do it all the time because everybody knows the punch line, except the freshmen.

I've never had anyone use the pass.

But I once had a kid ask, "Are we going to dribble the ball?"

Without giving away the ending, I dialed up the BS.

"Just use common sense. What do you think I'm getting loose for?"

He bites: hook, line, sinker. And I make my point.

The demonstration always raises awareness to the value I place on being a good passing team. Ballhandling is important, and you still need the dribble because there are times when you can't advance the ball through the air.

I just don't like it when a player gets dribble happy.

Neither did Doc Meanwell, a Hall of Famer.

***

When I was coaching in junior high, I wanted to expand my knowledge of basketball, so I went to the library and did some research. I was curious about the game and its history. As I was reading, I learned more about one of the early difference-makers: Walter E. Meanwell, who answered to "Doc" or the "Little Doctor."

He stood only 5-6.

But he was a giant in the sport.

Here I was just getting started in the business, not knowing if I would ever leave Pennsylvania or coach beyond the eighth-grade level, and I've got Doc Meanwell on my radar. I mean, who knew at the time that I would eventually wind up coaching basketball at the same school, Wisconsin, that is a part of the Meanwell legacy?

The more I read about him, the more I realized that he had a proven system that his players ran — a system that revolved around cutting patterns and ball movement; a system that allowed him to sustain success for a long period of time.

Walter Meanwell literally wrote the book on basketball: *The Science of Basket Ball.* It was two words in 1924, when the book was published.

I've still got a copy in my possession.

The Badgers, under Coach Meanwell, won eight conference titles and better than 70 percent of their games. In 1911, his very first team went 15-0 and was crowned as the Helms Foundation national champions. He retired in 1934 to practice medicine and turned the program over to one of his former players, Bud Foster.

Doc's game?

Pass and cut.

He really wasn't a big proponent of the dribble. But he brought structure, discipline and strategy to the game with the implementation of shorter passes and the zone defense. He was also credited with being the originator of summer basketball schools or camps. We can all thank him for the revenue stream that he created.

Over the years, I've corresponded with members of the Meanwell family — Liz Cooper and Honner Meanwell Cooper. They provided me with another book, entitled *Training, Conditioning and the Care of Injuries*, that Doc Meanwell co-authored with Knute Rockne, the legendary Notre Dame football coach.

In the book, they talk about staleness.

Right on.

Today, we call it burnout.

That's why it still has application to what I'm doing as a head coach. As the season moves on, you have to adjust and shorten your practices.

There's an inscription in the Meanwell book that's still very special to me.

It's from the family, and reads, "Bo, we think Doc would like you to have this."

I felt honored.

***

Some of the things that we were achieving as a program were matching or eclipsing some of the things that Doc Meanwell and his UW teams had achieved.

That, too, was an honor.

As we prepared for our third season at Wisconsin, some were pondering our odds of "three-peating" as Big Ten champs. But they were in the minority.

Most were saying that we were the third best team in the conference.

That was the consensus of the Big Ten writers and coaches in a 2003 preseason vote. Michigan State and Illinois were picked ahead of us.

None of that really mattered. I don't make predictions, and I don't put much stock into what is being predicted for us. That's what I reminded the players.

We went through two seasons where nobody thought we could do anything at a high level and now — on the heels of back-to-back Big Ten titles — some expectations had changed for the program. Most had not.

What really matters?

What the players are doing every day in every drill to get better.

Everyone has a sphere of influence and if they are around people who are driven, it's contagious, it's infectious. Does it start with the head coach? Not necessarily.

But it helps if everybody around your basketball program is driven — from the coaches to the players to the trainers. The athletic trainers, unfortunately, had to work overtime that season because of a rash of injuries — the most serious of which sidelined Alando Tucker with a broken foot.

Besides that, we had already lost a good scorer in Kirk Penney — someone that you could count on for points. Tucker was out and Penney had used up his eligibility, while Jason Chappell, who also had a foot injury, and freshman Brian Butch were redshirting.

So we had to rely more heavily on Devin Harris and Mike Wilkinson. Both started every game, averaged over 32 minutes and ended up as our scoring leaders. Boo Wade and Freddie Owens were also starters, and we got steady contributions from Zach Morley, Clayton Hanson, Ray Nixon, Andreas Helmigk and Dave Mader.

Have I ever thought about what it would have been like if Alando Tucker and Devin Harris had been able to play together for more than one season?

You can at least reflect on it. What if Alando didn't have to take a medical redshirt after his freshman year? What if Devin came back for his senior year? Imagine two more full seasons of Tucker and Harris playing on the same team?

I always felt they were compatible because they both had a burning desire to win and they worked so hard. Just talk to the security people at the Kohl Center. Who do they talk about being there all the time? Penney, Tucker and Harris.

You'd also have to put Mike Wilkinson in that category. Talk about a work ethic. Mike was all knees and elbows, and he never took a possession off. He was hungry and committed. He was the bacon in that meal of bacon and eggs.

You know what I'm talking about?

The difference between being involved and being committed?

(I use this one at most of my speaking engagements.)

If you're serving bacon and eggs for breakfast, you know the chicken was involved but when you look at the bacon, you know the pig was committed.

Mike Wilkinson was the bacon. He was committed.

Devin Harris was equally committed, especially with Tucker injured. Devin was our decision-maker, which is what you would expect out of a point guard. If you've got a good one, like Devin, there are so many things that he can add. He's the leader, the spokesperson, the energizer and the creator.

You can get some things from the post and some things from the wing. But when it comes to communicating and leading and directing everybody on the floor, you need to get that out of your point guard. Again, if you have a good one, like Devin, who also scores, plays defenses and handles the ball, it makes him that much more valuable.

When was the last time Wisconsin had the Big Ten's most valuable player?

Here's a clue: it was an era of strong accusations and McCarthyism.

That would be Senator Joseph McCarthy, not Packer coach Mike McCarthy.

I was 2.

The last time was 1950.

That's when Wisconsin's Don Rehfeldt won the award. The school's previous MVP winners dated to the '40s: Gene Englund, Johnny Kotz and Glen Selbo.

In 2004, Devin Harris bridged a 54-year gap. Not only was he the conference's player of the year, but he helped lead us to the Big Ten tournament championship in Indianapolis, where he was a unanimous choice as the most outstanding player.

How close did we come to a regular season "three-peat?" Real close. Illinois won back-to-back road games the final week. Both came down to one possession. Illinois won by two points in overtime at Purdue and by a point at Ohio State.

Had either the Boilermakers or the Buckeyes pulled off the upset, we would have gotten a piece of the championship. Give credit to Illinois. The Illini won it outright with a 13-3 record. They earned it. We went 12-4 and tied for second with Michigan State.

It was apparent that no one was paying attention on the NCAA tournament selection committee. We were 24-6 and ranked No. 10 in the media and coaches poll. We were also No. 12 in the RPI, but we got a No. 6 seed. Nothing justified that result.

I would have given up the home-court advantage — we played the first and second round games at the Bradley Center in Milwaukee — for a better seed.

We deserved one. Why the heck is the RPI even kept? If national rankings don't mean anything, why does the BCS exist in college football? The system is flawed.

Our seed was a joke, a travesty, an outright injustice.

***

I've been known to speak my mind. I've also been known to call out someone if they're lying or not telling the whole truth. That includes media people.

Anybody can have an opinion. But if writers or sportscasters are going to question something about basketball during the course of a game, I would hope that their remarks are based on some facts. If not, I'll call them on it.

I've always looked at dealing with the press as a necessary evil of my job as a head coach. At the same time, I don't have anything against media people doing their job.

Although I spent 15 seasons in the Division III ranks, it's not like I lived in the stone ages. When we were making our playoff runs at the end of the year, we would get some attention outside of the Platteville *Journal* and Dubuque *Telegraph Herald.*

We had our own TV show on the Platteville student station. The school had a communications major and everyone was practicing to become the next Matt Lepay, the radio voice of the Badgers, or Kevin Harlan, who has made a name for himself on CBS.

By the time I got back to Madison in 2001, the internet's presence and impact was being felt. The print media may have felt some competition, may have felt like it had to be a little more sensational or controversial or opinionated to get feedback from its readers.

That's my take.

But the topic came up during our 2008 Big Ten coaches meetings. We had a panel discussion with two respected sportswriters — *USA Today*'s Malcolm Moran and ESPN's Gene Wojciechowski — and a blogger. Yes, a blogger. That's how times have changed.

In many instances, I just think there's a lack of accountability with blogs. It almost becomes an obsession with some. And what follows is usually hearsay or an over-reaction, whether it's to one play or one game or one team. Where's the credibility?

Danny Murtaugh was the longtime manager of the Pittsburgh Pirates. He was also born and raised in Chester. (You knew I'd get that in, didn't you?)

I kind of subscribe to what Murtaugh once said:

"I would love to have a guy that always gets the key hit, a pitcher that always makes his best pitch and a manager that can always make the right decision. The problem is getting him to put down his beer and come out of the stands and do those things."

If you're fanatical about your team, it should be in a way where you really want to see the players do well. I know these young men feel better about themselves, and how they are perceived, when we accent the positives.

Trouble is, the fans only see the product on the floor. They see the exam, but they don't see the preparation. And that's understandable. Since they can't come to practice, they come to watch their school or home town team and they come to be entertained.

That's the business. Unlike the players, I'm an adult and I can handle the second-guessing, the critiques and whatever is thrown at me much better than they can. That's my job to handle those things.

When we win, it's great. When we take some bumps, everybody weighs in. That's why the game of basketball is so popular. More people have played this sport during some period of their life than any other sport. So they know the game, or think they do.

Same with the media.

I just see too many people who are weak at what they do and they get by with it. Some of their predictions are not even close, but they're not held accountable for them. Where is their won-lost record? I'm not saying everyone is that way. With some, though, there's too much speculation or innuendo and not enough information or facts.

Know what you're talking about.

Study the game.

Investigate, and talk to the right people.

Substantiate.

Is that asking too much?

During my weekly press conference, I'll say things to see if people are paying attention — to find out who really cares. Do they care about the welfare and development of the young people who are competing for the school that they're covering? I just never liked people trying to make themselves more important than the game.

You've seen my teams play.

We're all about team.

You will never hear me single out a player for criticism during my post-game press conference. I always thought that was a cop-out by some coaches.

I don't remember Coach Rainey ever ripping any of us at Chester High School or Wilkes College. I also don't remember him ever saying, "We weren't ready to play."

What the heck does that mean? How can you get away with saying that to the public or press or your buddy after a game? Our guys weren't ready to play? Nonsense.

I've always told players, "Guys, remember, we're in this together. If you ever hear me rip you or say anything about you in a negative context, I'm fair game."

I've talked to individuals after something has appeared in a newspaper, especially if what they've said reflected poorly on them or their teammates. I make them aware of their rights and freedom of speech. "But do you know how what you said was perceived?" I might ask. "Not probably in the way that you meant."

Here's something else that I tell them often:

"There are young kids and players who are going to listen to every word that you say. You've finally reached a point in your life — when you're 18 to 22-years old — where you can affect a 10-year old or a 12-year-old or even a 15-year old.

"What message do you want to send to them? What you need to do is spread the positive gospel of basketball and what the game has done for you. Talk about developing the discipline and the work habits that are necessary for being successful in life.

"Think back to when you were that age — when you were that 10-year old. Think back to the people you looked up to and how you felt about things they said."

You have to make your college players understand that they are role models, whether they want to be or not. We've been fortunate in that most of them get it. They've bought into what we're trying to pass on, and they're passing on good things.

Brian Lucas has been our basketball sports information director (SID) at Wisconsin. From the start, he understood that I had been around a little bit and I might have a little experience. It wasn't like a young SID coming in with a young head coach.

I pretty much knew where I wanted to go with some media-related things. I'm not a limelight coach — somebody who has to be the center of public attention all the time — and I conveyed that to Brian, along with some other thoughts.

"I'll let you do your thing," I said. "I'm not going to tell you what is a good story. But I'll give you an idea of things I don't like. We don't have to be in the news every day. We don't have to circulate a story just so they're talking about us."

In the long run, how the team plays is going to be the best story. Brian did a good job in that he fed the media some relevant human interest stuff about our players, and he minimized the time that I had to spend dealing with such things.

It's really simple. Nobody talks to one of our players without first going through the Sports Information Office. That's not that difficult, that's not unfair. I don't want people going to players' apartments or calling them at all hours of the night.

Do I have any other rules for the players?

Just one — do what's right.

I've lived by that one for a long time.

My general philosophy about the media can be best summarized by Cicero. I don't remember him coaching in the Horizon League. Or officiating in the Big Ten.

But I'm told he was a Roman statesman, who was known to be a flip-flopper. He would change his position depending on which way the wind was blowing — and then over-react. He might have been the world's first sports writer or blogger.

Whatever the case, a friend introduced me to this intriguing if not cryptic nugget from Cicero: "I know you believe you understand what you think I said, but I'm not sure you realize that what you heard is not what I meant."

I could not have said it better myself, and do so whenever I get the chance.

Welcome to my world — the world of Coachspeak.

Or Bospeak.

***

"We took North Carolina down to the wire."

"We had our chances to win the game."

"We're not satisfied because we know we could have won."

"We withstood a couple of blows, and threw a couple back."

"They survived the fight, but we left it all out there."

"We're not afraid to step on the court with anybody."

"We matched up toe-to-toe with the best in the country."

"Anyone calling us boring may have a change of heart."

Those were some of the comments from our players and assistants after we lost to No. 1-seeded North Carolina, 88-82, in the Syracuse University Carrier Dome. We were a No. 6 seed, and one step away from the 2005 Final Four. As it played out, North Carolina went on to win the national championship by beating Illinois in the finals.

"I haven't been around a team that's done what this group has done with what they've had," I remember saying afterward. "This group was unbelievable and made some of their own history. Some day, the statistics and numbers will all hit home with the players. All they know, for now, is they wanted to play another game."

From year to year, the roles change.

But the brotherhood continues.

After Devin Harris left for the NBA in the spring of '04, we returned five seniors: Mike Wilkinson, Clayton Hanson, Zach Morley, Sharif Chambliss and Andreas Helmigk. I've consistently said the same things about my teams, and this was no different: "Watch the players. Watch them develop. Watch them grow. Watch how they play together."

The amazing thing about young men on a basketball court is that they will figure out for themselves who's reliable, who's getting it done, who they can trust, and who will deliver. That all tends to emerge over time — over the length of a season.

In the NCAA tournament, Alando Tucker was the only underclassman in a starting lineup that included Wilkinson, Morley, Chambliss and Hanson. Kam Taylor was our leading contributor off the bench, followed by Ray Nixon.

Some of the younger guys didn't play much, but still benefited from the postseason exposure and experience. That included Jason Chappell, Michael Flowers, Greg Stiemsma and Brian Butch.

That was our fourth team at Wisconsin. Each of the first four, to some extent, had different personalities. But there were common themes and questions. Did they value the ball? Did they rebound well? Did they take away easy baskets?

If you get the right answers on a consistent basis, you'll always have a chance to compete with anybody. Except nobody gave us a chance against North Carolina.

We had more than our fair share of detractors before our game against the Tar Heels largely because none of the national pundits thought we matched up.

They didn't think we were worthy of the regional finals, I guess, based on who we had played or not played to get there. We beat Northern Iowa, Bucknell and North Carolina State, and that still wasn't good enough for some of the "experts."

They didn't like the Big Ten, and they didn't like us.

But I really didn't care what anybody else liked or disliked.

I was focused on our team and what we could do to win the game. We knew North Carolina was athletic because of their NBA talent: Scott May, Marvin Williams, Rashad McCants and Raymond Felton all went on to become first-round picks. We tried to counter some of the things that they did. Offensively, we felt that we could score. We just had to keep them from scoring.

Once we got comfortable with that realization — that we could run good offense — I just thought we needed to be better defensively. But they beat us to some spots on the floor because of their athleticism, and they executed a few more possessions than we did.

I never take too much from one game. I don't read too much into the outcome, whether someone plays us real tough or vice versa. You have never heard me say, "Aren't we good — because we just played North Carolina so tough?"

We had our chances to be the better team. But we weren't. The Tar Heels got it done over 40 minutes, and they were moving on to another two-game tournament.

That has always been our approach. Even when we're playing a first round game in the NCAA tournament, I don't stand up in the locker room and tell the guys, "Look, we need to get to the Sweet 16" or "Look, we need to get to the Elite Eight."

That's not the way we talk about it. Instead, we're talking about three two-game tournaments. The first and second round games make up one, followed by the Sweet 16 and Elite Eight games, followed by the semifinals and finals at the Final Four site.

You have to win six games. It's not like we get to a stage in the progression and we're jumping up and down and saying, "Oh, good, we've made it this far."

If I'm going to think about anything, I'm thinking. "How can I give our team a chance to win with five minutes to play in the national championship game?"

But somewhere along the line it has to register in your players' minds that you can't play that "next one" until you play and win "this one" — which can get you to the next one. After the North Carolina loss, I encouraged everyone to take the time to write or call or e-mail those people who had influenced their development as a student-athlete and helped put them in a Badger uniform.

"Make sure you thank them, especially if you're a senior," I said.

I bring that up to all my teams after the final game of a season.

When you're in the NCAA tournament, the finality is abrupt. Things can end so quickly and without warning in our sport. In football when you're in a bowl, you know that you've got one more game to play, and that's it.

In basketball, you have to deal with the one-and-done's.

Everybody wants to go on a run in the tournament.

That's academic.

Some runs are just longer than others.

***

Al McGuire liked reminding everyone that half the doctors in this country graduated in the bottom half of their class. You could make the same point about lawyers or journalism students or service academies or coaches. It was kind of like a Yogi Berra-ism.

When I was at UW-Milwaukee, I sat down a couple of times over coffee and bagels with Coach McGuire. He had some interesting stories about recruiting against Wisconsin in New York while he was still coaching at Marquette.

What a character. He was everything I pictured out of Al McGuire. You might not be quite sure where he was coming from on some of his thoughts. But you knew there was conviction behind everything that he was saying. That's how he saw life.

Fact is, I had uncles like him — they would do things in their own way with their own lingo. I know Wisconsin people made a big deal of Al's eccentricity. But he would have been just one of the guys in the neighborhood where I grew up.

Al McGuire liked saying, "The world is run by 'C' students."

I know a lot of business people whose success has been tied to their personality, their drive, their persistence and their intuitiveness. That outweighed what they might have remembered from studying for an exam or reading a book. But they would never imply that getting an education — their book-learning — was not important.

What does a 'C' grade mean? Literally, it means average. But the person who got the 'C' didn't create the system. Nor the parameters for the grade.

That came to mind when the NCAA decided to issue a so-called report card for schools by establishing the Academic Performance Rate or APR.

What the NCAA failed to do was involve some of the most important people in the equation: the basketball coaches. We live with the players every day.

Yet, the administrators didn't consult us when they devised the formula for Division I schools in 2005, and that was a mistake. It would be like someone talking about water safety and not having anyone on the committee who knew how to swim.

Here was the premise: the NCAA wanted accountability in the classroom — it wanted to go after schools that were performing academically in such an atrocious manner that it was an embarrassment. The NCAA wanted to put a number on graduation rates. But the NCAA needed to do more homework. The NCAA should have involved head coaches. The NCAA should have talked more to the student-athletes.

As a country, we've gone down this path before. It was called taxation without representation. It was centuries ago, but it didn't go over very big in the colonies. That said, I resisted the temptation to dump tea in Lake Mendota in protest over the APR.

In 2007, though, I got involved in the process when I was named to the NCAA's men's basketball academic enhancement group — a cross-section of athletic directors, faculty reps, league commissioners, school presidents and coaches.

I'm guessing that I was chosen because I'm not afraid to say what's on my mind. I was placed on a sub-committee along with Georgia Tech coach Paul Hewitt. Our undertaking was to determine the effect of transfers on the APR.

First of all, how are you going to stop people from transferring? Do you realize that over 25 percent of the faculty leaves the University of Wisconsin every year? Most of them don't give a reason why they're leaving, either. I get it. We're a mobile society.

One thing that we've found is that many prep basketball players are mobile. They move around a lot. College coaches didn't create that culture. That culture has been created by high school coaches and the accompanying influence of AAU coaches. Despite the denials, they have been recruiting players.

What are these players thinking? —"Let's see, I'm getting 10 shots a game, but if I transfer and go to this school, I can get 20" — and that's what they may be hearing, too.

Meanwhile, in reassessing how the NCAA is keeping score with the

APR, there are some different elements that factor into why players transfer from one college to another. Or coaches move on. For one thing, head coaches get fired and a player may want to leave that school and transfer because of a particular bond with that deposed coach.

Sometimes people find other priorities in college and basketball just isn't that important any more, so they leave the program. Happens in all sports. There are a lot of reasons why things change for athletes between the ages of 18 and 22.

The toughest part of the APR is trying to be fair. Points are awarded for athletes staying in school and staying eligible from semester to semester. Points are subtracted from a school's total if it doesn't meet predetermined standards.

An APR score of 925 is the equivalent to a 60 percent graduation rate under the formula. The NCAA initially sent out warning letters to schools that were guilty of poor classroom performance. But now sanctions can be applied and scholarships can be lost if a school falls below that number.

Here's the catch: there are some flaws in the APR process and how the scores are calculated. I'll give you two examples involving Wisconsin players.

Mike Wilkinson earned his undergraduate degree in December of his senior year. The following semester, he signed up for some graduate school courses. But at the completion of our season, he got invited to work out for some NBA teams.

That forced Mike to drop those classes. The intent was that he was going to come back in the summer or come back in a few years and pick up the courses and continue his pursuit of a masters. That would come after he was done playing for a paycheck as a professional basketball player. (So far, Mike has played in Greece and Russia.)

We still lost a point from our APR.

That infuriated me. He already had his degree and he was pursuing an occupation: basketball. And they were going to dock us for it? I made my anger known.

That loophole has since been closed by the NCAA.

The public has to realize that there are thousands of college students who drop out of school every year. Maybe they're gone for a semester or two because of financial reasons or other circumstances. But eventually many will come back and get their degree. Why shouldn't the student-athlete have the same opportunity?

Here's another example: Latrell Fleming was in our first recruiting class at Wisconsin, but he had to give up basketball after he was diagnosed with a heart ailment. Latrell stayed on scholarship, a medical scholarship, which meant that he was still subject to the APR standards for eligibility.

One semester, he was feeling sluggish and having trouble sleeping. Physically, he wasn't himself and he wound up dropping below the number of credits that he needed. Remember he was already on a medical, yet we lost a point from our APR.

We appealed.

At first, it was cut and dry with the NCAA. You could complain and clamor all you wanted, and you could make an argument, but it wasn't going anywhere. That has changed and there is a legitimate appeal system. The NCAA continues to tweak, too.

The APR is an attempt to measure all Division I schools by the same academic standards. I just don't know if you can really keep score because every institution has different resources. There is a clear financial delineation. Some have more money for summer school. Some have better academic support services.

Not everybody has the same assets. Not everybody has the same tools to work with. That's the problem. We're fortunate at Wisconsin that we have the funding to do some things. Others aren't as fortunate.

Maybe the six BCS conferences should be put under the same umbrella — academically — like they are in college football. These conferences have the money to commit to academic support, tutors and summer school. Maybe that would be the wisest thing to do since it's unfair to bracket funded schools with underfunded ones.

In the end, it still comes down to this: What is your institution will-ing to accept from its coaches? I've always felt that we were accountable for classroom performance before the advent of the APR. If nothing else, your school is going to hold you accountable. Or should. Some are more proactive in this area than others.

Personally, I will not go after kids who I do not feel will have a chance to make it academically at the University of Wisconsin. Sometimes, you will catch criticism for that attitude. But, in the long run, you've got to do what is in the best interest of your team, your institution and the student-athlete in question.

You're playing the percentages with some young people. You've got to take into account their academic record in high school and, to some extent, their scores on the standardized tests. You also have to factor in their willingness to work and how hungry they are to be successful in the classroom.

I know people change, but men's programs only get 13 scholarships. So at times, you have to make the best decision that you can based on the available numbers.

I'm going to take some kids who I might feel are somewhat of a risk. Why? Maybe I think they can get it done academically because of their personalities or because they're hard workers and they've steadily improved their grades in high school.

What should be understood is that the University of Wisconsin should have the face of Wisconsin and all of its different backgrounds. This institution should have the face of the kids from northern Wisconsin, it should have the face of the kids from Milwaukee and it should have the faces of the kids from the suburbs and the farms.

Just speaking my mind again.

***

After losing four of our top six scorers from our Elite Eight team, I knew that our returning players would have to play older than they were. Everyone was going to have to mature just a little quicker. Sophomores needed to play like juniors and juniors needed to play like seniors, while first semester freshmen needed to play like second-semester freshmen. That was the mandate for the 2005-2006 season.

Alando Tucker was the only returning starter.

We lost 22 years of college basketball experience. Mike Wilkinson had five years. So did Sharif Chambliss, three of them at Penn State. Clayton Hanson had four years, so did Zach Morley — including junior college — and Andreas Helmigk.

Besides Tucker, a redshirt junior, the only returnee who averaged more than 12 minutes was Kam Taylor, also a junior. Ray Nixon was our only senior.

Our team poster was "Watch us Grow."

How prophetic.

We got off to a great start by winning 14 of our first 16 games, including a 4-0 start in the Big Ten. But if you look at who we played and where we played them, you can see the schedule had something to do with our early success.

We didn't finish strong. Was it because of the missing players? We didn't have DeAaron Williams, Greg Stiemsma and Marcus Landry. Or was it possible our conference season might have ended up similarly even if we were at full strength?

You have to consider their inexperience. DeAaron had redshirted as a freshman. Greg had been in the system for a year but had missed time with an injury and saw limited action. Marcus was a true freshman. Still, their losses affected our depth.

DeAaron Williams left the program and transferred. Greg Stiemsma was struggling with things outside of basketball and was ineligible for the second semester. So was Marcus, who missed retaining his eligibility by a hundredth of a point.

Late in the season, when someone got into foul trouble or someone was a little fatigued, we weren't quite as deep as we needed to be. The amazing thing is that we still had a chance mathematically to battle for the top spot with two weeks to play.

If we would have won just one of our final two games, we would have finished 10-6 in the conference. And maybe that might have influenced our NCAA seed. The problem was that both of those games were road games.

On March 2, we played at Michigan State. We returned home and bussed to Iowa the following day and played the Hawkeyes on March 4. We lost both games.

Ohio State went 12-4 and won the league.

We went 9-7 and made the NCAA tournament.

We were a No. 9 seed. Our draw? Arizona.

That team was just better than us.

The Wildcats were the preseason favorite to win the Pac-10. But they had some issues during the season that prevented them from living up to expectations. Their leading scorer, Hassan Adams, had been suspended for the conference tournament for an off-the-court incident. But he was reinstated for the NCAA tourney.

Arizona's point guard, Mustafa Shakur, was a Philly kid, which meant that he was looking forward to his homecoming at the Wachovia Center in Philadelphia. Shakur was a McDonald's All-American at Friends Central High School. Another player who had been suspended for some games and reinstated was Chris Rodgers, another guard.

That was a very tough matchup for us athletically.

We needed some positive things to happen early in the game and when they didn't, and they hit some shots, we played from a hole throughout a 94-75 loss. But we got to the Big Dance and we had some guys play older than they really were. Maybe they weren't as consistent as they needed to be, but that was expected.

I liked the way the guys competed.

I also liked what Brian Lucas came up with after some research. He discovered that we were the youngest Wisconsin team to play a postseason game, dating to the '40s. That's the way I tried to look at the whole season — we were very inexperienced.

I really liked what we had coming back.

An experienced team.

CHAPTER TEN

Attention to Detail

While touring the spectacular ruins of the Colloseum in Rome, I couldn't help but think, "Wow, what a great home-court advantage."

Unless, of course, you were subject to the Emperor's whim and your life depended on a thumbs-up or thumbs-down signal.

Dealing with a Big Ten official seems pretty tame by comparison.

Coaches talk about how games are not a matter of life and death. Well, they were in ancient Rome. And you thought it was tough playing at the Breslin Center.

Our tour guide pointed out that the Colloseum could seat about 50,000. No telling what they got for courtside seats. I kept looking for Russell Crowe, but we didn't run into him.

Seriously, how could you not think about the movie *Gladiator* or Crowe, whose portrayal of Maximus won him the Academy Award?

Scanning the ramps and passages of the Colloseum, I could only imagine what the real combat was like when the participants made their entrance and the competition began: Gladiator vs. gladiator. Gladiator vs. lions. Talk about matchup problems.

All in all, it was a once-in-a-lifetime experience. Our guys wore smiles on their faces 24/7. They're still talking about the trip. And what a trip it was — 10 days in Italy, which included stops and sightseeing tours in Rome, Florence and Lake Como, which absolutely blew me away with its majesty and beauty.

What a tremendous way to start a season. During our August excursion, we played and won five games against Italian teams that were pretty Americanized. If you were a finesse player, you were out of luck. There was nothing timid about the play.

But the trip was about much more than just basketball.

Each of our guys appreciated the fact that they got an opportunity to do something that they realized the average 18- to 22-year-old doesn't get a chance to do. What I really liked is that they took advantage of the situation. They didn't sleep late or skip any of the things that we had planned for them. They absorbed everything.

Bottom line, they followed their leader, Alando Tucker.

I have said it before and I will say it again: Alando Tucker was by far one of the best team leaders I've ever had. Throughout the trip, he was always on the go — taking pictures, asking questions about what we were seeing, being inquisitive. Whenever your best player sets the best example, you know that you have something special.

There's no question that the trip brought our team closer together.

Two months later, we learned that we were ranked No. 9 in the *USA Today*/ESPN coaches' poll — the highest preseason school ranking in 44 years. Or since Little Eva was doing the "Locomotion" and Dee Dee Sharp was doing "Mashed Potato Time."

Even Chubby Checker was still doing the "Twist" in 1962 when the Badgers were ranked No. 10 in the first Associated Press poll of that season.

What did it mean? It meant the voters recognized that we had had a young team the year before and believed that our players would get better with added experience. It also meant the voters had respect for our program. Now, we had to justify the ranking.

But who could foresee us climbing to No. 1 in the country?

Nobody. That would be my guess.

But after winning 26 of 28 games, including 17 straight during one stretch, we made it to the top of the Associated Press national rankings for the first time in school history.

I never said it couldn't be done, but it isn't something that probably a lot of people thought would happen. It was a split decision, by the way. Ohio State was voted No. 1 in the *USA Today*/ESPN coaches' preseason poll.

Asked at my weekly press conference about my reaction when I got the news that we were No. 1, I detailed how I went to the closet and

CONDITIONS OF CONTRACT

In arranging for shore excursions for guests aboard our vessels, NCL(Bahamas) Ltd. d/b/a Norwegian Cruise Line and its respective agents do so as a convenience. NCL(Bahamas) Ltd. d/b/a Norwegian Cruise Line and it's agents have no ownership or control over the means of transportation or other services furnished in connection with such shore excursions. The owners or contractors providing such transportation or other services are independent and control the terms and conditions under which such transportation or other services may be provided. The guest agrees that he will be bound by all terms and conditions contained in applicable tickets and tariffs of the shoreside contractor. The guest by accepting the services of NCL(Bahamas) Ltd. d/b/a Norwegian Cruise Line, its agents or vessels in arranging for shore excursions, hereby agrees that NCL(Bahamas) Ltd. d/b/a Norwegian Cruise Line shall not be liable in any respect for any personal injury, death, property damage or any other liability arising from the selection of any shore excursion operator or otherwise arising out of or in connection with any shore excursion taken pursuant to this contract. Guest acknowledges that NCL(Bahamas) Ltd. d/b/a Norwegian Cruise Line cannot control the providers of shore excursions and releases releases NCL(Bahamas) Ltd. d/b/a Norwegian Cruise Line, its agents and vessels and agrees to hold NCL(Bahamas) Ltd. d/b/a Norwegian Cruise Line and its respective agents and vessels harmless from any loss, injury or damage to his personal property, however caused and of whatsoever nature, in connection with the shore excursions.

This ticket is subject to the cancellation fees as quoted in the shore excursion brochure.

Norwegian Spirit

Shore Excursion Ticket

Guatemala - Santo Tomas 2/25/2009

NORWEGIAN CRUISE LINE® TDEI0016 Las Escobas Waterfall Voyage

FREESTYLE CRUISING® Adult Ticket

NCL

MEETING POINT: ON THE PIER ASHORE

MEETING TIME: 01:50

HOLLER, SARAH LYNN - Cabin : 9566

20

Please Note:

48 hours notice prior arriving at port required to cancel. All tours run rain or shine. Operated by Grayline Tours

Wear a swimsuit & bring a towel. Hike is about 45 minutes.

pulled out a foam-rubber No. 1 hand and a New Year's Eve noise maker. I then tore up a newspaper and threw the confetti in the air while I was running around the house yelling and screaming.

That's my story, and I'm sticking to it.

But after going back to my office and watching a tape of Michigan State — our next opponent — crushing Iowa, I put the foam finger and party favor away, cleaned up the confetti and went back to work. That brought me back down to earth, I emphasized.

There was a lot of truth in that last statement.

Being No. 1 in the preseason is one thing.

Being No. 1 at the end of the season is another.

Being No. 1 in-season is fleeting.

One week, you're No. 1; the next week, you're not. We're not the only team that has gone through that cycle. It seems to happen every year in college basketball. The following season, in fact, Tennessee lost its first game after being ranked No. 1.

I didn't have to remind our guys, "Hey, they just picked us No. 1 and we're going to Michigan State and Ohio State and we're only as good as the next one."

They understood the challenge.

Nonetheless, whether you're No. 1 for a day or No. 1 for a week, you have to keep in mind that there are programs that never achieve a No. 1 ranking. I was so proud of our players — for their perseverance and what they had done.

You don't get to be No. 1 without having done something very special. It's not like I called someone on the phone said, "Would you please vote us No. 1?"

I don't even vote in the coaches' poll.

So I thought it was a heckuva statement on our players' behalf, and it had to be exciting for anybody who has ever worn a Wisconsin jersey and all of our loyal fans who have supported the program throughout the years.

But we were now wearing concentric circles on our back. We knew that we were a target, and our No. 1 status would be even more incentive for Michigan State.

It was. Their players said so.

After losing a tight game at the Breslin Center, I walked into the media room and tried to break the ice by saying, "Okay, if you start chanting 'overrated' I'm leaving."

In short, the Spartans were the better team that night.

But I was confident that our guys would show their resiliency five days later at Ohio State. I knew our seniors — Alando Tucker, Kam Taylor Jason Chappell — would bounce back.

I also knew that we would get the right answers from our juniors — Michael Flowers, Brian Butch, Greg Stiemsma, and Tanner Bronson.

Plus, I knew our sophomores and freshmen would be ready to play — Marcus Landry, Joe Krabbenhoft, Kevin Gullickson, Trevon Hughes and Jason Bohannon.

It was an historic showdown — No. 1 vs. No. 1 — in Columbus, and we came up a little bit short, losing 48-47 to an Ohio State team that featured three NBA first-rounders: Greg Oden, Daequan Cook and Michael Conley Jr.

Afterward Alando Tucker commented that it had been a heartbreaking loss for the players. But nobody hung their head. Alando wouldn't let his teammates dwell on the defeat.

The real blow was losing Brian Butch to an elbow injury. We're not the first team that has ever had to survive without a key player. We never belabored that point, or the injury, and we knew that we still had to find a way to get things done. But we could have used Brian. Especially going into the Big Ten and NCAA tournaments.

People talked about how top-heavy we were offensively that season: Tucker averaged 20 points, Taylor averaged 13 and nobody else averaged more than nine. But I've had other teams where the top two scorers were separated from the pack, so to speak.

In general, we tried to put Alando in scoring positions on the floor where he could use his skills to get us a point per possession. But we did the same things with Kam and Brian. We've done that for players ever since I started coaching.

I recall reading a story about some of the highest scoring duos in school history. The writer singled out three combinations: Michael Finley and Tracy Webster, Devin Harris and Mike Wilkinson, Danny Jones and Trent Jackson.

But statistically, none compared to Alando Tucker and Kam Taylor, who hit some big shots, game-winning shots. That those two were able to put up those numbers and win — and play in the NCAA tournament every year — was the important thing

Alando was very vocal. Kam was just a quiet guy who never said much. It was tough for me to read Kam. And he was not the first player like that I've ever coached. Some people are just easier to connect with than others.

The reality is that not all of your players are thinking, "Man, Coach Ryan is great. What a swell guy. He really knows what he's talking about."

That's okay. But you had better be doing the things that are helping the team be successful or you will have to deal with me.

***

About midway through that Big Ten season — late January of 2007 — we took a nostalgic trip back to Platteville and Williams Fieldhouse.

When I was first approached about attaching my name to the basketball floor, I suggested that they call it Pioneer Court to honor everyone who had practiced and played there. That made more sense to me than a Bo Ryan Court.

After all, I'm just one person who contributed to the end result.

Many others shared in the heavy lifting.

But then the light went on: maybe we could tie my name to a dedication and fund-raiser that would benefit the student-athletes by improving facilities at Platteville.

Everyone agreed that was the ticket. The next challenge was finding a date and time that would fit everybody's schedule, notably ours at Wisconsin. As a coach, you have to continuously remind yourself of one thing: never get distracted.

At my age, though, I figured I could juggle all of that and not get waylaid. So we went through our normal preparations leading up to our January 28 game at Iowa.

Since we were playing the Hawkeyes on a Sunday — and since we always travel by bus to Iowa City the day before a game — it all fell into place logistically for us to be in Platteville for the court dedication that Saturday.

Since I left for the UWM job in '99, it was only the second time that I had been back for a game at Williams Fieldhouse. As you might expect, just walking around that gym again gave me flashbacks to when I coached there. I remembered the big shots and big plays that were made by guys like Jeter, Theisen, Peavy and Van Wie.

Many of my memories were linked to the facility itself. During my first season, some construction work on campus resulted in cut power lines that left us in the dark during practice. I wasn't going to waste a day, so I opened the doors at one end of the building and we did what we could in the halfcourt.

There was another day where there was so much moisture on the floor from the humidity that there was no way in the world we could practice without getting somebody hurt. So I took our team to the outdoor courts.

That's another story.

When I first got to Platteville, they didn't have any outdoor courts. How can you be on a college campus and not have outdoor basketball courts? It was mind-boggling. But we worked hard to get them and we eventually put them to good use.

I wore a baseball cap to keep the sun off my head. It was just the weirdest day. The tape of our practice was picked up by a CBS affiliate and shown in other areas of the country with the voiceover, "You're looking at Platteville, Wisconsin, and the only team in college basketball that has to practice outdoors."

I thought about these things while waiting for the court dedication at halftime of the game between Platteville and UW-Eau Claire whose coach, Terry Gibbons, could not have been more gracious. Everyone was that way. The players from both teams stayed on the floor for the ceremony rather than returning to their locker rooms.

I felt so honored and touched to be a part of something like this, something I never dreamed would happen when I got started in the profession. Who would? Maybe the most touching thing was that our Wisconsin players wanted to be there.

When it first came up, I explained to Alando Tucker that I would be taking a detour to Platteville on our way to Iowa City, but I would catch up with the team later. When he found out what was going on, he stressed that he wanted to be there for the ceremony, and so did his teammates. You can imagine how that made me feel.

***

Alando Tucker was like family. He made you feel that way about him. When I was around him, I always felt like I was in the comfort of my home. And when he wasn't around anymore — after he left for the NBA — the media reaction was predictable.

We became a Big Ten afterthought.

Before the start of the 2007-2008 season, a writers' poll had us slotted fourth in the conference behind Michigan State, Indiana and Ohio State.

But remember, I never cared about predictions.

Whenever I was asked about the loss of Tucker and Taylor, and who was going to fill their scoring void, I said, "There are a lot of minutes to fill, and a lot of hungry guys. Let's find out who's going to rise to the top. But we have to do it as a group."

It was going to be a challenge because the year before about 90 percent of our players knew their role coming into the season. Now we were down to about 20 percent. But I was excited to see how they all meshed. I like challenges.

I always think we can be good. I'm always teaching players to maximize their potential. I knew we could be competitive. I knew we could play a lot of different people and get it done even though we lost Tucker and Taylor.

I just thought we would be better defensively. Alando and Kam were good defenders, average to good. But as a team, we were now good to really good — just by the way the guys rotated and played together. They were rarely out of position.

It was obviously the right mix.

Maybe it didn't look that way after we lost at Duke early in the season. How many did we lose by? Didn't matter. I never worry about point differential.

I just get ready for the next opponent. I don't panic after a bad game. I'm not going to kick the players out of the locker room or take away their practice uniforms.

Why would I?

What kind of message is that sending?

What I should do is punish myself and the assistants. Maybe I should ban the coaching staff from using our offices in the Kohl Center and take away everybody's golf shirts with the motion W on the pocket. If the team isn't playing well, that's our fault. I'm not going to punish a player for a bad practice or a bad game.

That's why I never blame a team for a defeat.

I've got smart kids. I didn't have to tell them that we just got our asses kicked at Duke.

The next day, we went back to work. There was no change in the routine. I've never needed players to reassure me that they understood what they did wrong and they would make amends. Show me — don't tell me — if you think you've learned something.

Every once in a while during practice, you might make a reference to what happened in a game: "Do you remember when this happened? Here's the reason why it happened. You needed to take a better angle."

Or you might show them a clip: "Do you remember when you were above the free throw line here — when you really needed to be below the free throw line?"

They'll usually go, "Yeah, I do remember that."

That's all I ever wanted as a player. Give me a frame of reference. You don't have to tell me that I'm a piece of crap. But, as a reminder, if you can tell me what can and can't work, or why it won't in certain situations, I'm going to be much better off.

Right after a game, I don't go over every possession with the players. They know the video clips are coming. My teaching focus is to ensure that no one leaves the locker room thinking that the loss was his fault. I don't let them leave that room with the notion that one guy let everybody else down.

It's a team game. And even when we win, we're teaching: "Hey, guys, it almost got away from us because we got a little sloppy or we didn't block out here."

The morning after a game, I'll watch video in my office at home. It's amazing how the officials always get better the next day. They're never as poor as you think.

I'm big into video. I always have been. If you can see images on a screen, if you can see the way something is being done, right or wrong, you have one way of learning.

I don't make the players watch a lot of video. What we give them is very much to the point because their time is precious, while I consider watching video a part of my job.

If not every head coach watches as much video as me, it's because they're a lot smarter and they don't need to. Or maybe they just figure they've got really good players and they don't have to worry about anything else.

When I'm on the treadmill, I'll throw in a tape. And it might go something like this: "Damn, that kid never once made a post move to his left hand. Every time he caught the ball, he drop-stepped and went to his right."

Some people brainstorm in the shower.

I do it while I'm working out.

We ended up using that clip as a learning tool on post defense.

***

After the Duke loss, we needed to get a couple of wins that would get our players to believe in themselves and what we were doing. We got one against Valpo at home, rallying from a second-half deficit. And we got another one on the road at Texas.

Up to that point, Trevon Hughes had been inconsistent largely because he was a sophomore and a first-year starter, still learning about the game. But when you look around the Big Ten, who would you rather have as a point guard?

The problem was that Hughes injured his ankle during practice the night before we played the Longhorns. We were long shots to begin with, according to the local newspaper. Did I have questions on how we might respond without him? I'm not an obsessive coach that way. I just reminded the team, "This is what we can do to win."

What Michael Flowers did in the closing seconds was beyond comprehension. Not only does he hit the game-winning shot (a 3-pointer to give us the lead), but he steals the inbounds pass and as he is going out of bounds, he has the wherewithal to throw the ball up in the air — knowing that the clock is going to keep running until the ball touches something.

That was the play of the year in my book.

That game served as a springboard, too.

And we just kept growing as a team.

As a player or a coach, I've always looked at things the same way: it's about the league, the league, the league. It was telling that we set a school record by winning 31 games, including 16 out of 18 league games with our only losses coming to Purdue.

But what was most telling about this team was that we won the Big Ten regular season championship and the Big Ten tournament championship. We got great leadership from our seniors: Michael Flowers, Brian Butch, Greg Stiemsma and Tanner Bronson (who was appreciated and respected by his teammates as much as any player I've had).

The leadership would manifest itself in a work ethic. All you had to do was watch Michael Flowers work — on the hill, in the weight room, at practice, on defense.

Overall, it was a resilient group. Whereas the year before it was Tucker and Taylor getting the headlines — which was great — we had different guys contributing. Nobody had to do it alone. If someone had an off night, someone else would pick him up. I liked the way they played together, and I knew my voice was being heard.

I figured these guys wouldn't be working as hard as they did in practice if they didn't want to listen and be in a position to get better individually and as a team. You know how you can be disrespectful as a teammate? Don't practice hard.

That wasn't the case with this group. They each had the mindset, "I'm going to beat you today on this drill or on this possession. I'm going to show you I'm better."

That's how I want players to be. But I want it every day, not just the first hour of practice or the second hour of practice. You want people to be consistent. They were, and I knew if they kept working at it, they would have a chance to do some good things.

Winning 31 games isn't easy. That says something for them right there.

I just found it very easy to identify with these players. If they had a tough game, they didn't make it all about them. Even when they won, they couldn't wait for the next practice. Each player had the attitude, "I know I'm better than that and I want to prove it."

It had a lot to do with their individual personalities. There were no mopers.

I've never had a team that I didn't like. But this group was easy to like.

In our NCAA tournament loss to Davidson, we got away from ourselves a little bit. We made some decisions with the ball that we don't normally make, especially after we lost Trevon Hughes to an injury. He had 25 points and was our leading scorer against Kansas State in the second round. I thought he had a heckuva game.

I truly believe some of our erratic play against Davidson was the result of some guys not having the same confidence without Hughes on the floor. That's how important he had become. One of the big things Davidson had going was the leadership of their point guard, Jason Richards, to go along with Stephen Curry's scoring ability.

Their role players did what they had done all year. Ours didn't. Their role players stepped up. Ours didn't — they didn't do what they had done in other games. That happens every year in the tournament, and that's how teams win or get beat.

I know it was a disappointing loss for everyone, especially our seniors. Michael Flowers and Brian Butch played in 133 and 124 career games, respectively.

Together, they were on the left-hand side far more than the right side. Flowers and Butch played on teams that won 105 games over the last four seasons.

I was pleased with how Michael stayed true to the task defensively — he was a chaser who bothered the heck out of good offensive players from other teams. As far as transition defense, he was one of the best I've ever coached.

Brian just took care of business, on and off the floor. I liked the way he handled everything around him — how he handled the tough news of his mom having cancer, how he handled the expectations that came with being a McDonald's All-American, how he handled his growth as a player and how he handled his academic workload.

Brian is all about the big picture. Whether or not he plays in the NBA, he'd like to — just like we'd like to win a national championship at Wisconsin.

Each year, we're trying to maintain the competitive level.

Each year, we're trying to be the best that we can be.

It will be no different next year, or the year after next.

When I decide not to coach basketball anymore, it will be because of a disconnect between me and the players. It will be because I don't feel as comfortable about how the young men are processing what I'm saying.

But as long as they're listening — as long as they want to be part of something positive and want to work hard and contribute as a team — I'll continue to coach.

What will I be doing 10 years from now? Check back with me in 10 years. I never worry about it. Maybe that's why I've been in coaching so long. There are always challenges out there. I don't know that you really have to look for them.

Sometimes they find you.

***

In life, there are choices. Once you've made a choice, you have to deal with the reality of the situation and handle it in your own way. Marcus Landry is treated the same as every other player when it comes to basketball. He has the same responsibilities on the court, even though he's married and has a wife and three small children.

You don't make concessions for anything in coaching. If something comes up, you deal with it accordingly. But you don't have a category of concessions for your players and start listing things under it. I don't know of any coach who does that.

I just expect things to be done a certain way. If I'm dealing with people who are rational, there isn't anything that I'm giving them that they can't deliver on. I'm not doing things just to try and get a reaction from someone. The things that I'm asking our players to do, need to get done for a reason.

Yet, we're talking about young people who are taking on life's responsibilities. So you're there for them, and you try to point them in the right direction. But you can't tell them how to live their lives because it's still all about the decisions they make.

In this context, we've always expected leadership from seniors. That will be no different for Marcus Landry, Joe Krabbenhoft, Kevin Gullickson or Morris Cain.

Some people made a big deal out of an exchange that I had once with Joe after an inbounds play. It was late in the game, and we were winning by a big margin.

But anybody who has ever played for me — anybody who has played a lot of basketball — knew exactly what I was doing. It wasn't that I was upset with Joe.

In order to be heard above crowd noise, you have to yell and when you do, your face is contorted in a way that it makes it look like you're angrier than you are.

That's my story, and I'm sticking to it.

My message? "Joe, don't give them another possession. They didn't earn it. Why take a turnover? Why not do the right thing?"

Here's what I'll say in the huddle: "Don't ever disrespect the game. We're not giving anything away. Don't do it. You've worked too hard."

And it doesn't matter who's on the floor. It doesn't matter if you're up by 25 points or two points, every possession counts and you have to try to do the right things. We don't let anyone get a wide-open shot in practice. Why would we do that in a game?

To reiterate, I tell them, "Stay true to the game. If you're giving up something during what other people call 'garbage time,' you're disrespecting basketball."

Joe Krabbenhoft plays the game the way you're supposed to play it. To lavish praise on a kid for hustling does not flow easily for me. But I've had a lot of guys who bring it every day, play hard and never take a possession off. I've had a lot of guys who have showed up early and left late — making sure to put in a little extra time.

Isn't that part of the model for success in any business?

There are other basic rules to being on the plus side: Educate yourself. Read more about whatever business you're in. Study the people who have been successful. Study the businesses that have had success. If you do this, you'll realize why some people make it and some don't. Some people take care of the little things in greater detail.

It seems pretty simple to me. Especially if you get the right kind of people, honest people, to work with you — not for you — but with you, in whatever business you have.

It works the same way in coaching.

Surround yourself with good people.

I have — starting with my assistant coaches and extending to our program assistants (Peg Cullen and Laura Strang), academic support and compliance.

Greg Gard is one of the hungriest guys in coaching. He has never let his ego or anything about himself get in the way of doing what needed to get done. He has handled every task imaginable, dating to when he started with me at Platteville and was basically working for peanuts. Today, he's one of the nation's standout assistants.

I know Greg will be a great head coach. He can communicate. He understands the game. He has a love for it. He's organized, and he can teach. What else do you need?

I've always thought Gary Close was ready to be a head coach, and I thought he was a perfect fit for the Drake job when it came open after the '08 season, but he didn't get it. Gary has a wealth of experience as an assistant, and I tap into it. He has coached in the Big Ten at Iowa and the Pac-10 at Stanford. He's a teacher, and he does a great job working with our players.

All of our assistants do.

Howard Moore has grown so much since he first got here. Today, he has a much better understanding of what's important, what's frivolous and what I like and care about. I don't like petty stuff or excuses. That's not part of our program. Howard has a much better grasp of the things that matter, like attention to detail.

I've had good people in the role of director of basketball operations at Wisconsin: Saul Phillips, Duffy Conroy, Will Ryan and now Joe Robinson, who was a former team manager. His familiarity with the program, combined with his tremendous work ethic and organization, made him an ideal fit for the position. He's always a step ahead.

What kind of advice have I given to my son Will, who's now on Saul's staff at North Dakota State? Not much. He grew up with a coach — same as his brother, Matt, the video coordinator on our UW staff. They've watched, listened and learned. They know what I go through. They know they'd better love the game, and it's obvious they both do.

I've been really fortunate in coaching to have athletic trainers and strength coaches who have understood what I wanted from them. That has certainly been the case here with Henry Perez-Guerra and Scott Hettenbach.

I didn't come in with the idea I knew their jobs better than they did. They each have their own areas of expertise. I just had some ideas on how I would like to see the players treated by the trainer and the strength coach. I've tried to get them raises because they deserve to be rewarded every bit as much as our coaching staff has been rewarded.

That's how much I think of them. They've been with me all along.

When I was at Platteville, I had a math teacher who made as many or more practices than any coach. His name was Frank Cheek, and he would keep stats or the clock or do whatever we needed. I've always allowed people to be around our basketball program as long as they were around it for the right reasons.

Otto Puls is a good example. Besides being an assistant equipment manager, he's our official scorekeeper and travels to all road games. Otto is a great guy. He's like an older brother at practice, even if he misses a few calls. I'm teasing. Otto is a Hall of Fame high school basketball official and former Big Ten football official.

Another guy whose heart is in the right place is Andy North. I like having him around because he knows and loves the game of basketball. After practice, he's always offering words of encouragement to our players. He's a friend, a confidant and someone who made it to the top of his golf profession by winning two U.S. Opens.

Andy and his wife, Susan, give back to the community in a lot of ways.

Speaking of giving, no one has given me more sage advice than Ab Nicholas, one of the most prominent donors to the program and school and a former All-Big Ten first-team basketball player for the Badgers in the early '50s. As philanthropists, Ab and his wife, Nancy, have deep-seated feelings for the UW.

Ab has been a mentor away from the game for me. He doesn't always offer advice, unless you ask. But he's wise in so many ways. When he talks, I listen. He has offered ethical support and information about my social life, my financial well-being and many things involving my parents and our kids.

Without family support, you can't do your job as a head coach. I'm able to do what I do because I've got the best thing going on the home front. I've got Kelly Ryan. That's why I've always viewed myself as a lottery winner. She's special more so than people know because she doesn't want to have a lot of people know about her.

She understands the profession. But she also knows that I'm not going to bring things home — like a tough practice or something that has happened with a player.

Our girls have always been in tune with that: Megan, who's married, and the two youngest, Brenna and Mairin, both of whom were very much into what we were doing at Platteville and UWM before we moved back to Madison as a family.

I have talked to other head coaches who have had their kids crucified on school busses by classmates who have overreacted to the outcome of a game. That has never happened to my kids. I've told them, "If someone says the Badgers stunk last night, don't worry about it. And don't get into a discussion or argument over strategy."

Leave that to me and the sportswriters.

I have never really thought about celebrity. I don't even know what it is. I would like to think when I go places and people recognize me it's as much from the charitable things I've been involved with as it is from my exposure on ESPN or CBS or the internet.

I have tried to use my "celebrity" to help other people. Maybe my signature is worth $500 dollars for some charity. That's great. But I've never tried to use celebrity to get something for nothing. That's not me.

***

I've had the opportunity to be around a lot of high-profile coaches through my work on various NCAA and Big Ten committees. That includes being a member of the National Association of Basketball Coaches' Board of Directors.

What's the most timely issue?

Early commitments have become a concern, especially after some schools have accepted verbals from eighth graders. As a result, there has been some momentum to pass legislation whereby a college would not be able to offer a scholarship to a prospect until he has finished his sophomore year of high school.

Question is, how are you going to control it? You can legislate the kid out of the equation. But his mom or dad or guardian or AAU coach or high school coach could tell you that he's committing. Nothing is binding until you sign a national letter of intent.

If you had asked me in the eighth grade what I wanted to be, I would have said, "a lawyer." If you had asked me the same question when I was younger, maybe when I was 10 years old, I would have said, "a fireman or a baseball player."

About 80 % of the players that we have signed to tenders, we have known about since the eighth or ninth grade.

But there are no sure things in life.

Especially in recruiting.

When the NCAA adopted the 8/5 rule — allowing programs to sign no more than five players in any one given year and no more than eight over two years — I pointed out how unfair the ruling was to a particular segment of our population: minority males.

I did some research and found out that hundreds of scholarships were going unused because schools couldn't take another player. Women have 15 scholarships, men have 13. Yet there were schools that were leaving tenders unoccupied because they couldn't give more than eight in a two-year period. That wasn't right.

Here we are in a society where we're working to help minority students and we were eliminating scholarship opportunities. The rule was rescinded.

And it was gratifying from the standpoint that you had the president of the NCAA — Myles Brand — realize that the rule was wrong and take action to do something about it. He moved swiftly to make a change, a great move on his part.

There has been some talk about changing the "kick" rule on defense. If I'm dribbling and throw a pass off your leg, it's called kicking. But why shouldn't you be able to use your body parts? Why should that be a penalty on the defense?

If they call kicking and there are five seconds left on the possession clock, it goes back to 15 seconds. It used to go back to 35. I've always felt that using your feet, your knees or your legs is part of being in the correct defensive position.

I don't think I'm alone on that.

Among the most recent changes, the NCAA rules committee has lengthened the 3-point shot — pushing the arc back to 20 feet, 9 inches from 19 feet, 9 inches. I don't think it will have a big bearing on the game. And if there is a decrease in 3-point shooting percentage I don't think it will be glaring.

I like the game the way it is today. No matter how much people talk about how it's too physical, they have to understand that these players are bigger, quicker and stronger while the court dimensions haven't changed.

It's tougher to get easy shots, it's tougher to score now. But if you take care of the ball and you get a shot every time down the floor, you can shoot 35 percent and win. That also applies if, conversely, you get people to take tougher and fewer shots.

How do you get better shots? Touch the post. Get closer to the basket. Be mechanically sound on each shot. Don't fade away. Don't shoot outside your range.

You can get more shots by not turning it over and getting on the offensive boards, and you can get better shots by getting to the free throw line. What's a better shot than a free throw?

I know what you're thinking. I sound like a broken record.

Am I dating myself?

Broken record? As in vinyl record?

Maybe I sound like a broken CD.

I don't have an iPod, but you know how I love my music: the Temptations, Marvin Gaye, anything Motown. I'll also listen to Outkast and Annie Lennox. But I must admit I wasn't prepared for the reaction that I got to my "Soulja Boy" dance video on YouTube. To say I was surprised would be putting it mildly. Heck, I'm old enough to remember the first "Soldier Boy," as sung by the Shirelles in the early '60s.

This past season, while I was going through the handshake line with the opposing team after a game, I can't tell you how many opposing players would say, "Coach, I saw you cranking dat 'Soulja Boy.' That was great."

Up until then, I saved most of my dancing exhibitions for wedding receptions. My specialty? Otis Day and the Knights from the movie *Animal House* — the Isley Brothers' hit "Shout."

You should see the looks I get when I drop down to the floor.

The dirtiest looks are from my own kids.

I've made a conscious attempt to try to stay young and relevant with my players. I've taken an interest in the movies that they watch and the music that they listen to.

Am I worried about getting old? No, I just worry about not being able to communicate — not being able to relate to people, whether they're young, old or in between. I want to be able to carry on a conversation with my generation as well as with adults who are a generation ahead of me and with young people who are generation behind me.

We have two grandchildren now. Megan and Matt had a girl, Aoife — pronounced EE-fah — which is a traditional Irish name. Will and Emily had a boy, Owen William.

In the old days, you'd probably think, "Oh, good, Owen will play basketball when he grows up." Instead, there's a chance that Aoife will be the athlete.

As a grandparent, I can't wait to start doing things with them, especially when they start to crawl and walk a little bit. Right now, there's a lot of holding and watching, which is okay. I'm glad someone held and watched me when I was that age.

A few years ago, I got hooked on doing crossword puzzles. I was reading about how people keep their minds sharp when they reach 60, and this is a pretty good way.

My old coach, Ron Rainey, has been doing puzzles for about 15 years. Out of the blue, he'll call on the phone and ask, "What's a five-letter word for ...."

I'm always checking out new words and the spelling of older words and that's why our dictionary is so beat up. I'm also a big fan of Sudoku, a puzzle based on placing numbers in boxes and rows. Some days, I draw a blank on a 4-star. Other days, I can knock out a 3-star in four minutes. It's not basketball. But I make it competitive.

Like I do most things.

***

Books are another outlet.

I'll read anything by David Maraniss, a Pulitzer prize-winner. I could read one of his books every day. He's from Madison, and I've had a chance to meet him. I also like James Bradley, whose *Flags of our Fathers* was so much better than the movie.

Rick Reilly is one of the most insightful, witty and intelligent writers around. He's now working for ESPN and *ESPN the Magazine* after years with *Sports Illustrated.* He's a character like Al McGuire is a character. They say that about me and my dad.

Rick is trying to make things better. He's not afraid to call things the way he sees them. What's wrong with that? If you believe it, say it, or write it.

I'm also a fan of Stephen Covey, a motivational specialist, and historian Stephen Ambrose, who was raised in Whitewater and got his Ph. D. from UW-Madison.

Ph. D. is one of my favorite acronyms.

Make it PHD — Poor, Hungry, Driven.

That's the way you need to stay. I remember a lot of the old school coaches on the East Coast, a lot of the guys my age using that expression. It's a mindset that you want to maintain. If a guy like me can make it, anyone can. How else can you go from coaching junior high ball in the Philly area to coaching a very successful program in the Big Ten?

Anything I've wanted to do, I've done at 100 percent. I decided to become a coach, and that's what I became, and I took on everything from A to Z. But I remind myself every day that you have to continue to find ways to get it done.

If I have to change course on something I've done, or work out a decision in a different way, I do it. Some people dwell on being wrong. You can't worry about that. You need to believe in what you're doing through study and instincts. If you were wrong, or something didn't work, make sure it wasn't because you were taking a shortcut.

What's the No. 1 life lesson I've learned?

That you don't have to get the last word in all the time.

That you don't have to win every discussion.

I think that's probably a Ryan trait, Butch and Bo.

There are times when you will agree to disagree. But you've got to move on and make something positive happen. Same with the players. Nobody agrees with everything. There's interaction. But they have to realize that this is the way it's going to be done.

It's like the army. Rank has its privileges, and there's always somebody above you. The key? When it comes time to make a move, you've got to have everybody on the same page because if they aren't, that's when something can go awry.

Bud Haidet, my athletic director at UWM, was military, he was a Marine. Meanwhile, George Chryst at Platteville and Barry Alvarez at Wisconsin had football backgrounds. Both were successful coaches. Pat Richter was a football guy too; a successful player. I'm a team-sport guy.

Whether it was George, Bud, Pat or Barry, I've tried to follow the same guidelines.

First, you find out what your AD expects — what he wants — and then you give it to him. And not only do you give it to him, but you give him maybe more than what he thought you could give. It's that old cliché: if they hire you for a nickel, give them a dime's worth. I'm trying to give Wisconsin a dime's worth.

Same thing in basketball.

I want to give everyone their money's worth.

We can have team meetings, we can have discussions, we can go over all sorts of things, but when it comes time to play, we all have to be on the same page. Some teams are going to have success because they have better talent. But if everything else is equal, the unified teams tend to win more games.

No detail, to me, is ever too small.

Ever write down a phone number without writing down a name next to it? I realize I'm dating myself again because we're in the cell phone era, but play along.

How many times have you picked up a scratch pad, seen a number and asked, "Who the heck is this?" You know what that means? It means the job was done half-way.

I tell our team managers, "Whenever you take down a phone number, make sure it's legible, and make sure there is a name attached to it."

It's a pet peeve.

Like small talk on the phone.

When we were kids and we got a phone call, my dad would grab an egg timer and turn it upside down. When the sand ran through to the other end, you had to be off.

I limit my small talk to about two to three minutes.

It's like always making sure you turn off the lights when you leave a room.

Or keys.

Another pet peeve.

It was a bigger deal at Platteville because I had a set of master keys. But even at Wisconsin, I still make sure that my assistants or managers hand the keys to me directly. Don't put them on a chair or desk. You always hand them to the person. That includes golf junkets. Before a person closes the trunk, I have them rattle the keys.

Why is that important? You can figure that one out on your own.

It's all about taking care of the little things. Just like it is in coaching: "Take care of the ball. Don't step into the lane too fast on a free throw because it might cost us a point," and so on. You don't micromanage. But no detail is too small.

If I have a legacy, I'm sure they will say that I was detail-oriented, which is fine. But I would hope they would also say, "He was firm but fair as a coach."

Every year, there's going to be another team, another group of young people who are going to be looking for guidance, another group of seniors who are going to be leaders.

Every year, there's going to be another hill to climb.

EPILOGUE

Never a Dull Moment
by Mike Lucas

There has always been continuity in the Ryan household.
Especially on game days. Kelly Ryan drives and frets. Bo Ryan rides and snoozes.

"Bo is into routine," she said of her husband, the rigidly structured University of Wisconsin basketball coach, "and we don't break routine."

The Ryans have been married since 1974. "And I have always driven him to the home games, and still do," Kelly said. "I've missed just one."

That was in 1989.

"I gave birth that day," she said.

What kind of an excuse is that for not driving? You've got to play through the labor pains, Kel. "So, you do know the story about Megan?" she asked.

An explanation followed.

Megan was the couple's first child. At the time of her birth in 1976, Bo Ryan was coaching a high school team in Sun Valley, Pennsylvania, not far from his roots in Chester.

"I was in labor all day, and I really didn't know it," Kelly said, picking up the play-by-play. "I was 12 days past my due date — you would have thought something would have clicked. But I was 23, what did I know?

"Well, late in the afternoon, I determined, 'Okay, this is the real deal.' My contractions were five minutes apart, and we lived five minutes from the high school. But I couldn't call Bo because they stopped answering the phone at 3, and now it was 4.

"So I waited to have a contraction and when I did, I picked up my little suitcase, jumped in the car and drove to the school. When I got there, I waited until the next contraction was over, and walked into the gym.

"Bo was playing intramural basketball with some of his students and when he saw me, he stopped the game and actually asked, 'Why are you here?'"

Kelly Ryan delivered the news to Bo Ryan: In case you haven't been paying attention, honey, I'm pregnant, I've been having contractions and the baby is on the way.

His response? "He wanted to know if he had enough time to take a shower first before going to the hospital," she related. "I said, 'Go ahead.' So, I'm in labor, sitting on the bleachers with some high school kids, and waiting for him to shower."

What happened next? "Bo still disputes this part of the story, but a woman in labor never forgets," she said. "After showering, he wanted to know if we could go back to our apartment and get something to eat, because he was really hungry."

Not really?

"Really," she said.

There was one more request on the way home.

"He wanted to know if he could take another shower because he had been sweating so much," she said, acquiescing to his wish. "So, I'm making him a sandwich and I reach up to get a glass out of the cabinet and I had the worst labor pain."

Her message to hubby now had some urgency.

"Bo, we're leaving," she ordered.

Hold the mayo, and get in the car.

"Because of the Friday night traffic, we didn't get to the hospital until about 6:30," Kelly said. "But the doctor was real nonchalant about the whole thing and told Bo, "This is your first baby, huh? You might as well go and get dinner.' So he did.

"On Fridays, all the teachers hung out at this particular bar and that's where Bo went. While there, he collected money for a baby pool — time of birth and weight.

"He got back to the hospital at maybe 8:30. Megan was born a little after 9. You can probably guess who he called first. He called the bar to notify the pool winner."

In recounting that story, Kelly Ryan was reminded of another Bo and baby tale. This time, she was in labor with child No. 2, Will.

"Bo was at a friend's house with a bunch of his golfing buddies and they were getting ready to head out," Kelly said. "I didn't know if they had left yet, so I called anyway and I got a hold of Bo and told him, 'I think I'm in labor.'

"He came right home and took me to the hospital. We got there at about 1:30 in the afternoon. For the next few hours, Bo paced the room. Finally, he said, 'Kelly, are you going to have this baby or not? I could have had nine holes in by now.'

"You talk about a woman in labor getting upset and wanting to scream. If there was ever a time I wanted to pick up something and throw it at him that was it."

But she resisted the urge to bop him. That's part of the beauty of Kelly Ryan: Poise under pressure. Always calm, always reasonable. Unless, of course, it's game day.

"I agonize over the games," she admitted. "I can be driving him to the Kohl Center and I'll feel like I'm going to be sick because I'm so nervous. I look over at Bo and he's either playing solitaire on his phone, or nodding off.'"

Zzzzzzzz? The coach of the Badgers?

"It's awful after a loss, too, especially if it has been a close game," Kelly went on. "I'll just lay awake at night and I'm replaying everything, 'If we would have just made a few more free throws or if we had just gotten a few more rebounds.'"

And Bo? "He's snoring away," she said. "He sleeps like a baby before a game and after a game and I'm the one who's wired — I'm the one who will get the ulcer."

She can't say that she wasn't warned about becoming a coach's wife. Kelly and Bo first met while Bo was an assistant to the late Bill Cofield at the College of Racine and Kelly was working as a secretary in the athletic department.

"There was a coach who used to say the three most important things in his life were basketball, golf and family — in that order," Kelly remembered. "I used to think, 'What a cad. How awful is that?' Now, I like to joke, 'I married someone just like that.'"

Bo and Kelly got married on the south side of Chicago. That's where

"Carol" Kelly was raised: 112th and Western Avenue.

That's another story: Kelly being a Carol.

"I was named Carol and brought home from the hospital on a snowy Christmas Eve," she recounted. "It was a lean year; and there was no money for shopping.

"My mom gathered the family and said 'Well, kids, here's your Christmas gift, here's your little Christmas Carol.' And they said, 'That's it, no gifts?'"

Carol Kelly was one of six children: Shelia, Mary, Jane, Rich and Phil. But she wasn't Carol to anyone in the neighborhood. She was just Kelly.

Her best friend was Louise Murphy and when they went out together, they were Murphy and Kelly. "Everybody went by their last name, and it just stuck," said Carol, er, Kelly.

When she was 10, she lost her father, who had heart-related health issues. "I was a daddy's girl — he was the kindest, dearest, funniest man," she said, holding back tears.

By her own admission, she has always been independent — never more so than after her father died and her older brothers went into the service. But she never flinched at having to fend for herself (which would bode well for her life as a coach's wife).

Along with her sisters, she did what she could to help out her mom, Mary, who returned the favor by hosting Bo and Kelly's wedding reception in her backyard.

"Oh, my gosh, it was probably the cheapest wedding in history," Kelly said. "My dress cost $40 dollars. It was a bridesmaid dress, but it was perfect. Bo's sister, Nancy, bought him his 'Great Gatsby' white suit. My mom and her friends made all the food."

There was one other matter — transportation — that needed to be addressed.

"My brothers were Chicago policeman and they took a lot of bodies to this particular funeral home," Kelly said. "The guy owed them a favor, so they asked, 'Can we get a limo and a driver for our sister's wedding?' Thankfully, it wasn't a hearse."

The wedding cost Kelly's mom all of $250 dollars. A few days later, Bo and Kelly started their new life together — that of an obsessive high school basketball coach, and an accommodating coach's wife.

Let the honeymoon begin.

"Honeymoon? What honeymoon? We spent two days driving a U-Haul to Pennsylvania," Kelly said. "And when we got to our apartment, Bo had me digging through our stuff for his old softball uniform, because he was playing that night."

They turned out to be the perfect match: a fiercely-proud and competitive Bo and a smart and savvy Kelly, who really did understand what she was getting herself into.

Still, there have been adjustments along the way.

When Bo was a UW assistant, and the family budget was tight, they never got around to buying furniture for the living room in their second Madison home. "Instead, we had a basketball hoop up for the kids," Kelly said.

That was a challenging period for another reason. Make that three reasons. "I had three kids in four years and Bo was never home because of basketball," she said. "I'd see other men in the neighborhood come home for dinner and I'd feel sorry for myself."

But not for long.

Kelly was always near family (her sisters) and she always rallied—even upon seeing Platteville after Bo accepted the head coach position. "I saw the size of the phone book," she said, "and I thought, 'Oh, my God, maybe we don't need to do this.'"

She quickly had a change of heart — falling in love with the people and community — while recognizing the benefits of living in southwestern Wisconsin. She also discovered how small a small town can be.

"It was funny, because I used to joke that he could never have an affair in Platteville," she said, "I'd go to the grocery store and people would tell me what Bo had for lunch: 'Hey, Kelly, saw your husband at Culver's today.' I'd ask what he had, so I'd make sure we wouldn't have the same thing for dinner.

"The first time his parents, Butch and Louise, drove to Platteville, they got lost on their way to our house. Someone spotted the out of state license plates on their motor home and pulled up to them and asked, 'Can we help you?'

"Yeah, we're looking for our son's house.

"Who's your son?

"Bo Ryan.

"Follow me.'"

The Ryans lived in the same Platteville home for 15 years before Bo took over the UWM basketball program. "I thought he would retire in Milwaukee, I really did," Kelly said. "I loved our home, the neighbors, the school. It was a fabulous two years."

But when the Badgers beckoned, Kelly agreed, "It was a no-brainer. We didn't even talk about it. Done deal. Besides, I adapt easily."

Even though Bo carries a high profile today as a Big Ten head coach, Kelly has still been able to slip under the radar. "People don't know who I am," she said, "and that's good because I can pretty much go to the store and look like a slob."

She still buys all of Bo's clothes. He has never set foot in West Towne or East Towne Mall. "He just isn't a shopper," Kelly reasoned. "But I did stop buying his shoes."

Kelly used to pick out Bo's game day attire. Not anymore. "He'll get feedback or he'll ask, 'What did I wear the last time we were on ESPN?'" she said. "And I'll say, 'If we don't remember, I don't think anyone else will, either.'

"One year, the W–Club gave him a beautiful red sports coat and after he wore it a couple of times, Bo's mother told him, 'You look like you ought to be parking cars.'"

Bo and Kelly laughed.

Life is good. She has taken an active role on recruiting weekends. "I love getting to know the kids and parents before they're officially Badgers," she said.

One thing to keep in mind about Kelly Ryan.

"I'm not a pushover," she stressed. "I do what I do by choice, because we benefit from his success. I don't want to live with someone who's losing ballgames.

"Therefore, he has always been free to do whatever he has to do to be successful, and he has never had to worry about the kids or anything at home.

"In many families, the kids aren't involved in their parent's career. Our kids are. Basketball has been a family job. Our two boys, Will and Matt, grew up in a gym."

She paused and added, "It's in their blood."

That also applies to her DNA.

Given the Team Ryan commitment, what's it like at home after a loss? "Quiet. Nobody talks for 24 hours," Kelly said. "But we don't lose too often."

The Ryans live on Champions Run; a fitting endorsement of the national championships at Platteville and Big Ten championships at Wisconsin.

But was it a coincidence that they build their home on that street?

"It was, but we'll take it," said Kelly Ryan, who will dutifully keep taking Bo to the home games — waking him up, if need be, just before they reach the Kohl Center.

She will then take her seat behind the bench; the same seat she has sat in for every game Bo has coached at Wisconsin. "And I won't leave my seat until the end of the game," she said, unwilling to break routine.

***

William Francis Ryan had a plan for his son, Billy.

You may know Billy as Bo.

You may know William Francis as Butch.

Butch?

"I was known as Butch all my life," he said proudly, almost defiantly. "I was a terror. When I was 7 or 8, I was fighting all the time. I fought for everything I've got. I was skinny, but I was rough and tough. You had to fight in those days to survive."

That's Butch being Butch. "You know what they always say?" he said, setting up his punch line. "Always make sure you spell it with a 'u' and not an 'i.'"

If you truly know Butch, you know that line is about as old as Butch. For the record, he was born on March 29, 1924. And he will tell you that he's of good stock: the County Donegal Ryans from northwest Ireland.

So what was his plan for Bo?

"I never let Bo win at anything — not at ping-pong, not at checkers, not at pool, not even when we played Cowboys and Indians," Butch Ryan said. "And when I coached him, I was harder on him than anyone on the team. Believe me, when I tell you that."

Believe this, too. Or, at least, believe most of what follows because it will give you some insight on Butch and maybe even more on Bo and his upbringing.

"When I got into the pool room, I could shoot a stick — I was good and I made money there," Butch said, carrying on. "I ran away from an orphanage when I was 11 and I raised my self. I was a street kid in the city of Chester.

"Mom died in '32. Dad was a vagabond. There was a fellow that I knew who owned a pool room and that's where I always used to hang out. I'd take care of the tables, fix the cues and mop up the floors. Got a room that way.

"I never robbed, I never stole. But I knew how to get money. Sold papers, shined shoes, worked in a mill. I was a pin setter at the bowling alley and worked on a milk wagon. Worked for everything I got. I'd be on the street corner at 12 at night, selling papers. Everyone knew me. My uncle was a cop, my grandfather was chief of police.

"I even used to sing for money when I was really young. Used to sing at amateur shows. One of my big hits was 'The Object of My Affection.' That's the one I really liked, and I'd win all the time because I'd open the side door up near the projector and let all my buddies sneak in and they would clap like heck for me and make the meter move.

"My junior high coach, Jack Crawford, took a liking to me and wanted to adopt me. He said, 'I'll give you a good home and send you to college.' But I told him that I didn't think it would work out. There was too much street in me.

"The only reason I went to school was to play sports. I was one of the biggest kids in town. But when the war broke out — February 2, 1942 — I dropped out of school and enlisted in the Navy. I lied about my age. I was 16 or 17. Spent four years in the South Pacific. During one of my leaves, I went back to Chester and met Louise at a dance.

"When I reached for her hand to help her out of the chair, I heard sirens and bells and sweet music. She was the one. I asked her to wait for me, and she did. I came home again in October of 1944 and we got married. It was tough going back to the war."

But he did, and he earned the Bronze Star for jumping aboard a sinking destroyer and assisting the injured — without being ordered to do so.

"There was two of us and our captain said he was going to recommend us for the Congressional Medal of Honor if the ship got back safe," he said. "But the captain died and they couldn't get verification. Doesn't mean the deed wasn't done."

After returning to Chester, he became a local coaching legend because of his success at the youth level. In football, his teams won five straight league championships. In Legion baseball, he coached the likes of Billy "White Shoes" Johnson, who later gained fame in the NFL.

But he gained most of his satisfaction and notoriety from his work with young basketball players, ages 10 through 12. His Biddy teams won four state titles. "I was known," he said, "as Butch Ryan, the Biddy League man."

Elroy Hirsch was his hero. As fate would have it, Bo Ryan's first job as a college assistant was at Wisconsin whose athletic director was the fabled Crazylegs.

"One time, Bo called me at 2 in the morning," Butch said.

"Yo, dad, where do you think I'm at?

"I don't know son. You been drinking?

"No, no. But I'm standing in Crazylegs driveway as we speak.

"You gotta be kidding me. Crazylegs Hirsch?

"That's right, THE Crazylegs Hirsch.

"Made my day," Butch recalls fondly.

Butch Ryan likes to tell the story about how his hometown Eagles got the best of Hirsch in one game. In fact, he enjoyed retelling it the most when Hirsch was around.

"Crazylegs says to me, 'Come here a minute, Mr. Ryan,'" Butch said. "If you ever tell that story again about me and Philadelphia, I'm going to get rid of you first and then I'm going to get rid of your son.' We laughed so hard. What a great man."

What a great story-teller.

In sum, did Bo Ryan inherit his street smarts from Butch Ryan?

"Bo has more than street smarts, he has smarts," Butch said. "I remember one day mom says to him, 'Bo, I'll give you a dollar to go out in the yard and pick the weeds.' Bo goes out and gets four kids younger than he is and he says, 'I'll give you each a nickel if you pick those weeds,' You can do the math, but he did all right.

"Louise, his mother, now that's where Bo gets his cool. Oh, yeah, she helped him in many ways, because that's the way she is — she's competitive. She applied to be the business manager at Widener, a college in Chester. But she didn't have her degree.

"They tell her if you take a half-dozen accounting classes and ace them all, then, the job is yours. Mind-you, she's in her early 50s. But she passed with flying colors. Smart lady. Like I said, she always plays it cool. Oh, God, yeah, I'm more of a hot head.

"Let me tell you about Bo. He's honest. He always speaks highly of people, or he won't speak at all. There's no in-between. Yet, at times, he's forceful at practices. Which is what you have to be as a coach.

"It just seems like when you're dedicated, you're dedicated and you don't leave any stone unturned. I know when I coached I looked for that angle or that edge that would give me a chance to win that game. Bo is like that."

So, why again did Butch never let Bo win? "Because I think that's what made me so competitive — I hated to lose," Butch said, "and I just passed it on."

***

Chester High School basketball coach Ron Rainey had a plan for his starting point guard, Bo Ryan. "I was probably tougher on Bo," he said, "because I coached the point guard more than I coached the other guys. If he made a turnover, he heard about it."

Rainey didn't hold back, either.

"My earlier years, I was goofy, I would really get on kids, scream and holler," he said. "Halftimes were sometimes really tough. But you never lose the good players. Bo would just listen to what I had to say, and play harder. Nothing phased him.

"From the start, I saw the leadership possibilities. Much of that had to do with his background and being in a situation where he always had to prove himself every day in and outside of practice. When you're on the basketball floor, you don't look at color. But he was one of only two white kids on the team.

"He was a three-year starter for me and the other kids knew I wasn't playing Bo because he was white. They knew I was playing him because he could play. He was my best point guard. He had street smarts and basketball savvy.

"The competition is what pushes him. He didn't ask too many questions. But he was a good listener. And if you'd tell him to do something, he was going to try and do it. He was fundamentally sound, and mentally tough."

Rainey also coached Ryan at Wilkes College. "I had him for seven years, including high school, and I'm not sure he learned anything from me or not," he said.

"But here's what I liked most about Bo as a player: he's going to refuse to lose. After the season, he had his teammates in the Wilkes gym playing every night, which none of them had done before. He'd organize them and coach them.

"We didn't have a hill to run at Wilkes. But in the gym, we had these 50 pound canvas bags of sand. And I made the players carry them when we ran sprints at the end of practice. Everybody hated the drill. Except Bo. Nobody could understand why.

"I'd say, 'We're running suicides tonight, everybody get a sand bag.' Bo would sprint out of the team huddle and be the first to the sand bags. You see, there were two bags that weighed 30 pounds instead of 50 pounds. Bo knew that. So, he'd race to get the 30-pound bag — unbeknownst to his teammates — and he'd be the first in line."

Rainey later coached with Ryan at Platteville.

"I was the head coach at Delaware but it was the wrong time and the wrong place and they asked me to leave," Rainey said. "That was very tough. That just about ruined me. I went back to Wilkes and we were winning some games but struggling a little bit.

"I was getting a little burned out and that's when Bo saved me by asking me to come out to Platteville. Coaching Midwestern kids is just the greatest experience. And it really rejuvenated me. Bo had complete control of the basketball program.

"Why was he so successful at Platteville? His game preparation is the best I've ever seen. He knows exactly what the other team is going to do. He knows exactly what his players have to do. So there are no surprises for the players during the game.

"He's doing the same things at Wisconsin: the preparation, the conditioning, the fundamentals. The most important thing that is the same? He's still winning."

***

Even as a freshman, Saul Phillips had no qualms about running the hill at Platteville — even when his head was throbbing and his stomach was queasy.

"I was one of the few guys on the team," Phillips boasted, "who could go to a keg party on Wednesday night and run the hill and finish first the next day."

Even as a freshman, Rob Jeter had no reservations about running the hill at Platteville — even when he had trouble breathing because of his asthma.

"When I went to college, I expected everything to be tougher and more challenging and difficult," Jeter noted. "So, when I saw the hill for the first time, I thought to myself, 'Wow, this is what it's all about.'"

Over time, they both learned the true meaning of the hill.

"It stood for mental toughness," Jeter said. "It kind of symbolized everything you do in life — where there are hills and mountains that you have to climb — and you have to be mentally tough to accomplish what you're doing to get to the top.

"The hill was a great equalizer. I saw some of the best athletes struggle and I saw some guys — who weren't very athletic — do fine on the hill."

Phillips saw and felt the same things.

"It was a shared suffering and the goal was to conquer something together as a team," Phillips said. "I knew there would be days where I would be running an extra hill or two just to drag a teammate — who was struggling — up that final hill.

"You can tell someone that you will be there to support him in time of need. But it's another thing to actually show him. There were times when the whole team would help somebody get up the hill, and Bo didn't have to tell anyone, 'Go help him out.'

"What was unique about the hill was that everybody who has ever played for Bo had a similar outcome — as far as what the hill did for them — even though so many of his players came from some very different backgrounds."

None were more different than Phillips and Jeter.

Phillips was from a small community, Reedsburg.

Jeter was from a big metropolitan city, Chicago.

Phillips' dad owned a hardware store.

Jeter's dad played for the Green Bay Packers.

Phillips, a marginal college player, was the captain of an unbeaten national championship team in 1995. "I wasn't that damn good," he said. "I was the human victory cigar. When I got off the bench, the game was over."

Jeter, an all-conference player, was the captain of Platteville's first national championship team in 1991. "That was a confirmation of everything Bo preaches," he said. "All the little things that he stressed are what will put you over the top."

In retrospect, none were more similar than Phillips and Jeter.

Both played on successful teams at Platteville. Both coached under Bo Ryan. And both are now head coaches: Phillips at North Dakota State, and Jeter at UWM.

Each has their own take on his influence.

"I remember the first time I sat down with him as a high school senior," Phillips said. "We talked for 10 minutes and I was mesmerized. He can really be persuasive one-on-one. What you find out about him is that he's just so damn smart.

"From the time I was in third grade, I wanted to be a basketball coach. Maybe I've got a screw loose, but that was my goal. So I went to Platteville to learn how to coach because I thought that I could learn more from Bo than anyone else.

"Looking back, it was amazing how much blind trust I had in his coaching. He could have led me into a burning building. The thing is, Bo has a comprehensive manual for how to have a successful basketball program. It not only has worked at different levels — Division III and Division I — but it fits everyone, all different types of players.

"What you come to realize is that he's got every scenario covered before it happens. That's because he's smart enough to have a vision on where he wants to go, and he's competitive and good enough to pull it off. I would say 85 percent of what I do as a head coach, or base my philosophy on, is a direct result of Bo Ryan."

Jeter, unlike Phillips, had no ambition to become a coach.

"I was working one of Bo's summer camps in Platteville," Jeter said, "and he asked, 'Ever thought about coaching?' I told him no. And he said, 'Well, if I ever have a position on my staff, I'm going to ask you to come back as an assistant. So be ready.'

"Sure enough, it happened, and I saw many of the same things as an assistant as I saw as a player. He's a tireless worker. He keeps it simple. And he's always trying to make you better. He starts with the person, not the athlete. He works on you becoming a man. Part of that translates into how you're going to handle adversity on the court."

Not that he always agreed with his head coach

"There were times when I was a player, where I'd think, "He's crazy. Why is this man always jumping on me?"' Jeter said. "Every player felt that Bo was on them more than anyone else. That's a sign of a good coach because he treated everyone the same, whether you were first team all-league or sitting at the end of the bench.

"The older I got, the more I appreciated what he was doing — the more I appreciated his attention to detail. There are a lot of different ways to do things. But he's doing it his way, and there's no questioning, no wavering, no going back and forth.

"He always says, 'This is what we're going to do and we're going to be the best at doing it, and, if you stay committed, it's going to work.' And it does. Everything I do as a head coach is somehow connected to him and how I was raised by mom and dad."

Jeter even found himself getting into a signature Bo Ryan catcher's crouch on the sidelines during a game. At the time, he didn't know that he was doing it. But when he thought more about it, he knew exactly why he was doing it.

"I've always looked at Bo as a father or a big brother," Jeter said, "and being a head coach is my way of paying him back and showing respect."

Jeter still chuckles at the memory of their first face-to-face meeting. "I pulled into the parking lot outside of Williams Fieldhouse in Platteville," he said. "There were three guys standing out front, and I asked if anyone knew where Coach Ryan's office was.

"One of them says, 'Does he owe you money? Has he done something wrong?'"

Weighing Jeter's response, the same guy says, "I'm Coach Ryan."

Welcome to the World According to Bo.

***

Wisconsin associate head coach Greg Gard has a fundamental working knowledge on how Bo Ryan gets his teaching points across to the players.

"He has made more positives out of negatives than anyone I've ever been around," said Gard, who also served under Ryan at Platteville and UWM. "He's always thinking a step ahead of everybody else. His mind just works that way."

There was the time in Milwaukee where the Panthers were getting ready to play a good Detroit team, right after having played an even better Butler team.

"Bo wanted to compare the different styles of the two teams," Gard said. "So he brought a boom box to practice. First, he played some John Mellencamp. It wasn't real fast, but it had a beat to it. He turns to the players and says, 'Fellows, this is Butler.'

"Then, he switched the boom box over to some AC/DC and he really cranked up the volume and he turns back to the players and says, 'Now, guys, this is Detroit.' He made his point and everybody knew what he meant."

Gard cited another motivational example.

"As a junior, Freddie Owens had a hard time moving without the ball and he had the habit of dribbling too much in place when he had the ball," Gard said. "I've got this battery operated megaphone that I used for summer camp to make announcements.

"Bo has me sneak up to the third level of the Kohl Center before practice. He told the players that I had gone on a recruiting trip. As soon as Freddie goes into his dribble routine, I'm counting them out on the bullhorn, 'One, two, three, four ...'

"Whenever Freddie starts to stand, I'm yelling, 'Freddie move.'

"Freddie has no idea what's going on, and Bo finally says to him, 'Freddie, did you hear that? It's the basketball gods, they're talking to you.'"

Not many have seen that side of Ryan.

Not many know him as well as Gard.

"He's never satisfied and I just think that comes from his background and how he was brought up," Gard said. "He's had to fight for everything he's gotten. That's where he gets his edge. Some coaches get to the 'I have arrived' status. Not Bo. And that's the way he wants his players. He wants them hungry.

"He sees different things in people — players, assistants, managers — and he cultivates their strengths accordingly. He treats everyone with respect. But he's demanding. If you're around him long enough, you'll see him stand up and go to bat for someone. You'll also see that he never throws a player under the bus with the media.

"It's a respect thing, 'I've got your back, if you've got mine.'"

But what about the personality conflicts that must surely exist with other coaches? What about his old relationships with Eau Claire's Ken Anderson or Whitewater's Augie Vander Meulen? What about the on-going Bo Ryan-Tom Izzo matchups?

"You look back at the rivalries we had at Platteville or now have at Wisconsin," Gard said, "and Bo has never brought personalities into it. Even with the assistants, when we meet as a staff behind closed doors, it's never about the other coach. He doesn't get caught up in it. He filters out all the nonsense and focuses on what his team needs to do."

What's it like to work for Ryan?

"He has always had people around him who have shared his vision for what he's doing," Gard said. "He can tell who's phony and who's for real. And he makes it so it's not just your job, but your passion. When you have assistants in the program with that sense of pride and ownership, you don't want to be the one to let it slip.

"You feel like, 'We're in this together. Let's roll up our sleeves and get after it.'"

There's a reason why you don't see a revolving door with his staff. "There's no way I'm where I'm at today without Bo," said Gard, echoing Phillips and Jeter.

***

Andy North knows something about approach shots. He also knows something about competition and basketball. His approach is not unlike Bo Ryan's.

"To be successful," said North, a two-time winner of the U.S. Open, "you can't be afraid to fail. Good God, I've failed all the time in our sport. In golf, you tee it up 600 times and win five tournaments, so you've failed a lot. Tiger Woods wins 27 percent of the time.

"I hated to lose. But I don't know that I ever feared losing. I've always used a bad performance to motivate me to work harder the next day. You won't find me feeling sorry for myself, or tucking my tail, because that didn't work in our household."

North is a coach's kid. His dad was a high school basketball coach in Tomah, Wisconsin. Stewart North later moved the family to Madison so he could work on his Ph.D. That's when Andy was exposed to Badger hoops at the Fieldhouse. From the upper balcony, he watched his favorites play: Dave Grams, Mike O'Melia, Ken Barnes.

Andy North had game. He was an outstanding prep basketball player at Monona Grove. "And I really considered playing in college," he said. "I went on some basketball recruiting trips. I looked at Wisconsin, Michigan State and Notre Dame."

North ended up at the University of Florida on a golf ride. Turned out to be a pretty good decision. "But I absolutely loved playing basketball," he said.

North and Ryan got to be friends in the late '70s.

Their bond has never been stronger than it is today.

The Norths — Andy and wife Sue — have made a generous financial commitment that will allow the athletic department to replace the basketball floor in the Kohl Center.

"Growing up in a household with a dad who was a coach, you understand how important team sports are," said Andy North, who attends many UW basketball practices when he's not on the road covering golf events for ESPN.

"One of Bo's great strengths is that the players understand that every day is pretty much the same. You go in Monday and practice hard and you do the same things on Tuesday, and the things that you practice are the same things you do in a game.

"I was a great free throw shooter and a great putter. You have a process and you do it every single time and you get to the point where you don't have to think about the ramifications. I loved having the ball at the end of game. I loved having that five-footer for some money. That's the fun part of all the work that you put in.

"Even if you don't want to be in that situation, you have to figure out a way to make yourself believe that's what you want."

The psychology of competition, 101.

"I can't ever imagine not being confident," North continued. "There are times when you're not playing very well. But it doesn't mean you're not confident in what you're trying to do. You might question yourself, 'Am I working on the right things? Or, am I ever going to play any good again?'

"Once you get out there and get in your process, I don't really think great players lose confidence. I think they're confident all the time or they wouldn't be in that situation. Now, can you get on a run where it's so easy and so simple? Yeah.

"Michael Jordan could go out and get nine points and he wouldn't be any different talking to him if he got 40. Bo is that way. After a loss, he's upset. But I don't think the losses grind on him like a lot of coaches.

"He's disappointed the guys didn't play well or didn't execute. Maybe he made some mistakes or whatever. You analyze that, and 12 hours later, it's gone and for Bo, it's always 'Let's move on to the next one.'

"I personally think Bo is the best coach I've ever been around. One, he has been successful. Two, he understands how he can get players to improve. If you look at his teams, the walk-ons improve as much as the stars do. That doesn't happen in a lot of programs. But he spends as much time trying to make them better as he does the No. 1 guy.

"I think he's as good of a fundamental coach as I've seen. Every drill, every moment they're on the floor, they're doing a skill that they're going to get better at. That's the essence of basketball.

"The reason you practice is to do things that are going to help you in the heat of battle. That's why he's such a darn good coach. I suspect the players think the games are not as tough or physical as some of the practices.

"There's not one perfect way to get it done. That's the beauty of athletics. You can take 20 different golfers and they've got 20 different ways they play. Likewise, you can take 20 different basketball players and each will have their own style and personality. It's the great coach who can take the players who are there and make them better."

What don't we know about Bo?

"I don't know," North said. "People know that he's compassionate and competitive and all those kinds of things. But I honestly don't know what people would think that they don't know about Bo. It's not like he's a great musician who sits at the piano and plays three hours a night. He's not hiding that from us."

It's not like anyone hasn't seen his cheesy "Hambone, Hambone" routine, either.

"Bo is pretty much what people think he is," North concluded. "He loves getting away from basketball when he can, but he's very dedicated to the sport. He's done a lot of great things for the game as far as the Coaches Association. He's terribly caring and loves the state and the community, which is underlined by the fact that he has been in Wisconsin for over 30 years.

"Bo is a regular guy and I think fans see him in that light. They love him because he's one of them. The neat thing about what he has accomplished is that his teams are good every year and they're going to continue to be good every year."

North has uncovered another Ryan strength that not everybody sees.

"He's a master at handling the media," said North, knowing the smoke and mirrors of a Bo Ryan press conference can rival a David Copperfield performance. "I tease him about it all the time. Basically, he can give them three or four thousand words and not say anything."

***

ESPN/ABC college basketball analyst Steve Lavin gets it all the time.

"Who are the handful of coaches who impress me?" he said, resetting the question. "I always say without hesitation, 'Bo Ryan.' There are others who have impressed me as well. But I'd put him right there at the top."

Lavin brings a coach's perspective to his analysis. For seven years, he was the head coach at UCLA — guiding the Bruins into the NCAA tournament six times, including five Sweet 16 appearances. John Wooden and Purdue's Gene Keady have been his mentors. Lavin was a Boilermaker assistant under Keady for three seasons.

Lavin is a teacher's kid. His dad, Cap Lavin, starred in basketball at the University of San Francisco, where he played for the legendary Pete Newell and Phil Woolpert. As such, Steve Lavin has a rich hoops pedigree, which impacts his insight.

"There are a number of dimensions to Bo Ryan's coaching that separates him as one of the best in the business," Lavin said. "One of them is his unique ability to inculcate his players with the ability to see and think the game the same way he does.

"You hear the cliché that a point guard is an extension of the coach on the floor. Or that the quarterback is the central nervous system of a team. It's easier said than done. Bo, though, has shown that he can get an entire team to buy into his philosophy and approach to winning games, while consistently developing player's basketball habits.

"I like to refer to Wisconsin as an old fashioned doughnut — no glaze, no sprinkles, no chocolate frosting. If you're a basketball purist, you love it because it's like watching an old fashioned pitching dual between Sandy Koufax and Bob Gibson.

"Yet, there's a great flexibility within Bo's thinking. This is old fashioned in the positive ways. This is not old fashioned as in dogmatic or stubborn or lacking flexibility or ingenuity or resourcefulness. So, for me, it's just a pleasure to watch.

"The Badgers have what I call the 'Green Beret or Navy Seal' training. Yet, Bo has been able to keep a looseness and child-like spirit, so there is a joy within the discipline. In this context, his assistants understand the Bo Ryan system and recruit with precision to ensure that they get the players who fit the marriage of talent and system."

Lavin documented the flexibility. "In back-to-back years, he won in two different ways," he said. "When he had a star — Alando Tucker — he surrounded him with role players and won 30 games. The following season, he doesn't have Tucker and he wins 31 games with a very balanced team that didn't have a star. That shows that he has been able to inculcate or instill into his players a level of confidence."

Not that Ryan hasn't frustrated Lavin, the interviewer.

"He's the walking contradiction that we all are," he said. "We're just more aware of it with our public figures because they're out in the open and so visible and so scrutinized and so dissected — like a frog in a biology class.

"On one hand, Bo has his straightforward approach and discipline and focus as a coach. But he also has a storytelling side. With the media, he's able to take an interview and control it and almost go into a stall like if one of his teams was protecting a lead and there wasn't a shot clock. So there's no time to ask another question or cross-examine.

"I marvel at it all, while I'm walking away shaking my head. But I kind of get a kick out of him because he is such a character — determined as he is to play it close to the vest and not give out any information that he thinks somehow could hurt his team's competitive edge or give an opponent any slight edge. He's one of a kind."

***

Brian Butch became known as the "Polar Bear" thanks to Lavin who came up with the nickname. Butch has a name for Bo Ryan: winner.

"The first time I met him, I could see the passion in his eyes," Butch said. "He was unlike some recruiters who came off as fakes. If you're a high school kid and you go into his office for the first time, you can see how much he wants to win.

"No promises are made. Nothing is handed to you. One thing that he emphasizes is that you're going to have to work for everything you get. As good of a basketball coach as he is, I don't think people understand how he gets players ready for life.

"When I was redshirting as a freshman, he told me, 'Listen, you made your decision, so now let's try to get better. Let's keep on improving so that by next year you're able to contribute to this team.' Some kids think a redshirt is a year off. But from our short little conversation, I took his advice and tried to progress every year.

"The first time I ran the hill, I wondered what the heck I was getting myself into. But by the time my senior year rolled around, I knew exactly what it was for. As a team, we knew that we were going to be in better condition than our opponent in the second half and over the last five minutes of a game. Not just physically, but mentally.

"There were times when I struggled tremendously with the hill when I was a freshman and sophomore and guys like Mike Wilkinson and Zach Morley and Clayton Hanson were there for me. That brings you closer together as a team."

Asked to describe his adjustment to the Swing offense, Butch said, "Indiana's D.J. White told me it was the hardest thing that he's ever had to defend. Not a lot of people like defending against constant movement because it's tough to do. But it does take time to get used to the Swing when you're making the transition from high school.

"That's why you need the right guys in the system, guys who want to accept the offense and learn it. During our summer pickup games, we're not like most college teams across the country. We're making sure everyone knows exactly what needs to be done with the Swing instead of freelancing. The older guys pass it down to the younger guys."

Why does the system work?

"Because he gets the players to buy into it offensively and defensively,"

Butch said. "And if you don't, you're cheating yourself. At first, you may think you're buying into it, you may think that you're doing the right things. It just takes some time, but once you do buy in, all 15 guys, then you can do some amazing things.

"The main thing is to really listen to what he's saying in practice. He's constantly giving advice and it's up to the individual player to use it. He's always emphasizing playing together and making smart decisions. Nobody wants to run sprints. But when we do make a mistake, the penalty is high, so we won't make the same mistake in a game.

"Ten years from now, I won't remember the basketball stuff as much as I will remember how he taught me to be a person and a man off the court. He taught me to be responsible for my actions and accountable. He's teaching you to be a better person, and he teaches everyone the same things: how to be successful, how to be a winner."

While he was practicing with the Utah Jazz summer team, Butch had a chance to visit with point guard Deron Williams, the former University of Illinois star.

Williams told Butch, "I hated your coach."

Not really, and here's why.

"You were the toughest team we played," Williams told Butch. "You were always ready for what we were doing and you always brought it. As an opposing player, you knew it was going to be a battle every single time you played Wisconsin."

Butch could understand where Williams was coming from.

Yet, he still has trouble understanding one of Ryan's idiosyncrasies.

"I never understood why coach always sits in the back of our chartered planes," Butch said. "I finally asked him one time, and he says, 'Have you ever seen a plane back into a mountain?' I'm thinking if the plane is going down, it's going down. Not him."

In the movie, *Dumb and Dumber*, there's a classic exchange between Lloyd Christmas (Jim Carrey) and Mary Swanson (Lauren Holly).

Lloyd: What are the chances of a guy like you and a girl like me ending up together?

Mary: Well, that's pretty difficult to say.

Lloyd: Hit me with it! I've come a long way to see you, Mary. The least you can do is level with me. What are my chances?

Mary: Not good.

Lloyd: You mean, not good like one out of a hundred?

Mary: I'd say more like one out of a million.

(Dramatic pause)

Lloyd: So you're telling me there's a chance?

Maybe, just maybe, Bo Ryan figures that by sitting in the back of the plane, if it does crash into a mountain, he would have that chance — just enough time, if only a split-second, to do something something about his predicament.

"That's exactly it," agreed Brian Butch, laughing. "That's him in a nutshell -- he'll always find a way to get it done somehow, someway."

NATIONAL CHAMPIONS
1990-1991   28-3

NATIONAL CHAMPIONS
1994-1995   31-0

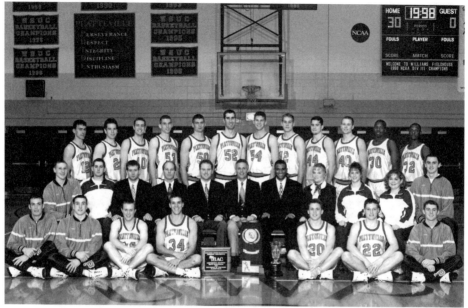

NATIONAL CHAMPIONS
1997-1998   30-0

NATIONAL CHAMPIONS
1998-1999   30-2

UNIVERSITY OF WISCONSIN 2001-2002

Big Ten regular season champions (11-5, tied Illinois, Indiana, Ohio State)
Note: Ohio State vacated record due to NCAA sanctions.

UNIVERSITY OF WISCONSIN 2002-2003

Outright Big Ten regular season champions (12-4)

UNIVERSITY OF WISCONSIN 2003-2004

Big Ten Tournament champions
(12-4, tied for second regular season)

UNIVERSITY OF WISCONSIN 2007-2008

Outright Big Ten regular season champions (16-2)
Big Ten Tournament champions

RYAN'S COACHING RECORD

Year	University	Record	Pct.	Conference	Record	Place	Postseason
1984-85	UW-Platteville	9-17	.346	WIAC	4-12	7th	
1985-86	UW-Platteville	16-11	.593	WIAC	8-8	5th	NAIA First Round
1986-87	UW-Platteville	14-11	.560	WIAC	6-10	T5th	
1987-88	UW-Platteville	24-5	.828	WIAC	14-2	1st	NAIA Third Round
1988-89	UW-Platteville	24-5	.828	WIAC	13-3	3rd	NAIA Third Round
1989-90	UW-Platteville	26-3	.897	WIAC	15-1	1st	NAIA Third Round
1990-91	UW-Platteville	28-3	.903	WIAC	13-3	2nd	NCAA Champion
1991-92	UW-Platteville	27-4	.871	WIAC	13-3	2nd	NCAA Third place
1992-93	UW-Platteville	24-4	.857	WIAC	13-3	T1st	NCAA Quarterfinals
1993-94	UW-Platteville	23-5	.821	WIAC	13-3	2nd	NCAA Sweet 16
1994-95	UW-Platteville	31-0	1.000	WIAC	16-0	1st	NCAA Champion
1995-96	UW-Platteville	23-3	.885	WIAC	15-1	1st	NCAA First Round
1996-97	UW-Platteville	24-3	.888	WIAC	14-2	1st	NCAA Second Round
1997-98	UW-Platteville	30-0	1.000	WIAC	16-0	1st	NCAA Champion
1998-99	UW-Platteville	30-2	.938	WIAC	15-1	1st	NCAA Champion
1999-00	UW-Milwaukee	15-14	.517	MCC	6-8	T4th	
2000-01	UW-Milwaukee	15-13	.536	MCC	7-7	5th	
2001-02	Wisconsin	19-13	.594	Big Ten	11-5	T1st	NCAA Second Round
2002-03	Wisconsin	24-8	.750	Big Ten	12-4	1st	NCAA Sweet 16
2003-04	Wisconsin	25-7	.781	Big Ten	12-4	T2nd	NCAA Second Round
2004-05	Wisconsin	25-9	.735	Big Ten	11-5	3rd	NCAA Elite Eight
2005-06	Wisconsin	19-12	.613	Big Ten	9-7	T4th	NCAA First Round
2006-07	Wisconsin	30-6	.833	Big Ten	13-3	2nd	NCAA Second Round
2007-08	Wisconsin	31-5	.861	Big Ten	16-2	1st	NCAA Sweet 16

24-year collegiate record		**556-163**	**.773**				
Record at Wisconsin		**173-60**	**.742**	**Big Ten**	**84-30**	**.737**	

BIG TEN WINNING PERCENTAGE

The following is a list of the coaches with the
best all-time winning percentages in Big Ten play (min. 5 years):

Coach (School)	Yrs.	Record	Pct.
1. Bo Ryan (WIS)	**7**	**84-30**	**.737**
2. Bob Knight (IND)	29	353-151	.700
3. Ward Lambert (PUR)	29	228-105	.685
4. Tom Izzo (MSU)	13	144-68	.679
5. Ralph Jones (ILL)	8	64-31	.674

ALL-TIME WISCONSIN COACHING RECORDS

Coach	Tenure	Yrs.	Overall			Big Ten			Titles
			Won	Lost	Pct.	Won	Lost	Pct.	
James C. Elsom	1898-1904	6	25	14	.641	—	—	—	
Emmett Angell	1905-08	4	43	15	.741	19	5	.792	2 Big Ten
Haskell Noyes	1909-11	3	26	15	.634	18	15	.545	
Walter Meanwell	1912-17, '21-34	20	246	99	.712	158	80	.660	8 Big Ten
Guy Lowman	1812-20	3	34	19	.642	19	17	.528	1 Big Ten
Harold "Bud" Foster	1935-59	25	265	267	.498	143	182	.440	3 Big Ten
									1 NCAA
John Erickson	1960-68	9	100	114	.467	52	74	.413	
John Powless	1969-76	8	88	108	.449	42	78	.350	
Bill Cofield	1977-82	6	63	101	.384	32	76	.296	
Steve Yoder	1983-92	10	128	165	.437	50	130	.278	
Stu Jackson	1993-94	2	32	25	.561	15	21	.417	
Stan Van Gundy	1995	1	13	14	.481	7	11	.389	
Dick Bennett	1996-2000	5	93	69	.574	39	45	.464	
Brad Soderberg	2001	1	16	10	.615	9	7	.563	
Bo Ryan	**2002-08**	**7**	**173**	**60**	**.742**	**84**	**30**	**.737**	**3 Big Ten**
									2 Big Ten Tourney
Totals		110	1345	1095	.551	687	778	.469	

500 WIN CLUB (ACTIVE)

Entering the 2008–09 season, Wisconsin head coach Bo Ryan owns the second-highest career winning percentage of any active coach with at least 500 career victories. Following is a list of the active Division I head coaches with at least 500 career victories (at all levels)

Coach (Current School)	Yrs.	Record	Pct.
1. Roy Williams (North Carolina)	20	560-134	.807
2. Bo Ryan (Wisconsin)	**24**	**556-163**	**.773**
3. Mike Krzyzewski (Duke)	33	803-267	.750
4. Jim Boeheim (Syracuse)	32	771-277	.736
5. Lute Olson (Arizona)	34	780-280	.736
6. Bob Huggins (Kansas State)	26	616-221	.736
7. Rick Pitino (Louisville)	22	520-190	.732
8. Eddie Sutton (San Francisco)	37	804-328	.710
9. Jim Calhoun (Connecticut)	35	774-337	.697
10. Pat Douglass (UC Irvine)	26	547-272	.668

CAREER HIGHLIGHTS

- Career record of 556-163 (.773)
- Seven-year record of 173-60 (.742) at Wisconsin (at least 19 wins in each of his first seven seasons)
- Big Ten record of 84-30 (.737)
- Best conference winning pct. in Big Ten history (minimum five years)
- Second-highest career winning percentage of any active Division I coach with at least 500 wins
- Has led UW to the NCAA Tournament in each of his seven seasons
- Has coached the five winningest teams in Wisconsin history, including school-record 31 wins in 2007-08
- 10 NCAA Tournament victories are most in school history
- Three NCAA Sweet 16 appearances in his seven years, including the 2005 Elite Eight
- Only coach in Big Ten history to win at least 11 conference games in each of his first four seasons
- Led Wisconsin to a share of the 2002 Big Ten title and the outright conference title in 2003
- One of four coaches in Big Ten history to win conference titles in each of his first two seasons
- Led the Badgers to first back-to-back conference titles since 1923-1924.
- Guided Wisconsin to first-ever Big Ten tourney crown in 2004
- Led UW to first No. 1 ranking in school history (Feb. 19, 2007)

- Won both 2008 Big Ten regular season and post season titles for the first time in school history, becoming just the fourth Big Ten team to win both crowns in the same season
- Has led UW to 107-7 home record, including 53-3 in Big Ten contests
- Owns 11 conference titles in 24 years
- All-time winningest coach in Division III history (353-76, .822)
- Led UW-Platteville to four national titles
- Has had just one sub-.500 season in his career (1984-85, his first season at UW-Platteville)
- 2002 Big Ten Coach of the Year
- 2003 Big Ten Coach of the Year
- One of just six coaches to earn Big Ten coach of the Year honors in consecutive seasons
- 2004 NABC Guardians of the Game Award for Service
- 2007 Clair Bee Coach of the Year Award
- 2007 Rupp Cup as National Coach of the Year
- 2008 Jim Phalen National Coach of the Year

"To get where I am today, it did seem like I was running uphill, at times, because of the route that I took. But life is like a road race: straight-aways, turns, climbs, and descents. In all cases, though, I knew that I wanted to teach and coach. It didn't necessarily have to be at this level, but that's how it has worked out, and I'm very fortunate. To the best of our ability, we're trying to impart our knowledge and experiences as adults to the young men that we're teaching and coaching. Friendships and relationships are formed in the course of doing our job, though we aren't always in a position to be their buddy. What we're passing along isn't always what they want to hear. But that's in keeping with the way all of us had to grow up. If things are done in a certain way, the percentages will pay off, and the good times will outweigh the bad. They have for me."

—Bo Ryan

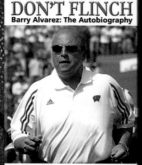
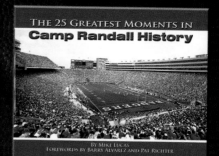
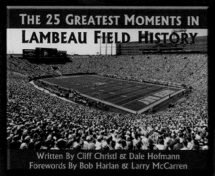

March 2009

Sunday	Monday	Tuesday	Wednesday	Thursday	Friday	Saturday
1	2	3	4	5	6	7
8	9	10	11	12	13	14
15	16 The Big Dance	17	18	19	20	21
22 The Big Dance	23	24	25	26	27	28
29 The Big Dance	30	31	1	2	3	4

HERE'S TO YOU COACH RYAN FOR GIVING BADGER FANS SOMETHING TO PLAN AROUND EVERY YEAR SINCE YOU CAME TO MADISON.